Strangers in This Land

STRANGERS

IN THIS LAND

Pluralism and the Response to
Diversity in the United States

E. ALLEN RICHARDSON

THE PILGRIM PRESS   NEW YORK

Photographs are by the author except where otherwise indicated.

Library of Congress Cataloging-in-Publication Data

Richardson, E. Allen, 1947–
    Strangers in this land : pluralism and the response to diversity
in the United States / E. Allen Richardson.
Bibliography: p. 245
    Includes index.
    ISBN 0-8298-0764-0 : $10.95
    1. United States—Ethnic relations.   2. United States—Race
relations.   3. Pluralism (Social sciences)—United States.
4. Religious pluralism—United States.   5. United States—Religion.
I. Title.
E184.A1R47   1988
305.8'00973—dc19   88-9634
                                                                    CIP

The Pilgrim Press, 132 West 31st Street, New York, New York 10001

for Mom and Dad

Contents

List of Illustrations

Acknowledgments

A number of people have made important contributions to the development of this volume. I am especially grateful to Theodore H. Erickson, General Secretary of the Division of the American Missionary Association of the United Church Board for Homeland Ministries, whose appreciation of the dynamics of American pluralism and support of the research led to this text.

Alfreda E. Meyers, whose knowledge of Asian history and religion as well as her years of experience teaching in the field, was a valuable asset to the project. Her suggestions for amplification of the text and numerous comments on each chapter were an important contribution without which the book would never have reached its present state.

Larry Kalp, Secretary for Publication, and Senior Editor Marion Meyer both were supportive of the effort from the outset. Under the helpful guidance of Meyer and with the careful attention of Consulting Editor Susan Converse Winslow, the manuscript was shaped into a finished text.

Paul Sherry, Executive Director of the Community Renewal Society in Chicago, provided valuable insight into the nature of pluralism in that city and, with his wife Mary, graciously shared their home during several research trips. Similarly, Richard McGuire's vision and understanding of American pluralism were always a source of inspiration.

A number of persons provided valuable insights as the research progressed. These included Herbert P. Rickman, Special Assistant to the Mayor of the City of New York; Lin H. Mo, Assistant Administrator of the New York Infirmary-Beekman Downtown Hospital; Hugh H. Mo, Deputy Police Commissioner of the City of New York; John T. Martin, Principal of Senn Metropolitan Academy in Chicago; and, C.T. Shen, Vice President of the Buddhist Association of the United States. In addition, I am indebted to the archivists and staff of the Amistad Research Center in New Orleans for their helpfulness in probing the history of the American Missionary Association.

I am also grateful to Joseph Carr, who shared his knowledge of Allentown, Pennsylvania, and Vivian and George Yoder, who·provided assistance in understanding the new religions. I owe special thanks to Sandra A. Johnson, who skillfully spent countless hours typing the manuscript, meeting deadlines, offering numerous technical suggestions, and tolerating what seemed to be endless revisions without hesitation or complaint.

There are many others, too numerous to list here, who provided valuable assistance as working on the text progressed. However, a group of friends, colleagues, and family deserves special thanks for their continued support. To the staff of the Penn Northeast Conference, who provided encouragement; to Linda Wilkens, who assisted in securing legal documentation; to Larry and Diane O'Connell, whose friendship helped see me through the work; to my parents, who provided numerous avenues of assurance and belief in the project; and to my wife, Betty, who helped with the manuscript and whose patience endured what seemed to be a limitless endeavor, I am continually grateful.

E. ALLEN RICHARDSON
Allentown, Pennsylvania

Preface

The idea for a text on American pluralism came about during a five-day consultation in 1982 sponsored by the United Church Board for Homeland Ministries in Deering, New Hampshire. Representatives of Hindu, Buddhist, Muslim, Jewish, and Christian faiths shared their experiences and perceptions about life in the United States.

Despite the fact that all of the presenters were American citizens and were either born in the United States or had been fully assimilated, most had known feelings of utter isolation and estrangement. With only a few exceptions, they had rarely been exposed to the religious or ethnic backgrounds of one another. Most had also experienced a lack of acceptance in the larger society.

For a brief interlude, the Deering Conference became a microcosm of pluralism in American life. The only difference was that the consultation approached diversity as an exercise, through schedules and presentations, from a consensus that we would agree to disagree. The atmosphere of the event was intentionally receptive and conducive to the expression of difference. Where persons and ideas were so dissimilar that there was no common "language," the beginnings of one were gradually developed.

In this sense, the conference was an anomaly. In most diverse communities in the United States, there are few opportunities to develop any common language. If communication takes place between persons from different backgrounds at all, it is usually occasioned by concerns about day-to-day life. It rarely includes the larger question of the structure of reality, the way the world works and makes sense.

Even for persons indigenous to the same society, communication about such basic meanings is difficult. However, for others who exhibit such extraordinary differences, there are even greater barriers. A Hindu, for example, may recognize a panoply of gods and may perceive reality in an ordered fashion through the impersonal processes of *karma* and rebirth. A Buddhist may hold a similar world view but may also understand existence to be transient and impermanent. A Christian may view life as a historical process in which an omnipotent God is innately involved.

When such different perceptions of life are housed in the same community, they may collide. The collision may involve confrontation, but more often it does not. What is more apt to occur is the mutual realization that since there can be no common experience of life, no common "language" or body of symbols, the only alternative is isolation.

This text explores some of the dimensions of this experience both in terms of the extraordinary level of diversity that can now be found in many communities and in relationship to the wider question of how such differences are perceived.

The book suggests that the experience of diversity in the United States has not been one of consensus. On the one hand, the designation "American" encompasses an array of persons from many ethnic and religious backgrounds. This understanding was the foundation of the diversity of the Fourth of July celebrations surrounding the one hundredth anniversary of the Statue of Liberty in 1986. On the other hand, the term "American" is ethnocentric, ignoring those Latin hemisphere countries that rightfully claim the same identification. By implication, the term also suggests a homogeneous national self-portrait that excludes diversity from matters of patriotism or identity. The cumulative push and pull in ideology that has resulted from these interpretations is particularly significant at a time when racial and religious plurality have escalated and when the experience of community is increasingly rare.

The question, then, of "Who are we?" cannot be adequately answered only by demographic means. It is a far larger issue with broader implications that really asks, "What kind of nation do we want to be?" We have proclaimed "In God We Trust." Now, when distant gods live among us, such a national credo cannot help but generate a moment of reflection. That moment is the agenda of this text.

"WHERE DISTANT GODS COLLIDE"

The appearance of the distant gods was not miraculous.

Its occasion was not the end of an age or an incarnation.

Instead, the gods came on the heels of immigrants, refugees and other seekers who followed the American Dream.

The gods came in uprooted altars and transplanted temples, not in chariots or riding on the backs of magical beasts.

They came from distant lands and once in America they collided as strangers.

Some made them welcome insisting that there were many gods and many ways of life.

Others insisted that America trusted in one God and had no room for many;

And the nation, and the gods, were confused.

CHAPTER **1**

Where Distant Gods Collide

In December 1982, a *New York Times* reporter interviewed the residents of a single floor of an apartment building in Elmhurst, Queens.[1] He found an environment so completely diversified that it defied the imagination. On the sixth floor of 87-30 Justice Avenue, forty persons from eleven countries were neighbors. Each was a current immigrant from a distant part of the globe. Natives of Korea, Haiti, Colombia, Nigeria, and Vietnam lived side by side, yet the level of isolation was so high that many residents lived with the terrible fear that they were the only foreign-born persons on the floor.

In the heart of Elmhurst with all of its vast differences in people, a variety of stereotypes about interracial neighborhoods are shattered. The area is not a slum. The majority of small businesses appear to be viable. The dwellings—a combination of rental apartment buildings, cooperatives, and a small number of privately owned homes—are well maintained and attractive. Some area residents appear to be upwardly mobile. While racial tensions may be a source of friction, the atmosphere in the community appears, for the most part, to be one of acceptance.

A walking tour produces endless surprises at the degree of accommodation of ethnic groups. A Japanese fast-food restaurant also includes a Chinese menu. Two restaurants each offer both Spanish and Chinese cuisine. A copy of the Chinese menu is printed in Spanish. A branch of the Bank of Ponce (Puerto Rico) is in sight of a variety of Asian-owned businesses. An Indian doctor's shingle hangs near that of a Hispanic physician. A grocery store in the same neighborhood advertises both kosher and nonkosher foods.

Elmhurst also exhibits extraordinary differences in religion. For example, every night a Buddhist family at 87-30 Justice Avenue burns incense in front of a small shrine.[2] The icons are placed on the wall above the family television set—an ironic mingling of Western mass media and Eastern spirituality. The daily regimen of prayer and offering incense before the shrine, however, is maintained for more than religious obligation. Behind it is the conviction that worship may bring religious merit in a world filled with endless, repetitive suffering.

Buddhism teaches that the cause of suffering is the craving for material possessions, power, sex, and a greater sense of "self." Buddhism understands these desires as forms of bondage that prevent the liberation of the human spirit. While monks are able to renounce the world and eliminate desire, the laity follow a different path. These two routes to salvation are further defined by a variety of Buddhist traditions encompassed by two schools (the Theravada and the Mahayana). While the total faith accommodates a variety of emphases, the basis of it all remains the conviction that the path to salvation leads away from suffering.

To a Muslim from Bangladesh living on the same floor, the world is entirely different. While Buddhism denies the existence of a creator God, Islam teaches that there is one permanent and pervasive deity, Allah. Sharing much of the same prophetic lineage of the Jewish and Christian faiths, Islam posits that the last, or seal, of the prophets was Muhammad. As the messenger of God, Muhammad is credited with receiving the revelations contained in the Qur'an, which is therefore understood to be the literal word of God. Through the teachings of the Qur'an and the example of Muhammad's life, Muslims have a model of an ordered existence, which is given meaning through God's judgment. As part of this structured life, Muslims are required to pray five times daily, an obligation that is a constant reminder of the role of religion in all that they do. Unlike Hindu or Buddhist worship, Islam imposes a strict prohibition against the use of images or the representation of God or humankind in any iconographic form. Roman Catholics from Central America and Hindus from India all living on the same floor perceive the world in yet other ways.

Each of these religions' understanding of existence, suffering, justice, and salvation differs from that of the other's. There is little agreement on the order of society or the role that each person is expected to play in it. Considerations of marriage, social relationships, and diet vary greatly, reflecting different presuppositions about the nature of the human condition.

The extraordinary fact about the residents of 87-30 Justice Avenue is that despite such vast differences, their situation is not unique. Rather, it represents a growing trend of pluralism in the United States. Pluralism is more than differing patterns of life-style or variations in belief. Instead, it is the convergence in a single area of people who are so completely different from one another in cultural orientation, religion, language, and a wide variety of other factors that neighbors do not have the conceptual or experiential tools to understand neighbors.

Pluralism is the existence of community within community and is focused, as Phillip Hammond suggests,[3] not on the heterogeneity of individuals but of groups. In Elmhurst and countless other pluralistic communities across the United States, a variety of ethnic and religious groups struggle for acceptance and success in an environment where the concept of "foreigner" is a way of identifying not those who do not belong but rather those who do.

The following pages explore some of the ramifications of this extreme diversity occasioned by dramatic changes in immigration law, illegal migration, and refugees—in short, by the continued appeal of the American Dream. While the level of diversity in Elmhurst greatly surpasses that of the majority of communities, the estrangement and lack of communication among different groups have become widespread. Following an exploration of the dynamics of American pluralism that affect this alienation, this chapter addresses a problem—the dualistic response to the issue of diversity in American life.

Religion and Ethnicity in American Pluralism

For most of the diverse residents of Elmhurst's Justice Avenue, who are thousands of miles from their place of birth, identity is supported in a number of ways. Traditional patterns of language, diet, dress, and social relationships help to retain ethnic heritage. Religion is equally important. It concerns not only acts of ritual or prayer but the way that the world is perceived and dealt with, including the interpretation of suffering, change, and death.

Religion and ethnicity are thus symbiotic expressions of group identity. They have also had a particularly close relationship in the United States. Andrew Greeley implies, for instance, that the interrelationship is so strong that the pattern of behavior that has evolved from it could be described as religioethnic.[4]

Greeley suggests that the linkage between religion and ethnicity has been an important component of denominationalism. From the earliest colonial times, denominations have been identified by regionalism and ethnicity. As the English Separatists brought Congregationalism to New England, so Germans brought the Reformed Church to Pennsylvania, and Norwegians carried the Lutheran faith to the upper Midwest. This historical linkage has been continued by the latest wave of immigrants, the Asian Americans.

A Buddhist Bon ceremony conducted in New Brunswick, New Jersey,

Figure 1.1   Buddhist Bon ceremony

in 1985 illustrates the close association between religion and ethnicity (see figure 1.1). Dating from the time of the Buddha, Bon is a rite in which the deceased are venerated. This particular ceremony incorporated some unusual elements. It lifted up the lives of seven young Japanese who studied in the United States in the late nineteenth century, possibly the first of their nationality to do so. The service was the first formal annual Bon celebration at the site of the seven graves. Three Buddhist temples from New York, New Jersey, and Virginia, each a member of or affiliated with the Buddhist Churches of America (a predominantly Japanese American Pure Land Buddhist tradition), participated.

Among the seven graves was that of Taro Kusakabe, the first Japanese to graduate from a North American university.[5] Kusakabe had come to the United States by ship, passing through Indonesia in what must have been a long and trying voyage. He enrolled at Rutgers University, finishing his course of study with honors in just three years. He also became the first Japanese to earn the distinction of Phi Beta Kappa at an American university. But soon before graduation, he died of overwork and tuberculosis. His degree and honors were awarded posthumously. Land for Kusakabe's burial was obtained by the Japanese consulate. Later, six other Japanese who had settled in the northeast were buried in the same site.

As the Bon ceremony progressed, the Japanese tradition of the veneration of ancestors was being played out in two worlds, one entirely Asian and the other in the United States.

Inquiries had been made in Japan and in the United States to secure as much information as possible about the identity of the six other Japanese, even to the extent of contacting descendents in villages in Japan. The brother of the second president of Keio University, a major institution in Kyoto, was one of the six buried in this tiny plot. Ultimately, a visiting professor from that school was dispatched to attend the rite.

As area residents, oblivious to what was happening, rode motor bikes and played disco music in their backyards overlooking the cemetery, a body of priests dressed in black ministerial robes and stoles began to chant. A small altar containing an image of the Pure Land (associated with nirvana) had been placed in front of the stone pillars marking the graves. A small bowl of burning incense stood in front of the altar and the graves (see figure 1.2).

For the forty participants who gathered on that hot June day, there was a strong link between their ethnicity, the history of Japanese in the United States, and Buddhism. A woman who had been incarcerated in a relocation camp in Wyoming during World War II quietly talked of her experiences and the manner in which, at the war's end, she sought a state in which to live that exhibited minimal prejudice.

Thus, the ceremony affirmed a particular ethnic identity. It affirmed education as an important part of the value system of the Japanese American community. It helped forge a link between the earliest Japanese immigrants, their descendants, and later émigrés. Finally, it reaffirmed for participants what it is to be Buddhist, to be of Japanese descent, and to be American.

As the Bon ceremony illustrated, the relationship between ethnicity and religion is so close it is difficult to examine one without the other. The focus of this text, accordingly, is pluralism within the religioethnic mix. The text assumes that religious and ethnic pluralism are so intricately related that they are virtually synonymous. Such an assumption has been affirmed by Phillip E. Hammond, who concludes, "And since modern societies commonly contain several religious groups, the notion of religious pluralism has been seen as analogous to or even synonymous with racial or ethnic pluralism."[6]

Multiethnic Communities: Elmhurst

Elmhurst, New York, is an example of a multiethnic community. It also illustrates a pattern of diversity identified as integrated pluralism. The term designates an area "in which there are many different groups that are also geographically intermixed."[7] An in-depth examination of Elmhurst

Figure 1.2   Altar for Bon ceremony

shows that the integration is so complete that there is little sense of ethnic neighborhood or of any one dominant group. Originally settled as a predominantly European community, the area has always been characterized by apartments and wood-frame houses. Following the dramatic ending of national quotas in U.S. immigration law in 1965, the community, like many others, began to experience significant change. Large influxes of Chinese, Koreans, Filipinos, Asian Indians, and Hispanics began to move into the area, augmenting the community's historic concentration of European people.

Some small businesses, such as the proliferation of Colombian shops and night clubs, cater to the new minorities. Still others look to an amalgamation of peoples, hoping to find a market in the potpourri of persons and ethnic groups. The city's Spanish-Chinese restaurants, for example, not only hope to attract Orientals but in addition seek to find clientele among the wide variety of Spanish-speaking (that is, Latin American) persons. Not only does such a unique configuration of languages meet the needs of several segments of the community, in many instances it also reflects the movement of Chinese immigrants from Central America to the United States. Other markets and small groceries have attempted to reach the same diversified market, offering well-stocked shelves of Chinese, Japanese, kosher, and Hispanic foods.

Since the 1965 immigration reforms, much of the growth in the Elmhurst area has been Asian American. The heart of the Asian community is focused in nearby Flushing, linked to Elmhurst by Roosevelt Avenue. There, large populations of Koreans, Chinese, Japanese, and Asian Indians have revitalized the inner city. The area now includes a wide variety of Asian-owned businesses and shops. On Bowne Street, two Hindu temples draw worshipers from several states. A variety of businesses including Korean-owned development firms, Chinese banks, and a host of restaurants and spice shops cater to the Asian population.

The rapid growth of Asian American communities in Flushing is illustrated by the density of Chinese, Korean, and Indian populations. Current estimates suggest that the three groups total more than 70,000 persons, and the resulting pedestrian flow has now been calculated at 10,000 persons per hour, equivalent to that in midtown Manhattan.[8] The number 7 Flushing train is popularly called "The Orient Express."

Signs of Asian influence are becoming part of Flushing's self-image. A community-development brochure (figure 1.3) is printed in English, Spanish, and three Asian languages. A local architect who now designs structures to appeal to Asian Americans has proposed erecting an apartment building containing two hundred condominiums, each with two or more bedrooms.[9] Among Koreans, Chinese, and Indian families, it is common practice to provide accommodations for relatives, including

SHOPPING IN FLUSHING
A Word Guide to Shopping

HACER LA COMPRA EN FLUSHING
Una guía de palabra para comprar

在法拉盛區購物

購 物 用 語

후라싱 지역 샤핑.

샤핑을 위한 상업용어 안내.

फ्लशिंग में खरीददारी

खरीद करने का शब्दकोष

Downtown Flushing Development Corporation
136-56 39th Avenue, Flushing, NY 11354 (718) 445-0020

Figure 1.3   Brochure demonstrating the diversity in Flushing, New York

grandparents and even distant cousins who wish to emigrate to the United States.

With the increase of Asian Americans in both Flushing and Elmhurst, one of the major service industries, Elmhurst Hospital, has had to find ways of coping with the tremendous variation in language. Accordingly, the hospital has developed an extensive translation program in which three hundred volunteers have assisted patients speaking more than twenty-one different languages.[10]

The extent of the diversity in Elmhurst is the most dramatic when examined in a single block. The accompanying graphs based on the 1980 census (figures 1.4 and 1.5) show the ethnic variation within two adjacent blocks.[11] Both are residential neighborhoods, marked by high-rise apartment houses and a few older wood-frame homes.

Judge Street (block 201) and Ketcham Street (block 202) both include a Caucasian population that is the largest ethnic group on the block but is under 50 percent of the population. Because there are so many ethnic groups, no single one can correctly be identified as being in a majority on either block.

The second-largest group of persons on Judge and Ketcham streets is Hispanic from Central and South America. Yet, within this group is diversity. Persons from Colombia, the Dominican Republic, and other

Figure 1.4 Census tracts near Elmhurst, New York

Block 201, Tract 269, Judge Street
Total Population (1980 Census)—
  918 Persons

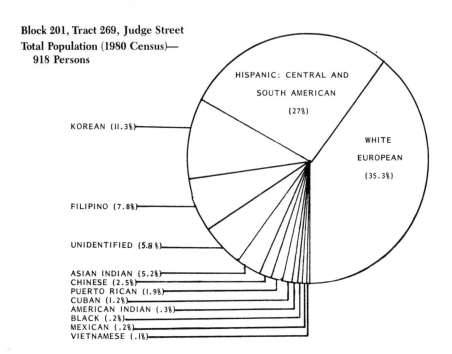

HISPANIC: CENTRAL AND
SOUTH AMERICAN
(27%)

KOREAN (11.3%)

WHITE
EUROPEAN
(35.3%)

FILIPINO (7.8%)

UNIDENTIFIED (5.8 %)

ASIAN INDIAN (5.2%)
CHINESE (2.5%)
PUERTO RICAN (1.9%)
CUBAN (1.2%)
AMERICAN INDIAN (.3%)
BLACK (.2%)
MEXICAN (.2%)
VIETNAMESE (.1%)

Block 202, Tract 269, Ketcham Street
Total Population (1980 Census)—
  462 Persons

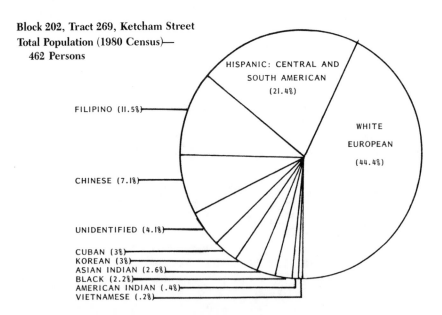

HISPANIC: CENTRAL AND
SOUTH AMERICAN
(21.4%)

FILIPINO (11.5%)

WHITE
EUROPEAN
(44.4%)

CHINESE (7.1%)

UNIDENTIFIED (4.1%)

CUBAN (3%)
KOREAN (3%)
ASIAN INDIAN (2.6%)
BLACK (2.2%)
AMERICAN INDIAN (.4%)
VIETNAMESE (.2%)

Figure 1.5   Ethnic diversity on two adjacent blocks in Elmhurst, New York

countries are united by a common language but separated by culture and national origin. Their separate loyalties are apparent in the proliferation of clubs and restaurants in the area that cater to particular clienteles.

Included in the remainder of the population on both blocks are groups of Koreans, Filipinos, Asian Indians, Chinese, and blacks. The percentage of persons in each ethnic group, however, differs from street to street. For instance, only 2 percent (14 persons) on Ketcham Street are Korean. Yet, on Judge Street, Koreans are 11 percent (104 persons).

The differences in the ethnic makeup of the two blocks are reflected not only in linguistic but also in cultural and political diversity. Among Indians, for instance, language is indicative of regional identity and is part of a cultural complex that includes dress, diet, caste, and religion. Each of these elements may be a source of profound division among persons from the same geographical area. When all these forms of diversity are taken into account, there is little sense of true "community" in an area like Elmhurst. The area allows for individual expression but provides few natural connecting links between persons or traditions or belief systems.

Ethnic Neighborhoods: Chicago

In other cities, diversity is regionalized in a pattern identified as segregated pluralism. In this pattern "there are many different groups, but . . . each group inhabits its own geographical area."[12] Metropolitan areas of this type are characterized by distinct configurations of peoples. The ethnic neighborhood is the norm.

An example of segregated pluralism is Chicago. Chicago's population is a unique clustering of groups including European, Hispanic (Latin American), black, and Oriental.[13] The largest of these minorities is black, a large proportion of whom live in the inner city. The European population includes older groups of Germans, Polish, and Irish, as well as a variety of other smaller ethnic communities. Each of the major Latin American populations in the nation is represented in Chicago.[14] Of these, the largest communities are Mexicans and Puerto Ricans followed by clusters of Cubans and persons from Central and South America. Chicago's Oriental population includes Chinese, Japanese, Koreans, and Indians as well as a variety of refugees from Indochina (Thailand, Cambodia, and Vietnam). In addition to these groups, the city contains some small numbers of American Indians.

Chicago is a city of ethnic neighborhoods where the lines of demarcation between them are strong. One resident, for example, speaks of specific times on weekdays when the elevated trains carry chiefly white riders and other times when they contain mostly blacks. Another speaks of a physical barrier on a city street where the neighborhood changes from black to white.

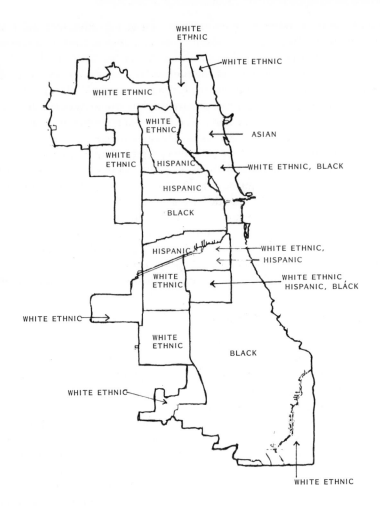

Figure 1.6 Ethnic diversity in Chicago

This composite map shows the dominant racial groups in different parts of Chicago and demonstrates the highly segregated nature of the city. Other minorities in smaller concentrations may also be found in many areas and often reside in tightly concentrated ethnic neighborhoods.

The designation "White" includes persons of German, Irish, Italian, Greek, Polish, Russian, Swedish, English, Dutch, French, Croation, Lithuanian, Czech, and Slovak descent. "Asian" refers to Japanese, Chinese, Filipino, Indian, Korean, Vietnamese, and other groups. "Hispanic" includes large populations of Mexicans and Puerto Ricans as well as the widest variety of other groups from Central and South America and the Caribbean.

Data for the map were obtained from the 1980 census and appeared in an article, "Where we're from, where we live," *Sun Times* (Chicago), 6 February 1983. Also consulted were The Chicago Fact Book Consortium, *Local Community Fact Book Chicago Metropolitan Area Based on the 1970 and 1980 Censuses* (Chicago: The Chicago Review Press, 1984) and issues of *The Chicago Reporter*.

As the map (figure 1.6) demonstrates, the sizable Hispanic and black minorities in Chicago are ringed by clusters of whites (many of whom are of European extraction), increasing their isolation. This is particularly significant for large populations of Puerto Ricans and blacks who are among the poorest groups in the city.

This high degree of separation and segregation among racial groups has resulted in incidences of violence. Tensions are often high, and considerations of zoning and racially motivated politics have fueled the increasing isolation of ethnic groups. The segregation is so strong that even among ethnic groups speaking the same language there may be substantial separation. The Puerto Rican and Mexican populations, for instance, have historically been independent of each other and have in some cases even clustered in distinct ethnic neighborhoods.

Finally, it is important to note that while Chicago is in many ways an example of segregated pluralism, integrated sections may also be found in the same metropolitan area. One diverse yet integrated community is Uptown in northeastern Chicago. This community, which will be described in more detail later, is an intake or resettlement area for many immigrant groups, most notably for Asians. It is much akin to Elmhurst, New York, in its often overwhelming level of ethnic plurality.

Mixtures of Integrated and Segregated Areas: New Orleans

Some cities are thorough mixtures of integrated and segregated sections. This is the situation, for example, in New Orleans. The city is known for its rich Creole culture and quaint French neighborhoods. Beyond this traditional heritage, other groups have added to the mix. The metropolitan area now includes significant numbers of Chinese, Japanese, Koreans, and Indo-Chinese.

An examination of sections in New Orleans shows both neighborhoods that are segregated and other sections that are quite integrated.[15] For example, Pontchartrain Park in the northern part of the city was listed by the 1980 census as 99 percent black.[16] Marigny in the inner city bordering on the Mississippi River is 66 percent white, 22 percent black, 10 percent Hispanic, and 2 percent Asian.[17] A contiguous area, Bywater, shows population of whites (42 percent) and blacks (53 percent) that are only eleven percentage points apart and smaller numbers of Hispanics (5 percent) and Asians (5 percent).[18]

The movement of population groups in the greater New Orleans metropolitan area has affected the character of still other regions. The most fully integrated and probably the most pluralistic of such areas is Jefferson Parish. The parish, which is south of the city across the Mississippi River, has become attractive to large numbers of Asians and Hispanics alike, many of whom left the inner city. Jefferson Parish offers an environment where rents are cheaper, crime is reduced, public schools are better, and employment is easier to secure than in ethnic enclaves in the heart of New Orleans. The parish also includes a significant Arab population.

With its combination of integrated and segregated areas, New Orleans has a unique ethnic heritage and identity. It is defined more by its minorities than by a traditional Anglo-Saxon majority. Older, aristocratic Spanish populations are in positions of prominence. Newer groups of Central Americans do not enjoy the same status but have sizable populations. The New Orleans metropolitan area, for example, is said to include more Hondurans than many cities in that country. In addition to these well-defined groups, a confusion of ethnicities is frequently encountered among white, black, and Hispanic populations who have intermarried over long periods of time. Persons of this combination of ancestries frequently identify themselves with a particular heritage, depending on their families and the communities where they have been raised. With such extreme and highly personal traditions of self-identification, the character of both integrated and segregated areas becomes highly individualized.

Pluralism Outside the Cities

In May 1987, two thousand people gathered at a Tibetan Buddhist center in the tiny northeastern Vermont hamlet of Barnet for a most unusual event[19]—the first cremation in the United States of a Lama, a monastic leader in this ancient, highly mystical tradition. For members of the Tibetan community who participated in the funeral and for the faithful who came from all over the United States to watch, the Green Mountains provided a serene backdrop for the rite. For residents of Barnet, whose traditional Yankee community was smaller than the crowd, the ceremony was an anomaly.

This example of diversity in a rural area seems startling because the word pluralism often connotes images of densely populated urban areas. Diversity, however, is frequently part of life outside the cities. This occurs both because of the spillover of population groups from metropolitan areas and, as the following example illustrates, because of the search for privacy.

Chuang Yen Monastery   In New York's rural Putnam County, the older Protestant, Catholic, and Jewish religious groups have a new neighbor. Within a few miles of scenic Bear Mountain, near the town of Kent, is the Chuang Yen Monastery. The complex is a project of the Buddhist Association of the United States and was dedicated in May 1985.[20] The association, which is predominantly Chinese American, established its first temple in New York City soon after it was organized in 1964.

The construction of a monastery in upstate New York is not an unusual phenomenon for Chinese Buddhists. Some temples located in urban areas, often in the midst of heavy concentrations of Chinese people, have sought to construct larger facilities in rural areas. The nonurban locations have become ideal sites for retreat centers, just as they have for Protestants, Catholics, and Jews. They provide a residence for monks in a location where the daily regimen of the *Sangha* (the monastic order) can take place unhampered. Not far from the Chuang Yen Monastery, for example, is Temple Mahayana in South Cairo, New York, which houses several monks from East and Southeast Asia.

The Chuang Yen Monastery is an ambitious project and is indicative of the energy that has gone into the construction of Asian religious institutions by immigrants in the United States. As with many projects of other faiths, the effort is entirely supported by devotees now living in North America.

The Buddhist Association of the United States claims only 380 members. Yet the monastery, which is its second major project, includes a large meditation center, dining hall, and residence for an abbot. The meditation center, which houses a porcelain icon of the bodhisattva Kwan-Yin, is precisely constructed in the architectural style of the T'ang dynasty in China fourteen hundred years ago (see figure 1.7). In addition to the image of Kwan-Yin, housed in a carved wooden structure especially designed to fit the space, the building contains a large bell. Looming well above the heads of most devotees in its temporary resting position on the floor of the great hall, the cast bronze bell was crafted in Taiwan and brought to the United States as the gift of a devotee.

The Chuang Yen Monastery is grounded in the T'ien T'ai school of Chinese Buddhism. The abbot is a direct descendant of the historical patriarchs of the faith and holds a position of distinction among devotees. Yet, despite the monk's qualifications and the deep sense of roots in a popular school of Buddhism, the institution advocates participation in all forms of the faith. (This approach is also taken by Hindu temples in an attempt to reach a broad segment of devotees in the United States from different sectarian traditions.) Thus, the Chuang Yen Monastery not only is grounded in the T'ien T'ai tradition but also teaches elements of Ch'an (the precursor in China of Zen Buddhism in Japan) and Taoism.

Perhaps the most intriguing part of the Chuang Yen complex is a mausoleum identified as the Thousand Lotus Memorial Terrace (figure 1.8). Erected on a wooded knoll, the terrace overlooks the meditation hall and dining hall. It contains five sections of specially constructed niches for ashes of the deceased. Each niche is covered with a bronze plaque embossed with the symbol of the lotus, a common iconographic representation of the faith (figure 1.9). Space in the Memorial Terrace can be purchased by devotees for donations of two thousand dollars.

The terrace helps devotees who may want to secure the remains of loved

Figure 1.7   Meditation Hall, Chuang Yen Monastery, Kent, New York

ones in the United States rather than at a great distance in China. It also
has become a place of honor not only for the deceased but for all individuals who wish to acquire merit. The continued presentation of the *dhamma*
(teachings) of the Buddha on an altar at the site provides a constant flow of
merit. For Buddhists, the acquisition of merit or demerit is the product of
the positive or negative acts in this life and has lasting effect into future
births. One Buddhist monk purchased a niche in which he placed cuttings
taken from his hair during a fourteen-year period. The act not only
assured that the monk's name would be in a place of honor but that he
would vicarously receive the benefit of the regular repetition of the
dhamma and would acquire additional merit.

Like other institutions, the Chuang Yen Monastery stresses the importance of both religion and culture as contributing parts of a unified
experience. While the primary purpose of the center is to provide housing
for a resident monk and a setting where he may worship and teach,
cultural activities are also routinely scheduled. Lectures and demonstrations on Chinese acupuncture and classes on Chinese vegetarian cooking,
Chinese art and painting, and Chinese language have all been offered
periodically by the monastery.

Unlike many other Asian religious groups that have sought the solitude
and isolation of rural locations, leaders of the Buddhist Association of the
United States have not tried to protect their institution from the community. Instead they have welcomed it. Foregoing the traditional nonprofit, tax-exempt status of a religious institution, they have voiced a

Figure 1.8 Memorial Terrace, Chuang Yen Monastery, Kent, New York

readiness to pay taxes benefiting the community nearby. In addition, they welcomed residents of the area to participate in the meditation classes and demonstrations of Chinese culture offered by the monastery.[21] As a result of this openness, the venture appears initially to have been highly successful. Community leaders speak warmly about the monastery, and a rapport is developing with residents of the area.

This example in Kent, New York, has focused on religious pluralism in a rural community. It came about not so much as a result of population movements as of the transplantation of a mainstream Chinese Buddhist institution into a rural area.

Oak Park An example of the transformation of a nonurban area into a highly pluralistic community because of population movements is Oak Park, Michigan. A bedroom community near the Detroit metropolitan area, Oak Park has evolved into a potpourri of ethnic groups. "One in every five residents is foreign born. Within a single block a shopper can browse in a Vietnamese bridal shop, eat in a Greek restaurant, visit a black-owned ice cream parlor and sample what is believed to be Michigan's only freshly baked kosher pizza."[22] Merchants commonly advertise in Arabic as well as English.

Oak Park is not a thriving metropolis, nor is it an inner-city area of the type usually associated with extreme differences in ethnicity or religion. The community's population has been estimated at 31,000[23]—hardly com-

Figure 1.9   Niche with lotus at Memorial Terrace, Chuang Yen Monastery,
              Kent, New York

parable with the dense neighborhoods found in the borough of Queens in
New York City. Yet, the diversity contained within Oak Park's five-mile
square limits is equally great. It contains a sizable black population, the
largest Orthodox Jewish community in the metropolitan Detroit area, and
a small number of Russian Jewish émigrés. It also contains 5,000 Chaldean Arabs.[24]

Such a dramatic increase in diversity is related to national trends. Oak
Park's black population grew, for example, when their improved economic
situation enabled many to move out of the inner city to seek a suburban
life-style. The Arab population followed much the same pattern, becoming one of the fastest-growing minorities in the area. Detroit is often
recognized as containing the largest Chaldean community outside of
Baghdad, about 40,000 persons, and a total Arab population of more than
100,000.[25]

Together, Oak Park and Kent represent two very different patterns in
which religious and cultural diversity have dramatically affected areas that
twenty years ago were homogeneous. In Kent, the transplantation of a
religious institution created an awareness of vast new differences in religion and ethnicity. In Oak Park the movement of many different types of
people into the same community brought about a fresh consciousness of
the importance of language and culture. In both situations, the new

pluralism has not been perceived as a threat but as a way of broadening the life of the community.

A Note on Regional Variation

Regional variation refers not just to the distinction between urban, suburban, and rural areas but to the variation between comparable locations.[26] A Puerto Rican in New York City, for instance, may be part of a population with a different composition than that to which a Puerto Rican in Allentown, Pennsylvania, belongs. Although both persons retain the same national origins and speak the same language, they may differ in a number of ways including variables such as age, marital patterns, generational distribution, household composition, number of children, and religious affiliation.

A number of important considerations help to distinguish minority populations in one area from those in another. The most obvious is the size of the minority community itself. Larger communities may tend to reinforce ethnic, religious, or cultural traits. They may be more cohesive and may exhibit lower rates of intermarriage with other populations. These variables have been noted in studies of Hispanics:

> . . . the tendency to marry outside of one's group varies considerably by region . . . (thus) Cubans in Florida and New Jersey, where there are large concentrations, have much lower rates of outgroup marriage than do those that live in New York and elsewhere where their numbers are smaller and their settlement pattern is more dispersed. Similarly, Puerto Ricans in New York, their area of principal concentration, are considerably less likely to intermarry than are those that reside elsewhere. And Mexicans in the Southwest are much more likely to marry others of Mexican heritage than are those who reside in other regions.[27]

Other regional differences are also apparent. The questions of socioeconomic status (class), education, and age at marriage have been demonstrated to influence the number of children that families will have.[28] Similarly, regional differentiation and patterns of assimilation are also clearly related. For example, a Chinese American living in San Francisco's Chinatown may feel few pressures to assimilate into the larger fabric of American life. The same person living in a suburban community in the Midwest where there are few others of the same minority may feel greater pressures to meld into the larger society.

Stereotypes and Diversity

These considerations suggest that unless approached carefully, with attention to regional differentiation, ethnicity can become a stereotype.

This is particularly true for population groups whose designation as black, Hispanic, or Asian is in itself a sweeping generalization that includes a wide variety of racial and cultural groups.

For example, the designation black may be used by the general public to refer to a North American black of African descent or a Caribbean black who is a first-generation immigrant. It may also refer to persons from any of several Spanish-speaking countries (Nicaragua, Honduras, for example) where dark-skinned populations and lighter-skinned peoples coexist. The designation may also apply to recent immigrants from Nigeria, Senegal, Ghana, and other African countries. In the United States, many blacks are also part American Indian. Similarly, the designation Hispanic may refer to persons from a widely divergent variety of cultures and races in as many as seventeen different nations in Central America, the Caribbean, South America, Mexico, and Spain. In each country, while there is a common understanding of Spanish and important common identifications as Hispanic peoples, there are also very different expressions of culture.

To describe an ethnic identity as Asian or Asian American is also misleading. The designation implies a uniformity among the most diverse of cultures and racial groups where none necessarily exists. The term implies a commonality among cultures that are entirely different. What, for instance, are the linkages between the Thai and Filipino peoples other than the fact that they both lie in the Eastern Hemisphere?

Even to describe the ethnicity of an Asian Indian can be stereotypical. In India where any one of fifteen languages may be spoken and where there are extreme differences in religion, caste, cultural orientation, and color, the generalization still fails to be specific enough. While there are characteristics that are readily identifiable as Indian and a certain distinct "Indianness," the designation still fails to be adequately descriptive. Moreover, it fails to distinguish between individuals of different national origins from the same cultural backgrounds such as persons from India, Pakistan, Bangladesh, or Sri Lanka.

The ambiguity of the designation Asian has been addressed by Harold Issacs.[29] Issacs discussed prevailing stereotypes of persons from the wider civilizations of India and China. He also described the confusion that has frequently arisen from the designation Asian, particularly as it has been applied in public education:

> In the last ten years or so, American map makers have begun to take a somewhat more patriotic view of the world; instead of Europe, they place North America in the world's center. The effect—besides moving the center of the world from Greenwich to the longitude of Peoria, Illinois—is to leave Japan and a chunk of eastern Asia visible on the west, with the remainder of a truncated Asia reappearing far, again, in the east. . . . The literal-minded schoolboy, shown this map and asked to define the "Far East," would look carefully and reply: "Iran, Pakistan,

and Afghanistan." He might then, quite logically, call India the "Far West." China would then become, no doubt, the "Middle West" and Japan the "Near West." In the interests of simple consistency one could not stop here with adapting the old terms to the new arrangement. If Iran and Pakistan become the "Far East," then surely Athens and Rome must fall within our new "Middle East," and this, of course, places the "Near East" smack down on the Place de la Concorde and Piccadilly Circus.[30]

Issacs explores the variety of stereotypes about Asians that lead to the kind of ethnocentrism that he humorously attacks. Images of "yellow peril" that were so frequently applied to both Chinese and Japanese in the early twentieth century were one manifestation of the fear that accompanied stereotyping and the national malaise that came to surround an increase in diversity. Both Chinese and Asian Indians suffered at the hands of Hollywood, which portrayed them at different times as sinister and untrustworthy. In different historical periods, images of both peoples changed according to international relations, immigration policy, and the impact of the media and public opinion. Portrayals of Muslims as aggressive and warlike, of Sikhs as militant, and of Buddhists as other-worldly are all images that are descriptive of a few individuals but are applied to many. They have blocked communication and have effectively repelled any attempt to penetrate beneath them.

Two Visions of American Life

The preceding pages have suggested that the demography of the nation is changing—that an increasing level of diversity is being experienced not only in urbanized metropolitan areas but even in rural and suburban regions once characterized by a homogeneous population. With the increase in diversity, has come an increase in isolation and alienation in community life.

These problems are compounded by a dilemma. Both historically and currently, the nation has been unable to resolve a basic contradition. The quandry is a clash of values that are deeply engrained in the nation's identity—the confrontation of two visions of American life characterized by diversity and homogeneity, pluralism and assimilation.

At the simplest and most personal level, the two visions are a continuing source of tension for the families of some immigrants. There are many instances, for instance, of one set of grandparents who urge their children to cling to customs of language and religion that derive from the country that the older generation has left behind, while the other grandparents of the same ethnic background value assimilation, conforming to the societal mainstream. For the grandchildren who experience such a philosophical tug of war, ethnicity and religion can become confusing and frustrating issues. As a far broader, societal dilemma, the contradictory values emphasize on the one hand freedom of racial and religious expression and the tolerance of diversity and on the other hand, conformity.

Accordingly, this text suggests the existence of two broad, pervasive visions of American life, one of homogeneity and the other of diversity. Since the earliest colonial times, they have been associated with the nation's identity, and they have affected attitudes toward both ethnicity and religion and the way that minority groups have been perceived and treated (figure 1.10).

The two contradictory views of America have had no single cause nor have they proceeded from any one ideology. Rather, the continuing contradiction is the result of a variety of historical currents and eddies. Specifically the two views have been formed by utopian philosophies and by perceptions shaped by history (i.e., colonialism).

The two views have been encouraged by symbiotic understandings of religion and ethnicity. In the Massachusetts Bay Colony, for example, Puritan theology governed attitudes toward the entire settlement including the question of ethnic diversity. Conversely, in Jamestown, as Benjamin B. Ringer has convincingly demonstrated,[31] the entrepreneurial attitudes of the Virginia Company of London, consisting of white, English, chiefly Anglican citizenry, dominated society.

The purpose of this text in demonstrating the contrasting visions is to show their pervasiveness in American life. Because the contradiction applied to the foundations, the cornerstones, of the American experience, its later expressions have affected a wide variety of social issues and led to conflict.

"The New Colossus" and The Melting Pot

The idealogies of diversity, or plurality, and homogeneity in American life have had two powerful national symbols at their forefront in the late nineteenth and early twentieth centuries. One was an intentional symbol of "the American mosaic"—the Statue of Liberty and a poem. The other was a curious combination of a playwright's vision of the melting pot process and an island in the New York harbor that became its metaphor. Both symbols emanated from the Jewish experience in the United States.

Emma Lazarus, a Portuguese Sephardic Jew, penned an image of receptivity to religious and racial differences and freedom from tyranny. Her poem, "The New Colossus,"[32] was affixed to the Statue of Liberty's pedestal and gave the national icon its focus.

> Not like the brazen giant of Greek fame
> With conquering limbs astride from land to land;

> Here at our sea-washed, sunset gates shall stand
> A mighty woman with a torch, whose flame
> Is the imprisoned lightning, and her name
> Mother of Exiles. From her beacon-hand
> Glows world-wide welcome; her mild eyes command
> The air-bridged harbor that twin cities frame,
> "Keep, ancient lands, your storied pomp!" cries she
> With silent lips, "Give me your tired, your poor
> Your huddled masses yearning to breathe free,
> The wretched refuse of your teeming shore,
> Send those, the homeless, tempest-tost to me,
> I lift up my lamp beside the golden door!"[33]

"The New Colossus" had followed a large number of poems in whch Lazarus spoke of her Jewish identity.[34] The statue as the Mother of Exiles, a beacon for the diaspora, welcomed both Jew and Gentile from every shore, from every measure of tyranny and from imposed conformity. The poem extended the statue's image as a beacon of liberty to a new, unbridled tolerance of diversity. The wedded symbols—the poem and the statue—continued to convey this image over the next century. They portrayed the immigrant as the seed of a nation rather than as the catalyst of its demise. It was in keeping with this imagery that the country's most dramatic emphasis in immigration and plurality was affirmed in 1965 when President Lyndon Johnson signed an amendment to the Immigration and Nationality Act into law at the statue's base.

"The New Colossus"[35] was a very different image from the one that another Jewish émigré, Israel Zangwill, conceived. Just twenty-five years after Lazarus's composition, Zangwill looked somewhat closer at Manhattan for his dominant symbol, not of diversity but of the fusion of differences into a new, composite whole. In his play *The Melting Pot*[36] he focused on Ellis Island, which became a powerful image of the crucible in which old traditions were boiled away and in which a new, homogeneous, uniquely American identity was refined.

As voiced by the play's central character, David, the melting pot was seen as divinely ordained:

> America is God's Crucible, the great Melting-Pot where all the races of Europe are melting and re-forming! . . . when I see them at Ellis Island, here you stand in your fifty groups, with your fifty languages and histories, and your fifty blood hatreds and rivalries. But you won't be long like that, brothers, for these are the fires of God you've come to— . . . Germans and Frenchmen, Irishmen and Englishmen, Jews and Russians—into the Crucible with you all! God is making the American![37]

Although Zangwill was fully aware of the inhumane treatment received by some on Ellis Island, which he never sanctioned, the immigration center

Diversity or Pluralism	Homogeneity or Assimilation
Diversity is part of the American heritage as expressed in the Constitution and in the ideal of a liberal constitutional state.	The American experience emanates from the concept of the virtuous republic, which, as expressed in the Declaration of Independence, promotes the equality of its citizenry and by implication a desirable uniformity.
Religious freedom is guaranteed by the state.	While religious freedom may be an important principle, it is superseded by the value of a homogeneous Christian civilization, which was emphasized during the Great Awakenings.
The colonial experience in settlements such as Rhode Island, Pennsylvania, and New Netherland emphasized freedom of religion.	The colonial experience in settlements such as Massachusetts Bay, Connecticut, and Jamestown emphasized conformity to Christian ideals.
Freedom of expression includes areas of individual moral choices such as temperance, abortion, and speech.	Part of the duty of a republic is to promote a uniform level of morality and to actualize a public conscience through the concerted actions of individual citizens. This informs issues such as temperance, abortion, and speech.
In the frontier, Americans found opportunity for freedom and self-determinism.	The frontier provided an opportunity for the nation to reach its manifest destiny and for the advancement of Christian civilization.
Dialogue between different religions and cultures often leads to unity through diversity.	America holds the possibility of realizing its fullest potential as a Christian nation in which religious values and patriotism (civil religion) guide the republic.
The United States is best identified as a mosaic of religions and cultures.	American identity is defined by a larger national fabric, an amalgam of religions and cultures—the melting pot.
The nation's unique identity is derived from the interaction of diverse religions and cultures in the mosaic.	The nation's unique identity is derived from the amalgam of religions and cultures that is refined in the melting pot.
The most powerful symbol of the mosaic and of the freedom inherent in it is the Statue of Liberty.	A once-viable symbol of the melting pot was a point of arrival in the United States, Ellis Island.
Immigration is a historical process that has strengthened the mosaic.	Immigration is properly subject to the ongoing process of Americanization, or assimilation. However, if extended too far, it can jeopardize the process and the character of American society.
The American Dream is based on the exercise of free choice in a society that rewards perseverence and individualism.	The American Dream is innately related to the Protestant work ethic and rewards those who contribute to the common good.

Figure 1.10 A twofold American ideology

became a vivid symbol of America. As names were shortened or changed, so cultures and races were merged in a new, purified form.

"The New Colossus"[38] and *The Melting Pot*[39] came to symbolize the push and pull that some members of the Jewish community had experienced as they struggled both to retain their identity while living in a diaspora, and at the time to become American. The images conveyed in the poem and the play also came to be a metaphor of the struggle of other groups and of the clash of values that had become part of the American experience.

The notion of contradictory understandings of America is supported by a number of social theorists. The differences between a utopian vision of America and the plural characterization of race was stated by Gunnar Myrdal in *An American Dilemma*[40]

> The "American Dilemma" . . . is the ever-ranging conflict between, on the one hand, the valuations preserved on the general plane which we shall call the "American Creed," where the American thinks, talks, and acts under the influence of high national and Christian precepts, and, on the other hand, the valuations on specific planes of individual and group living, where personal and local interests; economic, social, and sexual jealousies; considerations of community prestige and conformity; group prejudice against particular persons or types of people; and all sorts of miscellaneous wants, impulses, and habits dominate his outlook.[41]

Myrdal talks of a sustained level of exploitation of minorities by the dominant white culture (and an "American Creed") that has been "legitimated by the legal-normative order of the larger society."[42]

A similar construct has been applied to the historical treatment of race by Ringer. In a comprehensive volume, *"We the People" and Others: Duality and America's Treatment of Its Racial Minorities*,[43] he suggests that the idea of plurality was the product of colonial leaders, who developed it as a means of subjugation. He suggests that racial minorities were viewed as having less status than the white citizenry. He states his central thesis:

> Through . . . colonial conquest, subjugation and forcible importation of nonwhites . . . the white European has characteristically imposed upon the nonwhite a racially-segmented Plural Societal Structure which he has dominated through the raw exercise of power. And in his quest for a permanent abode, he has characteristically created a colonist society in his own racial, religious and national image for himself and his fellow whites. The character of these dual structures, their linkage and relationships have varied with the national identity of the white European, the racial identity of the nonwhite proportions of each race, and historical circumstances.[44]

Ringer delineates two understandings of American society. The first is the notion of the People's Domain.[45] Its premises are conquest, paternalism, and an equation of citizenship with the best interests of Anglo-Saxon colonizers. The second understanding of society is pluralistic. It is defined by diverse minority groups, which are excluded from participation in the People's Domain. In making these assumptions, Ringer draws on the earlier work of a number of theorists including J.S. Furnivall, M.G. Smith, John Rex, Frantz Fanon, Pierre L. van den Berghe, and others.[46]

From the vantage point of the sociology of religion, Robert Bellah has argued in a similar vein for the role of two ideals in American history.[47] The first is the concept of the *Virtuous Republic*, which, as expressed in the Declaration of Independence, generates a homogeneous understanding of society. This is in sharp contrast to the second ideal, the notion of the *Liberal Constitutional State* expressed in the Constitution. The state, in this sense, encourages individual expression and assumes that individuals "would somehow be harmonized by the 'invisible hand' to produce the good society."[48] He concludes:

> Though formulated by some of the toughest minds in the history of modern philosophy—Hobbes, Locke, Hume, and Adam Smith—this tradition gave rise to what would appear to be the most wildly utopian idea in the history of political thought, namely, that a good society can result from the actions of citizens motivated by self-interest alone when those actions are organized through the proper mechanisms. A caretaker state, with proper legal restraints so that it does not interfere with the freedom of the citizens, needs to do little more than maintain public order and allow the economic market mechanisms and the free market in ideas to produce wealth and wisdom.[49]

For Bellah, the thread that has historically prevented sustained conflict between the two visions is the assumption that religion would provide consensus, holding the fabric of the nation together.[50]

The Pluralist Vision

As occasioned by these theories, the pluralist vision has emphasized the self-determinism of races and religions. It is the stepchild of the rationalist philosophy of the Enlightenment, in which human freedom was a cardinal principle. It is equally the offspring of Bellah's interrelated notion of the Liberal Constitutional State.

The pluralist position was also born of the experience of the early colonies. When a despotic director general, Peter Stuyvesant, recognized only one religion, Dutch Calvinism, in New Netherland, the managers of the Dutch West India Company refused to support him, wisely surmising that religious uniformity would not result in a thriving economy. Instead, they reasoned, a free marketplace based on the unhampered expression of diversity was a far better economic risk.

The thinking of the Quaker William Penn, the Baptist Roger Williams, and the Roman Catholic George Calvert, Lord Baltimore, was very different. As religious dissidents from the mainstream Anglicanism of the English Reformation, they had experienced persecution. But the result was the same as in New Netherland. They founded the colonies of Pennsylvania, Rhode Island, and Maryland based on religious freedom.

Another layer of ideology that was fused onto the pluralist position (and ironically onto the assimilationist position as well) was the utopian significance attached to the frontier. As Frederick Jackson Turner observed, the frontier was a vision of America that began with the arrival of the *Mayflower*.[51] The ideology was not a preconceived cargo that the *Mayflower* and the *Susan Constant* carried in their holds but rather a symbol of the expansiveness and opportunity that flourished in the new wilderness. The frontier offered escape from tyranny and, above all, greater opportunity for individual expression free from the oppressive expectations of traditional societies.

Yet another contributing element to the pluralist view was the American Dream. That dream, rooted in the seedbed of the frontier, emphasized pragmatism and individualism and recognized the right to be different as intrinsic to the American experience. (Ironically again, much like the frontier, it also contributed to the assimilationist position in that it united an image of limitless opportunity on the frontier with a religious zeal to build a uniform Christian civilization.)

The pluralist position, then, drawing on the Enlightenment, the imagery of the frontier, and the American Dream, sought freedom of expression. It envisioned a government that would allow diverse religious and ethnic groups to reach their own accord. Some of its seminal documents include the Virginia Bill for Establishing Religious Freedom, the Flushing Remonstrance, and the Constitution. Its most powerful symbol is the Statue of Liberty, which, as framed by Emma Lazarus's words from "The New Colossus,"[52] conveys a sense of receptivity for diverse and oppressed peoples.

In later expressions, such as Horace Kallen's theory of cultural pluralism,[53] the pluralist view has sought unity in the midst of diversity and has not assumed that consensus must be found in conformity. In this sense, it has suggested that the confluence of religions and cultures is not a divisive force in American life but instead is the very matrix around which the nation was conceived.

The Assimilationist Vision

The assimilationist vision of America as a homogeneous society had different origins from those of pluralism. Espousing the rhetoric of civil religion (whose symbols are those of God and country), the assimilationist ideology drew from the classical understanding of the republic as found in both Greek philosophy and, later, the Enlightenment. The customs of the republic were "public participation in the exercise of power, the political equality of the citizens, a wide distribution of small and medium property with few very rich or very poor—customs that will lead to a public spiritedness, a willingness of the citizen to sacrifice his own interests for the common good."[54] Because the republic is committed to equality and to the establishment of a principle of economic moderation in which there are no exploiters (the very rich) or exploited (the very poor), a level of homogeneity is assumed.

The homogenous view of America was like the pluralist position in that it also developed from direct experience, in which utopias were altered to suit political expediency. This experience capitalized on the process of colonial expansion. The colonial empires in North America were built as transplanted segments of European society. They assumed a subjugation of minorities and the establishment of an order in which the nature of the citizenry was uniform. The clearest examples of this domination were in the colonies of Massachusetts, Connecticut, and Virginia, where differences in race or religion were discouraged.

As Ringer suggests, America became the arena of the colonial mindset—that of the sojourner elite—in which the homeland was often not left fully behind.[55] At the same time, the new world became the home for the colonizer who decided to stay. Both the colonizer and the colonialist subjugated minorities and the expression of diversity to suit their own preconceived ends.[56]

The argument for homogeneity was given dynamic life by the two Great Awakenings of the eighteenth century. These religious revivals stirred American Christianity as no other movements had been able to do, instilling a fresh pietism and enthusiasm.

Sidney Ahlstrom suggests that the First Awakening, which flourished in the 1730s, had a unitive effect.[57] This came in two areas. The first was theological, a regeneration of the Puritan understanding of conversion. Conversion grew to transcend theological disagreements and became a focus around which the American experience of Protestantism could grow. The second area was demographic. The First Awakening united a diversified colonial empire and cemented it with religious zeal.

The Second Great Awakening, which began between 1790 and 1800, built on the fervor for revival of the first. It also continued to have a unifying effect by convincing the churches of the need for a Christian presence from coast to coast. In addition to inspiring this westward expansion, it generated yet another form of religious organization, the voluntary association.[58]

Because both Awakenings rallied a sense of unity that had hitherto been unexperienced and because they also emphasized conversion and pietism, their focus was not on freedom of religious expression or diversity. Instead, they nourished seed that had been planted long before in Europe. This was the utopian vision of a new land that had the promise of becoming the zenith of Christian civilization. This idea became the core of an assimilationist and amalgamationist position that America was not to lose.

The quest for homogeneity not only gained momentum in the churches where the two Awakenings inspired a zeal for conversion, it also found expression in Enlightenment rationalism. Steeped in Enlightenment thought, Benjamin Franklin spurned popular notions of evangelism. Nevertheless, he called for the establishment of a "public" religion.[59] The dominant characteristic of this new faith was to be a strong Protestant presence and the absence of competing beliefs that Franklin understood as superstitious. As a "public" tradition, his vision of a single, homogeneous faith was an early expression of what was later understood as civil religion.

The arguments for assimilation and amalgamation were expressions of a desire for a uniform or homogeneous society. Each was an ideology (or a utopian vision) that also became a social theory.[60] The assimilationist position sought a melding of differences to conform to the wishes of the majority. Its major historical expression was American nativism.[61] The amalgamationist position sought a process of fusion through which differences were realized in a new form stronger than any of its composite parts. The major expression of the amalgamationist position was the utopian vision of the melting pot. In the public eye, both ideologies shared a desire for societal uniformity and homogeneity that often did not distinguish between the different theories that composed them.

The desire for homogeneity, as has been suggested, also drew heavily from the ideology of the frontier. However, instead of understanding the frontier as a place where individualism and freedom of expression could reign unhampered, the homogeneous ideal saw the American wilderness as an expanse of opportunity for the advancement of Christian civilization. Its image was America's manifest destiny, and its God-given duty was to reach a pinnacle of Christian promise that traditional societies in Europe had been unable to achieve. Proponents of homogeneity have not focused on the question of religious or ethnic differences but on the homogeneous identification of an American. The homogeneous view drew support from the ongoing evolution of the American Dream, from the amalgamationist vision of the melting pot, and the assimilationist understanding of Americanization. It has emphasized the value of monoculturalism and monolingualism and the vehicles by which American identity is best perceived. Its symbols are those of the civil religion—God and country.

The argument for American homogeneity has insisted that the United

States has primarily been a Christian (if not a Protestant) nation. This condition, it has claimed, has been divinely ordained. While religions outside of the mainstream may be allowed to exist in a free republic, they are not associated with the nation's unique calling to exhibit a progressive Christian civilization.

Comparisons

Both the pluralist and the assimilationist/amalgamationist positions have shared a common assumption. Each has emphasized the importance of a single national identity and has based that identity on its own belief system.

Each position has also accepted some of what the other has had to say. For instance, even the staunchest advocate of religious and cultural pluralism would rarely deny that an American represents at least to a small degree, a mixture of cultures. There are unique accents, patterns of behavior, and even dietary traditions that are defined by regionalism and are part of the nation's still-evolving sense of identity. In the same way, few assimilationists would deny the validity of religious freedom as an important principle. Thus, in response to criticism. Israel Zangwill was quick to claim the Statue of Liberty as a symbol of the same freedom that the image of the melting pot conveyed.[62] In reality, this association did not apply; the imagery inspired by the Statue of Liberty remained quite different from the monoculturalism of the melting pot.

The two views have borrowed from each other because they both were influenced by three seminal ideologies in U.S. history: American individualism, the frontier, and the American Dream.

The association of American individualism with the pluralist position, which hinges on an understanding of freedom of expression, is well known. Such pivotal thinkers as John Locke were quick to underscore the importance of the individual—an idea that was easily adapted to the American experience of democracy and diversity.[63] In *Habits of the Heart: Individualism and Commitment in American Life*, Robert Bellah et al. have shown how individualism was also part of the understanding of the classical republic, which "evoked an image of the active citizen contributing to the public good."[64] Individualism was thus applied equally to the ideal of freedom of expression and to the role of a virtuous citizenry. The ideal of a virtuous citizen linked the individual with public service, moderation, and hence with a desirable uniformity.

The concept of the American frontier relied on an understanding of individualism to inform its own utopian interests. The frontier became a locus of opportunity for individual expression, for minority groups that sought it as a refuge, and for those who out of self-interest sought its riches. At the same time, it also became attractive to a homogeneous view that saw the geographical expanse as an opportunity to construct a fuller Christian civilization.

The American Dream became a funnel through which ideologies of individualism and the frontier were poured. The dream relied on the notions of individualism and freedom of expression for its appeal, especially in traditional societies in Europe and Asia where the role of the individual apart from family, clan, and caste was virtually unknown. At the same time, the dream also became the locus of the Protestant ethic in a society where conformity to the principles of hard work, ambition, and personal initiative promised to yield success. The dream was tied to the notion of the frontier and offered a vision of an expansive wilderness with endless opportunity both for those who sought refuge and security in which to express their diversity and for those who sought to build a homogeneous civilization.

In short, the American Dream evolved with a breadth that could not be the exclusive property of either those with a homogeneous view of a societal melting pot or of those who found value in a pluralistic mosaic. Because each ideology could find support in it, the dream became a confused portrait of American life. It did not resolve the differences between the two understandings of society but merely provided an outlet through which they could both be poured. The dream itself thus became a symbol of the continuing difficulty of the American experience to cope with the pervasive contradictions in its self-image and character.

Finally, the suggestion of this text that the two views of society are pervasive in American life is supported by points of similarity between two major theories—Ringer's concept of "We the People" and Bellah's understanding of the republic both emphasize the role of a citizenry that participates in the life of the state. For Bellah, citizens of the republic avoid the extremes of either wealth or poverty and by implication come to exhibit a certain level of uniformity. In Ringer's understanding of "the People," uniformity is a political device, established in a colonial environment to ensure continued prosperity and well-being.

Similarly, Bellah's understanding of a liberal constitutional state and Ringer's notion of a plural society share a basic assumption. In both cases, pluralism is understood as an intentional ordering of society. Diversity is not an accidental experience but an aspect of life that is accepted in order to achieve a particular end. An important difference in the arguments is that for Ringer the "plural society" is an invention of the colonial state to serve its own ends and to legitate the subjugation of minorities. For Bellah, plurality results from the ability of a liberal constitutional state to affirm the freedom of individual expression.

Yet, in the difference in these arguments is still another contradiction—

America's self-image as housing a utopian view of tolerance and freedom of expression and at the same time the reality that much of the nation's history has, as Ringer concludes, used plurality as a means to an end.

For this discussion, what matters is the unavoidable conclusion that the two ideologies of American heterogeneity and uniformity have had a variety of significant causes. They have shared some of the same origins and are broad and pervasive enough to house theories drawn from both the history of events and of ideas. What Bellah has defined in terms of philosophy and utopias, Ringer has continued in a historical context where ideologies frequently were bent or broken to suit the needs of those in power. What this text hopes to add to the discussion is an understanding of the way in which the two visions of America hold a continuing, pervasive influence in a variety of avenues of American life.

The Influence of the Two Visions on Social Issues

In the religioethnic mix, the contradictory visions of diversity and uniformity have influenced the treatment of minority groups. They have affected such divisive national issues as the treatment of Roman Catholics and Mormons in the nineteenth century as well as the struggle over slavery. They have been especially visible in disputes over immigration. The contradiction has also been important in a variety of other current issues that impinge on the nation's continuing identity.

Affirmative Action

The most obvious and the most heated of these concerns has been civil rights. The reforms in the area of equal rights for black Americans and the accompanying societal upheaval were typical of the conflict that the contradictory views have historically produced. The conflict raised queries of identity, both for the minority groups that have sought equal status in and access to public life and for the society as a whole.

An example of a particular civil rights struggle debated in the context of the contradictory views is affirmative action. In the mid 1970s, the debate was focused on a case in California that eventually reached the Supreme Court.[65] Allan Bakke, a thirty-two-year-old mechanical engineer, applied to medical school at the University of California at Davis. His grades were good, and he was optimistic of acceptance.

The university's newly formed medical school wrestled with the question of admission of minority students. The number of minority students in the first entering class was extremely low, and the school resolved to create an affirmative action program to remedy the situation.

In spring 1973, Bakke learned that he had been rejected. Claiming reverse discrimination as the reason, he contended that because sixteen seats in the entering class had been reserved for minority candidates, he had been prevented from applying for all one hundred openings. Applying once more, he was rejected again. Subsequently, a lawsuit was filed with the Yolo County Superior Court charging that he had been discriminated against.

The premise of Allan Bakke's attack on affirmative action was a vision of a homogeneous society where equal opportunities were available to all persons regardless of race. Discrimination was perceived as an iniquity not because in the past it had prevented minority students from gaining admission to the medical school but rather because it was being used as a determining factor in selecting students at all. Bakke thus contended that the inequity of a racially induced quota system had prevented him from gaining admission to a school that he was well qualified to enter. The school's contention that minority students had been denied an equivalent preparatory education, and therefore did not score as high on entrance examinations was, in this view, irrelevant, since the university had chosen to discriminate in order to correct the inequity. In the end, what mattered was not the needs of diverse minority groups but the larger principles of the society itself, which, in Bakke's view, must be color blind, treating all Americans as essentially the same.

Opponents of Bakke's position lauded affirmative action as an appropriate means of insuring the rights of minorities to equal opportunity. In so doing, they supported the premise that racial differences were an important means of identification in a society that was founded on the freedom of individuals and groups to express their uniqueness. The preferential treatment of minorities was not only seen as a way of redressing discrimination in the past but also by implication was an affirmation that society was never uniform or homogeneous either by birth or opportunity.

Bakke's suit in California was ultimately won. The eventual decision of the Supreme Court to review the decision symbolized the fervor that came to surround the debate as reverse discrimination became a national issue. The Supreme Court's decision was ambiguous and attempted to settle the issue by ruling that, as a principle, affirmative action was valid. It also held that Bakke had been treated unfairly and should be admitted. For the public, the ruling increased the confusion on the issue, which remained a subject of ongoing debate.

Following the Bakke decision and the popularization of the argument for reverse discrimination, a landmark case was decided by the Supreme Court in 1986.[66] The Court denied the right of the Jackson, Michigan, school board to lay off teachers to give preference to minority applicants. But, in so doing, it also affirmed the principle of affirmative action as long as it was narrowly applied to cases where actual discrimination could be demonstrated.

The decision reflected the Court's attempt again to temper the contradiction and a vociferous national debate. While the decision of the school board to implement a quota system was rejected, the principle of racial diversity was affirmed. This was demonstrated by a partial concurring decision of Justice Sandra O'Connor, who wrote:

> Although its precise contours are uncertain, a state interest in the promotion of racial diversity has been found sufficiently "compelling," at least in the context of higher education, to support the use of racial consideration in furthering that interest.[67]

Thus, much as in the Bakke decision, the Court's stance on the debate in Jackson reflected an ongoing struggle with the contradiction of homogeneity and diversity. The decision, as argued by O'Connor, affirmed the principle of diversity in American life. Yet, it also created confusion, since it left the particular issue unresolved and the Jackson school board racially homogeneous.

On July 2, 1986, the Court brought greater clarity to the issue of affirmative action when it ruled in favor of a lower court order that required a sheet metal worker's union to meet a quota for minority membership.[68] The Court ruled that racial preferences for minorities were justified even if they benefited persons who had not actually been discriminated against.

The Court also approved an affirmative action plan of the city of Cleveland.[69] An organization of black and Hispanic fire fighters had sued the city for discrimination in hiring practices. Ruling against the Reagan administration, which had supported the city, the Court held that Title VII (of the Civil Rights Act of 1964) "permits employers and unions voluntarily to make use of reasonable race-conscious affirmative action."[70]

While both decisions showed clearer support of affirmative action than had been true in the recent past, they still held a certain ambiguity. This was particularly true of the consideration of how strong a case the Court would require to allow affirmative action as a remedy. Moreover, as in other affirmative action cases (see also *United Steelworkers v. Weber*, 1979, and *Memphis Firefighters v. Stotts*, 1984)[71] the Court was divided, reflecting the ongoing struggle with the issue and the diverse philosophies that have informed it.

In April 1987 the Court again ruled on affirmative action. In a 6 to 3 decision the justices argued that the Santa Clara County Transportation Agency in California could consider sex and race in its employment practices.[72] The Court's decision went against the claim of Paul Johnson, a white male, who claimed that he had experienced reverse discrimination when a road dispatcher's position was awarded to a female, Diane Joyce, despite the fact that Johnson had scored higher than Joyce on a examination.

Although the Santa Clara decision further clarified the affirmative action issue, the debate continued. In a dissenting opinion, Justice Antonin Scalla argued that the goals of a society that did not discriminate on the basis of race or sex and that also observed proportional hiring practices on those bases were incompatible. Scalla's dissent not only represented an important reaction in the Court but also affirmed a significant measure of public opinion.

Immigration

As the civil-rights movement in the 1960s achieved more and more victories, both in law and in public attitude, so at the same time the nation dealt with another significant change in its experience of diversity, a change resulting from a new policy toward immigration. The United States has a long history of statutes and court decisions restricting immigration. Among the most influential were the Immigration Acts of 1917, 1921, and 1924, which for the next four decades effectively barred Asian peoples from emigrating to the United States. A Supreme Court decision, *The United States v. Bhagat Singh Thind* (1922), reinforced the exclusion of Asian Indians. Thind, a Sikh, had contended that he was of Aryan descent and could therefore be considered Caucasian. Subsequent decisions, most notably *Porterfield v. Webb* (1923), *Terrace v. Thompson* (1923), and *Webb v. O'Brien* (1923), upheld state alien land legislation that had barred Orientals from owning property or from entering into contracts with citizens who did.[73]

A significant new law, the McCarran-Walter Act, had been passed in 1952 but had not altered the admission of only token numbers of Oriental immigrants. In 1965 President Lyndon Johnson signed into law the first major change in United States immigration policy since 1924. The amendment to the National Origins Act succeeded in opening the nation's doors much wider to persons from the Eastern Hemisphere.

In the wake of the Vietnam War, additional changes in the requirements for the entrance of refugees into the nation again raised the level of diversity. Vietnamese, Cambodians, Laotians, and numbers of tribal peoples entered the country.

The reaction to such a dramatic increase in diversity has been predictable and has been well within the historical pendulum of thought that has both welcomed diversity and then sought ways to eliminate it. Thus, in years following the amendment to the Immigration and Nationality Act and the Refugee Act of 1980, a significant backlash has developed. Perceiving the need for limiting immigration, supporters of this position lobbied for yet a new law, which became the Simpson-Mazzoli Bill. After considerable debate, the bill became the Immigration Reform and Control Act of 1986. It significantly changed immigration policy by granting amnesty to some illegal aliens and requiring documentation for employment of aliens.

Abortion

Another national struggle that has become a volatile issue for the religious community and that reflects the same contradictory views is abortion.[74] Significantly, neither the freedom-of-choice nor the pro-life position is solely concerned with a moral issue. Rather, each argument is also deeply embedded in the continuing debate between advocates of homogeneity or diversity in American society.

Linkage between the debate about abortion and the contradictory views of American life is also demonstrated historically by other issues of moral reform that have been advocated by religious groups to bring Christian civilization to America and, in the process, to create a homogeneous society. The clearest example is the Christian drive for temperance in the nineteenth century, which sought a homogeneous national policy. An Episcopal bishop in Ohio expressed the prevailing public sentiment on the issue when he proclaimed that "no effort can be effectual without being universal."[75] Following the rise and wane of the Depression, the issue's spector still reappears in the difference between those states that seek to control distribution of alcoholic beverages and those that do not.

The similarity of the arguments is not a contrast between the issues of temperance and abortion, which would be a ludicrous comparison. Rather, what is very much the same is the insistence of a religious body that an overwhelmingly important issue of morality be decided universally with no room for diversity of opinion or expression. This has been a characteristic of American Christianity in its zealous search for the complete realization of a Christian civilization. The debate over abortion reflects this same dynamic, which is locked in a struggle with the equally zealous concern for the maintenance of individual rights and self-determination.

Thus, persons advocating the pro-life position are also insistent that abortion not only be rejected by the church but by society in general. As a result of this conviction, the pro-life argument has sought the passage of a constitutional amendment that would compel the nation to adopt a single point of view.

It is important, however, to note that the ideology or vocabulary of a "pro-abortion" stance has not been a dominant argument on the other side. Instead, the opposition to the pro-life argument has been conceptualized as freedom of choice. Leaders argue that abortion should be permitted because it is a religious issue, which by virtue of the Constitution, cannot be legislated. Supporters of the women's movement also suggest that the freedom to choose abortion is a basic right that is connected with the rights of individuals to have control over their own bodies.

While the intensity of debate over abortion reflects vast differences of opinion on the moral issue, it has also become volatile because of the contradictory views of American society. It is the struggle between advocates of a societal reform considered so important that it cannot be compromised and advocates of self-determination. Because the debate is perceived in this extreme manner, a middle ground has rarely emerged. Instead, supporters of each point of view have vigorously continued to argue their position, which for each is historically linked to questions of the separation of church and state and the role of the individual in American society.

An Official Language

The contradictory views have engendered profound debate in education focusing on the question of language. Following the popular debate surrounding bilingual education, its most heated source is the proposed amendment to the Constitution to legitimatize English as the nation's official language (see figure 1.11). In 1986 a similar measure became an amendment to the California state constitution. Twelve other states have adopted laws making English the official language. Thus the movement is not an isolated California phenomenon but has become national.[76]

This debate has had important historical precedents. In Pennsylvania, for example, at the turn of the century, public reaction to the proliferation of German newspapers in the state produced a heated argument. At issue was the use of German as a medium of instruction in public education. Proponents of German in the Pennsylvania German parts of the state lost ground. In 1905 Pennsylvania passed a law that forbade the use of any language other than English in public schools.[77] The anti-German sentiments in the United States during World War I ended further debate.

Today, while the focus of the issue has shifted from German to Spanish, with the presence of large numbers of Spanish-speaking peoples in the United States, the dynamics remain much the same. The debate is not only a source of popular discussion but is also the subject of professional debate among two organizations—the National Association for Bilingual Education and Teachers of English to Speakers of Other Languages.

The debate has involved profound differences in theory. Discussions have focused on the importance of offering students who have emigrated to the United States, and whose primary tongue is not English, continuing instruction in their native languages. On the one hand, propo-

99TH CONGRESS
1ST SESSION

H. J. RES. 96

Proposing an amendment to the Constitution of the United States establishing English as the official language of the United States.

IN THE HOUSE OF REPRESENTATIVES

JANUARY 24, 1985

Mr. SHUMWAY (for himself, Mr. BADHAM, Mr. HANSEN, Mr. HYDE, Mr. KINDNESS, Mr. MCCANDLESS, Mr. MCCOLLUM, Mr. NIELSON of Utah, Mr. PACKARD, Mr. PORTER, Mr. RUDD, Mr. SUNDQUIST, and Mr. WHITEHURST) introduced the following joint resolution; which was referred to the Committee on the Judiciary

JOINT RESOLUTION

Proposing an amendment to the Constitution of the United States establishing English as the official language of the United States.

Resolved by the Senate and House of Representatives of the United States of America in Congress assembled (two-thirds of each House concurring therein), That the following article is proposed as an amendment to the Constitution of the United States, which shall be valid as a part of the Constitution if ratified by the legislatures of three-fourths of the several States:

"ARTICLE —

"SECTION 1. The English language shall be the official language of the United States.

"SECTION 2. Neither the United States nor any State shall require, by law, ordinance, regulation, order, decree, program, or policy, the use in the United States of any language other than English.

"SECTION 3. This article shall not prohibit any law, ordinance, regulation, order, decree, program, or policy requiring educational instruction in a language other than English for the purpose of making students who use a language other than English proficient in English.

"SECTION 4. The Congress and the States may enforce this article by appropriate legislation.".

A similar resolution has been introduced in the U.S. Senate by Senator Steve Symms (S.J. Res. 20), and co-sponsored by Senators Quentin Burdick, Jeremiah Denton, James Abdnor, James McClure, John East and Ed Zorinsky.

Figure 1.11 A joint resolution to make English the nation's official language, an expression of the argument for homogeneity

nents of bilingual education contend that instruction in their native language assists students in obtaining the education to which they are entitled. On the other hand, supporters of English as a second language suggest that instruction in a student's native tongue cannot always be assured, particularly in the case of esoteric languages in nonmetropolitan areas. But, they claim, such instruction is also beside the point, as it retards a student's ability to be assimilated and to become part of the mainstream.

The debate has also been highly politicized. The support of the Reagan administration for English as a second language has rapidly placed bilingual education in a secondary position. Particularly, for bilingual teachers, the issue has become one of economic survival.

Free Speech in Shopping Malls

A less visible issue that incorporates much of the same contradiction and that has a direct bearing on the character of public life has been the issue of freedom of speech in shopping malls. As public life has narrowed, "the mall has become the equivalent of the village green in colonial America."[78] As "main street" shopping areas are rapidly becoming antiquated and attract fewer shoppers, so in the same way there are increasingly fewer places where public life can be experienced. An emerging option to replace "main street" is the shopping mall. Increasing numbers of teenagers, elderly, and persons who have been deinstitutionalized find the atmosphere of the mall to be a place where they can experience community life.

Shopping malls are remarkably homogeneous institutions. A visitor to any two cities can, without much difficulty, find malls that are remarkably similar. While stores may differ in name, the mixture of small shops, specializing in exotic cookies, men's and women's wear, sporting goods, and a variety of other attractions, combined with large department store chains, typifies the environment. Differences in decor are of minor significance when compared with the uniformity of the overall atmosphere, which maybe climate-controlled and unaffected by changes of night or day.

This remarkable degree of conformity is the result of a national marketing phenomenon. Marketing uniformity and the development of chain stores and franchises have produced not only a remarkable similarity in products but in the environment within which they are purchased. However, the issue of conformity in the marketplace is not just the result of Madison Avenue planning. Rather, at its root, it is the degree to which Americans are more comfortable in a uniform environment where differences of opinion (or environment) are reduced and where the "norm" is a clearly perceived part of American life.

The interest of political groups in distributing leaflets or demonstrating in malls is an expression of diversity. To some mall owners, this has been perceived as a threat to the uniform atmosphere of the mall, which is in their view most conducive to commerce.

In several states, the issue has been taken to court. Malls have not just limited access to political organizations but have also opposed the use of their facilities by other apolitical groups that nevertheless are an expression of diversity. In some cities, mall owners have experienced conflict when different segments of the community have sought to use the mall as a place to congregate. Gatherings of senior citizens, persons who have been released from mental institutions, and others wishing to assemble may be viewed as a threat. Mall owners have perceived such gatherings of persons who exhibit significant differences as a hindrance to the "normal" flow of commerce. The issue thus raises the far larger concern about the segregation or mainstreaming of such persons within the society.

Interdenominational Divisions

Finally, it is important to note the struggle within the denominational system. One form has been the continued plurality of American Christianity, which is nurtured through splits, schisms, new movements, and transplanted religions. The other is the trend in some Christian circles toward merger, consolidation, and homogeneity.

The issue has been internalized in a number of mainline Protestant traditions as well as in American Catholicism. The discussion has been evident particularly in the Southern Baptist faith, where the conservative evangelical appeal and the desire for biblical literalism have produced a profound division from members of the faith more inclined to accept diversity. This debate is often interpreted as a dispute between theological conservatism and liberalism. Yet, its roots are far broader and extend back to the deeply seated struggle about pluralism in American society.

The Two Visions as a Global Issue

Pluralism is a global phenomenon. In many countries, as well as in the United States, extreme diversity is becoming a common experience, leading to tension between the pluralist and assimilationist positions. A few countries have attempted to resolve the tension by adopting multiculturalism as public policy. This has been true in Canada and Australia, where dramatic ideological shifts were precipitated by changes in government.

Canadian Policy

In 1971, the Canadian House of Commons proclaimed that the nation was officially a multicultural society.[79] This affirmation had come after the publication of the Royal Commission Report on Bilingualism and Biculturalism a year earlier. The report and the issue itself reflected the desire of then Prime Minister Pierre Trudeau to create a national ideology rooted in the premise of cultural diversity. The ideology reflected the historical role of French and English cultures and the struggle for their coexistence in a pluralistic society.

The official multiculturalist policy included a number of concerns— "Prime Minister Trudeau envisioned a society in which: members of all cultural groups would have equal economic, social, and political opportunities; the distinctiveness of a number of separate cultural groups would be encouraged . . . national unity would be brought about by interaction among diverse cultural groups."[80]

Trudeau's vision of a pluralistic society was one in which minority groups would enjoy cultural autonomy and have their distinctiveness supported by the government. He expected the autonomy of each group to be balanced by their willingness to interact and to contribute to the nation's spirit and identity. A sense of national unity would, he posited, be a tangible result.

The ramifications of the Trudeau policy were felt throughout Canadian society, all the way from the creation of new offices of government to the way in which religious denominations perceived interfaith relationships. The United Church of Canada, for example, created the position of interfaith officer, who had major responsibilities in developing networks among adherents of all major religions in the nation. Successful dialogue projects involving such diverse groups as Hindus, Muslims, Christians, Buddhists, and Jews evolved in major cities such as Vancouver and Toronto. Such efforts were warmly received by the government as an apt expression of an officially sanctioned multiculturalist policy.

Australian Policy

In 1972, a year after the Canadian experiment had begun, Australia experienced a dramatic shift of national response to ethnic diversity.[81] With the election of the Edward Gough Whitlam labor government in December of that year, decades of assimilationist policies were overturned.

Prior to the Whitlam victory, there had been little doubt about the government's disapproving attitude toward pluralism. The minister of immigration had been quoted as saying:

> We must have a single culture—if immigration implied multi-cultural activities within Australian society, then it was not the type Australia wanted. I am quite determined we should have a monoculture, with everyone living in the same way, understanding each other, and sharing the same aspirations. We don't want pluralism.[82]

The change in governmental attitude toward multiculturalism was crafted
by Minister of Immigration Al Grassby. Although he was defeated in the
parliamentary election of 1974, he laid the foundations for the more
defined multiculturalist policy of the new John Malcolm Fraser government of 1975. In so doing, he made a variety of changes:

> [He] . . . had introduced the new points system, extended the assisted
> passage scheme to all races, abolished discrimination in trans-Tasman
> travelling, reduced the five-year naturalization period to three, made
> things easier for non-European students, allowed free overseas travel by
> Aborigines and abolished all race statistics and special records of non-
> European migration.[83]

Grassby had been recognized as a champion of ethnic affairs and had
become a symbol, through his policies and his personal response to
diversity, of a new attitude. One accolade left little doubt about the
contrast of his policies with those before him:

> . . . when he spoke to a migrant he did take trouble to pronounce his
> name. He also learned something of the historical background of Aus-
> tralia's ethnic groups and acquired a smattering of languages.[84]

Following Grassby's initiative, a Department of Immigration and Ethnic Affairs was established under the Fraser government. An ethnic affairs
unit was also established under the Department of the Prime Minister.
The word ethnic quickly became part of popular jargon.[85] Moreover, the
government let it be known that instead of understanding immigration as
a threat to the economy, it saw immigration only as an asset. Claims that
an influx of foreign laborers would result in a loss of employment were
contested and not sanctioned as official policy.

These positions were affirmed in the Galbally Report, in which a
variety of recommendations were made for the further implementation of
a multiculturalist policy.[86] Teaching English as a second language was
encouraged, as was the creation of local multicultural centers. Ethnic
broadcasting was touted along with a variety of other programs all designed to stimulate the government's stated ideological position.

The Fraser multiculturalist philosophy firmly recognized cultural pluralism as a national philosophy. However, the policy was carefully crafted
so that it included significant references to "integration" or assimilation.
Members of migrant cultures were urged to integrate and to adopt Australian patterns of life but not to forgo their heritage. The policy thus
internalized the contradiction rather than anchoring its position in one
philosophical extreme, which could be easily attacked. At the same time it
left ample room for the historical pattern of Anglo-Saxon dominance. This

was indicated by the failure of the multiculturalist policy to recommend or receive adequate financial support.[87]

Problems of Multiculturalism

Unlike either the Australian or Canadian experiences, the United States has never evolved a unified policy that has allowed it to affirm pluralism or cultural assimilation as a national ideology. This is not to suggest, however, that societal problems surrounding the issue of diversity will be resolved by the adoption of a single ideology. Rather, it is to imply that a reduction in tension resulting from the elimination of the two conflicting visions can yield a greater possibility for approaching the issue of diversity constructively. Even in such a case, however, there are other problems to consider.

The success of multiculturalism, for example, has been shown to be relative to a number of factors, not the least of which is the political environment. In Australia, the multiculturalist policy of the Fraser government became politically expedient and in many instances was poorly implemented. In Canada, the experience has been more successful and has been helpful in creating a national understanding and acceptance of diversity.

Also it should not be implied that public policy by itself can eliminate the tension between conflicting ideologies with long histories. Perhaps the most obvious example of the failure of public policy in this regard is apartheid. As the official policy of the government of South Africa, apartheid has sought to maintain a homogeneous level of societal control by economically, politically and geographically segregating diverse elements. Because the policy has been that of a white government with a colonialist mindset and not that of the black majority, it has led to unrest and has precipitated revolution. This is in sharp contrast to the Canadian experience in which a multiculturalist policy met the needs of the government and of large segments of the society.

Each of these national situations has some similarities to the struggle over the question of diversity or homogeneity in different periods in the United States. Yet, they differ in that in the United States, while a variety of elements of public policy have affirmed both pluralism and homogeneity, they rarely, if ever, have claimed either as the nation's only official, ongoing means of self-identification. Since the earliest colonial times both in public policy and in dominant societal attitudes, the United States has linked both the assimilationist and pluralist positions with its national self-image. At the same time, it has developed powerful ideologies to bolster each point of view. Because the issue of diversity and identity has not been resolved and has repeatedly been associated with the nation's very reason for being, the debate has had a significant role in the continuing

American experience. The remainder of this text will explore the dimensions of its impact in a number of ways.

Chapter 2 demonstrates some of the historical foci of the debate, which have had important consequences for the ongoing history of the nation. Chapter 3 examines the ideological presuppositions of the discussion. It shows the ambiguity about diversity in the American Dream and the nature of subsequent ideologies, including the melting pot and cultural pluralism. These ideologies have crystalized historical understandings of unity and diversity in the nation's history. They have also been simultaneous expressions of national identity. This dynamic, in particular, has made the debate between the nation's self-image as a homogeneous American amalgam on one hand and a rich, diversified mosaic of religions and cultures on the other, intense and acutely volatile.

Chapter 4 examines the nature of the debate in the denominational milieu. It shows how the denominational system has assimilated diverse religions and their struggle to retain important aspects of identity and diversity.

Chapter 5 examines the effect of the debate on community conflict. It suggests that because the nation has affirmed both a vision of religiocultural conformity and an often simultaneous and conflicting vision of diversity, there has been a great deal of confusion on a local level. This is not to suggest that the debate has caused community conflict but that it has created a vacuum in which conflict has frequently been allowed to flourish. As a result of this vacuum, society has been unable to provide mediating structures between the mainstream and persons and groups who are most different from it.

Finally, chapter 6 examines a variety of models of mediating agencies and structures. It offers these as examples of ways in which the society can not only become more aware of its stereotypes about minorities but can also submerge the conflict to prevent it from becoming confrontational. The models are drawn from a variety of areas including education, health care, and interfaith dialogue.

CHAPTER 2

One Nation-Divisible

The history of ethnic and religious diversity in North America reflects the conflict between divergent ideologies. Crystalizing in the colonial period, two opposing visions of a civilized world became dominant, as described in chapter 1. One, drawing on Enlightenment philosophy and the notion of the liberal constitutional state, was pluralistic and incorporated an understanding of society where a variety of religions and races were not only welcomed but expected. The other, influenced by the Greek and Enlightenment understanding of the republic, was homogeneous and was nurtured by a profound insistence that society be of a single, undifferentiated type. That second view saw North America as the logical extension of Christian civilization in a renewed and purified form. [1]

As both ideologies developed during the colonial period, they vigorously shaped the history of the United States. The curious result of their combined and often conflicting influences has been a national self-image that is muddled and confused.

After demonstrating the ways in which the colonial period helped forge the two contradictory understandings of America, this chapter examines several of the public issues on which they have focused: slavery, anti-Catholicism, and the subjugation of the American Indian. The chapter then explores the dynamics surrounding immigration and the public reaction to the nation's increase in diversity from 1820 to 1924. It concludes with a description of a brief interlude in an expanding drive to limit plurality—the 1893 Parliament of Religions—and the legislation that shut the nation's door to further Asian immigration thereafter.

Pluralism and the Colonial Experience

The experience of pluralism differed greatly among the various European colonies in North America. These included the Spanish in the south and west and the northern European settlements on the east coast and in the Ohio and Mississippi valleys.

The Spanish Colonies and the Indians

The earliest Europeans to come to the Americas in any numbers were the Spanish. Initially they were conquerors and priests. In the wake of the Spanish Inquisition, in which thousands of religious dissidents had been tortured or killed, the Spanish conquistadors brought with them a vision of conquest and conversion that tolerated diversity only if it was not an obstacle to absolute cultural dominance.

From 1540 to 1542 Don Francisco Vásquez de Coronado led an expedition into what is now New Mexico.[2] Coronado's lust for gold and his search for the legendary seven cities of Cibola resulted in little more than frustration and defeat. When an initial venture failed to turn up either Cibola or the gold, Coronado pushed farther into what is now Kansas. Although he was soon forced to end his quest, he left behind a trail of missionaries, who initiated a more tolerant approach to the Indians in the land that was their new home.

The priests who established missions after Coronado departed did so for a variety of motives.[3] Foremost was the urge to colonize those areas that had just been "conquered." Second was the desire for personal recognition, often at the cost of martyrdom. Third was an intense desire to baptize and convert the Indian population. While such a view could not be considered pluralist, it did recognize the Indians as a people who, once baptized, could be assured of salvation.

In some quarters, there was a stronger insistence that the Indian was not only to be converted but also to be treated with dignity and respect. The Dominican friar Bartolomé de Las Casas was perhaps the most outspoken representative of this point of view.[4] Early in the sixteenth century, he openly advocated fair treatment of the Indian population in Honduras, where he was a missionary. Subsequently, he was scoffed at by members of the government, the Spanish aristocracy, and the church, who dismissed his views as absurd.

While Las Casas's views were not accepted at the time, they came to symbolize a new and even more tolerant position among the conquistadors and the clergy, which coincided with the wane of the Spanish Empire. By the end of the sixteenth century, the fortunes of the Spanish in Europe had begun to fade as had their quest for dominion in the Americas. As the zeal for settlement replaced the vision of conquest, so the Spanish began to perceive the colonial empire in a new way. They now came to North America not so much to seek victory or gold to take back to Spain as to live in the new land. This changed understanding was dramatized by a new type of leader, the colonist who established settlements rather than waged war.[5]

A case in point was the expedition of Don Juan de Oñate, who in 1598 with a small band of soldiers marched north from Chihauhua, Mexico, into what is now New Mexico.[6] Oñate's men had few intentions of subduing or even fighting the numerous tribes of Pueblo Indians they encountered. Even if conquest had been a primary objective, their numbers surely prohibited such a useless venture. Instead, Oñate brought a new vision of colonization that sought to implant Spanish rule by decree rather than by the sword. Indigenous Indian cultures, in this new view, were understood as part of the expanding colonial empire rather than as an enemy who was an obstacle in its way.

Perhaps the strongest evidence of this new view was the readiness of Oñate's band, and others who followed, to intermarry with the indigenous Indian population. Such a consideration had rarely been part of the design for control that the conquistadors had followed even a century before. But Oñate's men, unlike those of his predecessors, carried the implements of an extended stay—"plows, seeds, sheep, and axes."[7]

Northern European Colonies and the Indians

The tolerant Spanish view of colonization differed remarkably from the views in the majority of the other European settlements that were soon established in the seventeenth century on the East Coast. There the Indians were often ignored unless they became a menace to the process of colonization.[8] In other instances, they were seen as potential military allies. This was especially true in such conflicts as the French and Indian War in the eighteenth century. Algonquins, Hurons, and Mohawks became important sources of warriors in the dispute, which contested the claim of both the French and English to parts of North America. Although Indians in this instance were viewed as a tactical commodity, in other situations they were seen with much less concern and often exterminated outright. The comparison with the level of tolerance of such colonists as Don Juan de Oñate is startling:

> Looking at . . . [Oñate's] tiny column through the perspective of history helps one understand why the Indian cultures in its path survived while those of Eastern America did not. The English brought with them the concept of racial superiority and the metaphysics of Puritanism, Calvinism, and the idea of "salvation of the elect and damnation of the many." Among the English and Dutch there were no niggling,

time wasting doubts and arguments about the Indians. Unless they got in the way, they were let alone. If the white man wanted their land, they were driven out or exterminated, with neither malice nor intended cruelty. Lord Amherst, representing the British Crown in the English colonies, suggested that smallpox be spread among the savages to clear the land for more rapid development by the Christians, but germ warfare had not yet been perfected and nothing came of the idea. The English colonists moved slowly and left no Indian cultures behind them. They would have found the expedition of Oñate hard to understand.[9]

Most of the English, Dutch, and Germans who settled the original thirteen colonies on the Eastern Seaboard would indeed have had little patience with Oñate's vision of life.

Colonies That Welcomed Religious Diversity

If there was little argument in the Eastern Seaboard colonies about the role of the Indian, there was far less consensus about the level of tolerance that was to be extended to diverse religious groups. As the colonies became more established, profound differences in the visions of society developed. Some colonies from the beginning were havens for religious and other cultural diversity. Other colonies were founded on a close interdependence between church and state that reflected a homogeneous world view.

The northern colonies that welcomed religious and cultural diversity (in different periods in their history) were New York, Rhode Island, Pennsylvania, and Maryland. In each of them, however, tolerance for diversity evolved for very different reasons.

In New York for a brief thirty-eight-year period, beginning with the purchase of land in 1626 until the English took it in 1664, the Dutch had dominion. From the outset, the interests of the Dutch West India Company were entirely commercial. They saw New Netherland as a profitable venture, unhampered either by other European interests or by hostile natives. In addition, they believed that in order to secure the best possible trading economy, all forms of religion must be tolerated.

This precedent in the new world was challenged both by Dutch clerics and by director generals who insisted that the Dutch Reformed Church must become the official religion of the land. This insistence became particularly strong under the often despotic rule of the famed director general Peter Stuyvesant. Stuyvesant became irate when any religious group that he considered at all unorthodox tried to settle in New Netherland. Included in this category were Jews and Quakers, who, when they ventured into the port city of New Amsterdam, were treated with either contempt or physical abuse.[10] Ultimately, in support of the colony's inherent diversity, the citizenry pressed their demands for change in the policy of the settlement toward newcomers. Their concern was voiced in the Flushing Remonstrance, which has since been viewed as one of the seminal documents in the history of religious freedom in North America. In the end, both the Dutch West India Company and public pressure overruled Stuyvesant, who was forced to allow diversity to thrive. By the time the colony was appropriated by the English in 1664, its level of diversity and its thriving commercial economy had become well established.

Unlike New Netherland, which saw diversity as a component part of a successful commercial venture, the smaller colony of Rhode Island began as a sanctuary for religious dissidents. Founded by the Baptist Roger Williams in 1654, the tiny settlement quickly became a haven for persons who were persecuted because of their religious beliefs. It was an outgrowth of Williams's own battles with the courts of the Massachusetts Bay Colony and with the Puritan Reformers of the Church of England, who controlled it. Williams argued for a separation of church and state, purging the corruption that in his view came about inevitably through the church's association with government. This view led him to become a staunch advocate of religious freedom for all persons, Christian and non-Christian alike.

It is noteworthy that, while pushed by his own convictions in this liberal position, Williams's own theological bent was extremely conservative.[11] He advocated a biblically based way of life that included the express wish that the true Christian would dress and behave exactly as the Bible, in Williams's view, specified.

Rhode Island attracted persons from many religious traditions; it included Jews, Baptists, and Quakers, all of whom had been treated with disdain and even outright hostility in the other New England colonies. The settlement was soon regarded as a refuge for scoundrels and misfits and was popularly identified as "Rogues Island." It remained, however, one of the clearest examples of a distinctly pluralist ideology as the founding principle of a new world settlement.

Like Rhode Island, both Pennsylvania and Maryland developed as sanctuaries for religious diversity. Of the two, perhaps the more noteworthy, was Pennsylvania, which under the leadership of William Penn, became a refuge for groups that were identified with the left wing of the Reformation. It especially welcomed Quakers, who practiced a faith that many New England Puritans thought to be immoral and depraved. At the same time, it created a diverse cultural environment that attracted great numbers of Germans and enabled their strong cultural identities to be perpetuated.

Although Pennsylvania was more tolerant of diversity than the vast majority of colonies, it is important also to remember that some groups did experience discrimination. For example, Jews in Philadelphia did not enjoy the same civil rights as Christians. A rabbi concluded in 1783: "No Jew can be a member of the General Assembly [of the Representatives of the Freemen] of Pennsylvania. . . . But there is no impediment of a Jew, being an Officer of either Judicial, Executive or Military Departmts. [sic.]"[12] Despite such inequities, the population as a whole remained less restricted than in colonies where the linkage between church and state was more rigidly defined.

Like Rhode Island and Pennsylvania, Maryland was established with an emphasis on religious freedom. The colony was the ambitious project of an established Roman Catholic family whose head, George Calvert, Lord Baltimore, sought a suitable environment where his family could continue to enjoy a privileged position unhampered by prejudice or persecution. While the colony's response to the Catholic population eventually changed drastically, it remained in its inception a haven for members of the faith who had been discriminated against in other areas.

Colonies That Insisted on Religious Homogeneity

In the Massachusetts Bay and Connecticut colonies quite the opposite was true. Organized under the shadow of Puritan Congregationalism, they tried, as John Calvin did in Geneva, to create monolithic bastions of Protestant orthodoxy and consequently were profoundly antipluralist. The colonies left no doubt that while church and state were not unified, they were strongly interrelated. In Massachusetts under the leadership of John Winthrop and in Connecticut under Thomas Hooker, the linkage between church and state was so strong that one could not become an established, successful citizen without being a member of a recognized church.

The Puritans themselves were dissidents from the Church of England. Yet, in their zeal for reform, they established a norm for expected behavior that was rooted entirely in the Bible with stringent standards of behavior and dress that did not allow diversity.

In the Massachusetts Bay Colony, the relationship between church and state was so strong that the notions of being a citizen and a church member were one in the same.[13] While the leaders of the colony did not attempt to initiate a theocracy or to replicate the kind of church and state ties that had existed in England, they did make it clear that in matters of religion the state had ultimate authority to remedy any ills. This intent was clearly stated in the Cambridge Platform of 1648, which boldly proclaimed that it was "'the duty of the Magistrate to take care of matters of Religion, and to improve his Civil Authority' by seeing to it that the commands and prohibitions of God as made clear in the Word were observed."[14]

As Puritanism evolved in strength and influence, similar understandings of the "correct" role of religion developed in New Hampshire. These traditions, once implanted, were to last well into the nineteenth century.

In Virginia, an equally homogeneous point of view early became public policy. It was rooted in the economic dominance of the Virginia Company of London, and it resulted in an understanding of religion that left little room for diversity:

> Any attempt by colonists to pursue any other religion . . . was to be punished severely. In building this internal moral and religious order, the Company insisted, the colonists were also to use the Anglican faith in the proselytization and conversion of the heathen Indian, a charge explicitly made by King James in his charter of 1606.[15]

Jamestown thus became an exercise in the ability of a colonial empire to maintain, in entrepreneurial fashion, a company settlement. In such an environment, it was expedient to maintain a homogeneous religious atmosphere so that the welfare of the colony's citizens, the accumulation of their profits, and the blessings of the company and the crown would be maximized.

The establishment of some colonies that were tolerant of diversity and others that were opposed to it meant that there was little attempt to reconcile the two visions of America. Thus, the "solution" to the nagging issue of religious pluralism was a natural, self-selected division between those colonies that welcomed diversity and those that did not. People who preferred freedom of expression—more often Quakers, Baptists, Jews, Mennonites, and others who were not welcomed by the New England Puritans or who did not favor Jamestown's rigidity—sought the more tolerant atmosphere of New Netherland, Rhode Island, Pennsylvania, and Maryland. People of more orthodox belief stayed in the other New England colonies and Virginia, where religious affiliation determined status and privilege.

Pluralism as a Societal Struggle

As the infant nation grew older and as patterns of immigration among states developed, the geographical and political lines that had separated the two ideologies began to fade. What emerged in their stead was a more confusing national image in which pluralism became profound societal struggle.

In the thirty-year period before the Civil War, two attacks on diversity became national issues. Both had had a long history of turmoil well before the birth of the republic. The first issue was slavery. The second was an increasingly heated attack on Roman Catholicism.

Each issue had a significant impact on the nation's still fluid identity. The country was forced to decide not only if it would be tolerant of racial and religious diversity but if the accompanying pluralism would be treated consistently with its frequently espoused democratic ideals. Abolition of slavery carried with it a dramatic change in the appearance of racial diversity in public life and was a gateway to the more complicated and potentially even more threatening issue of pluralism. At the same time, a vision of a homogeneous Protestant nation gathered increasing momentum and posed still another question of religious identity as the number of Catholic immigrants escalated and a formidable backlash developed.

Both the debate over slavery and the debate over Catholicism had strong religious and ethnic components. Abolition was argued pro and con, with the Bible as the motivating force on both sides.[16]

The opposition to Catholicism was debated as a matter of ethnicity as well as religion as the number of Irish immigrants swelled. Both discussions, as the following pages demonstrate, were strongly dialectical and pulled the nation in very different directions. Ultimately, the severity of the struggle over slavery eclipsed the issue of Catholicism as the country prepared for civil war. Pluralism had matured as an issue that was not to be solved simply by one's choice of a colony or state in which to live. Instead, it had been translated into a profound national struggle and a major public-policy issue that threatened the very existence of the republic.

Abolition as a Racial and Religious Issue

Of all the issues related to the question of pluralism, slavery was perhaps the most divisive. It divided the nation and it divided the churches. The struggle over slavery helped precipitate civil war and for four years contributed to the disintegration of the union.

As abolition was an argument for racial equality and individual liberty, so it also had strong implications about the nation's identity and pluralism. The eventual defeat of the South, the Emancipation Proclamation, and the Fifteenth Amendment to the Constitution were important components of a movement toward a more pluralistic society. They affirmed that states did not have the right to decide the issue of slavery for themselves, and by implication since abolition had become federal law, racial plurality was no longer defined by the geography of only those states that chose to accept it.

The churches' response to the abolitionist movement was as varied as the nation's. One of the most dramatic reactions came from a group of Congregational leaders who became involved in a court case resulting from an unusual incident on the high seas. In the spring of 1839 a band of African slaverunners kidnaped a group of fellow Africans.[17] The band of fifty-three Mendi (from Sierra Leone) were sold to a Portuguese trader. Later, they were transported in irons to Cuba, where they were resold.

On board the ship *La Amistad*, the Mendi were transported to the Cuban city of Guanaja. During the course of the voyage when the crew jokingly informed them that they were going to be murdered, the slaves rebelled, took control of the ship, and proceeded to attempt to change its course. However, after two crew members managed to correct the compass heading at night, the *Amistad* eventually landed near Montauk Point on Long Island, instead of its original destination. The Mendi slaves were subsequently taken in custody and brought to New Haven for federal trial.

The debate in the courts that followed sought to answer the complex question of the ownership of the small band of slaves and the larger consideration of their right to be free. The case reached international proportions when a claim was made that the slaves rightfully belonged to Spain. The case repeatedly caught the public eye, and by the time of its conclusion involved important national leaders. "Before it ended, the affair involved Presidents Martin van Buren and John Tyler, former President John Quincy Adams (who acted as defense attorney in the final appeal before the Supreme Court), the possibility of war with Spain, and the establishment of the Mendi Mission in Sierra Leone."[18]

The defenders of the Mendis' right to freedom won their case. The slaves were released and eventually returned to Sierra Leone. However, the drama of the court battle had produced another result—a group of religious leaders who, in forming the Amistad Committee, became the motivating force for the formation of an abolitionist organization within the Congregational Church—the American Missionary Association. As an abolitionist association within a tradition that had varying points of view on the issue, the AMA exemplified the struggle within the churches, which had cut deeply into denominational life.

Church leaders argued the issue pro and con referring to the Bible to justify both views. Abolitionists insisted that equality of opportunity and basic human rights were part of the biblical understanding of justice. Defenders of slavery argued that they too were vindicated by scripture and held their position as a moral absolute. This tenet was expressed by Bishop Mead of the Protestant Episcopal Church, who urged that slaves accept their role as divinely ordained. He wrote, "Almighty God has been pleased to make you slaves . . . which you are obliged to submit to, as it is His will that it be so. . . ."[19]

As emotions flared and preachers exhorted their congregations and denominations to accept slavery or to seek its demise, structural divisions arose in the churches, which led in some cases to outright schism. The Presbyterian Church divided over the issue (and other concerns) in 1837 and 1838, forming new denominational bodies in the South and the North identified as Old School and New School. Similar splits arose between northern and southern Methodists and Baptists. The divisions in the Baptist churches arose in 1836 when the General Conference refused to elect a bishop because he held slaves.

New denominations were also organized among blacks. One of the most significant of these was the African Methodist Episcopal Church organized by Richard Allen, who had been born a slave.[20] Others included the National Baptist Convention.

Beyond ecclesiastical divisions and the formation of new churches, some of the most dynamic activity over the question of slavery occurred within religious organizations. There the debate led to active missionary movements whose primary targets were the freedmen. One of the most significant of these bodies was the American Missionary Association. In typical Congregational fashion, the AMA became an independent association, which, while supported by members of the faith, was not a part of any hierarchy. This was in keeping with Congregational polity, which greatly feared ecclesiastical control. While far smaller than other Congregational bodies such as the American Home Missionary Society, the AMA was far more active on the slavery issue and became a leader within what historians have identified as the Tappan wing of the abolitionist movement.[21] Its history and its polemical debate with other organizations of the same church, including the American Home Missionary Association, the American Board of Commissioners of Foreign Missions, and the American Bible Society, illustrated the plurality of opinions about abolition within a single religious tradition.

The importance of the AMA for this discussion is that it utilized the abolitionist issue as a springboard for organizing missionary activities among a wide variety of ethnic and racial groups in the United States. The concern of the AMA was not paternalistic—rather, it sought to become in itself a multiethnic society.

The primary evidence for this assertion comes from the fact that the AMA cultivated black leadership within its ranks.[22] Both in helping to develop its overseas missions and in initiating schools in the South, the racial integration of its own organization became an important asset.

In addition to its role in the churches, the AMA also engaged in a variety of antislavery activities in the secular world. It supplemented the work of the American Anti-Slavery Society (also led by Louis Tappan, a founder of the AMA) and the political organization that championed the abolitionist cause, the Liberal Party.

The AMA espoused a belief in self-determination for black Americans. Its leaders wrote, "We owe him the best education—in art, science, and religion—which our civilization affords, and he will repay us by intelligent toil, by cultured art, and above all, and richer than all, in the example of a religion that is emotional, spiritual and practical."[23] This vision was expressed by a variety of leaders within the organization and contained at its heart an understanding of cultural pluralism in which black, white, and all racial and ethnic groups could live in harmony and understanding of one another.[24] Both in helping to develop its overseas missions and in initiating schools in the South, the racial integration of its own organization became an important asset.

The AMA's strong abolitionist activities precipitated a variety of changes in the Congregational churches that supported it. One of the most important of these changes was the transfer of support by some churches from the prestigious American Board of Commissioners for Foreign Missions to the AMA. The board, in the face of the abolitionist movement, had continued to support missionaries who were slaveholders, although in theory it had voiced opposition to slavery and had forbidden its clergy to hold slaves.

The difficulties that the difference in philosophy of the two organizations posed for relationships with local churches, which were important sources of funding, is illustrated by a letter from Corresponding Secretary Michael E. Strieby to his colleague George Whipple in 1864. Strieby wrote of a conference with a representative of the American Board to help find a remedy to the problem that faced both organizations. He described the issue:

> . . . Some of *our* friends, in the various churches, still insist on giving their *Foreign* Mission Contributions to our association instead of to the Board. This of course diminishes the Board's collections, and deters the Board's friends from consenting to a regular church contribution for the association.[25]

The problem that both organizations in the same denominational tradition faced was illustrative of different understandings about the issues of slavery and abolition. The larger context of disagreement that they represented, however, was a variation in philosophy about the significance of racial diversity and the manner in which it should be addressed.

The American Board was similar to other religious organizations and secular groups who by design, or because of their inactivity on the issue, continued to allow slavery to exist. The American Bible Society, also of Congregational origin, had refused to provide slaves with Bibles, a decision that infuriated leaders of the AMA. The American Home Missionary Society, founded in 1826, developed numerous mission churches on the frontier through an agreement with the Presbyterian and Congregational churches and was much larger than the AMA. The society frequently addressed the issue of slavery as an urgent concern. Yet, much like the American Board, it equivocated and accepted a position that allowed the practice to continue even under the auspices of its members. The vehicle for this position was the society's refusal to intervene in its ministers' affairs. A report of an arm of the society in Missouri in 1850 thus agreed: "Now, in reference to the subject of slavery, this Society deems it to be the province of the missionaries as ministers of Christ, . . . to determine for themselves the occasions and the way in which they will bring the Gospel to bear on this and every over evil."[26]

Perhaps the greatest contribution of the AMA to a vision of cultural pluralism was its work with schools in the South. This effort began even as the Civil War raged. Following the Union armies into the South, AMA teachers established hundreds of schools. Schools were open to any child in need of an education regardless of race or religion and were not segregated. The scope of the association's work was unprecedented and unequaled, both during the Civil War and directly afterwards. It had a significant impact on the work of the Freedman's Bureau:

> . . . in 1867 almost one third of all the teachers reported by the Freedman's Bureau at work in the South were commissioned by the AMA. Several of its superintendents served on Southern boards of education. . . . In the list of organizations—political as well as benevolent—that contributed money toward black education, the AMA's donation stands second only to the aggregate sum disbursed by all the southern states and cities, the AMA having spent in that endeavor by 1893 more than twice as much as the Freedman's Bureau had expended during its existence.[27]

Teachers for the schools initiated by the AMA were recruited from the North. Later additional blacks in the South were recruited to help with the teaching.

Schools were begun in little more than mud huts in some rural areas. In the cities, where feasible, large buildings were purchased that could accommodate sizable enrollments. One correspondent wrote from Montgomery, Alabama, in 1866, for example, of an enrollment of three hundred children.[28] Another wrote to the AMA from Mobile during the next year to suggest that a building in that city would make an excellent school and had several floors, each of which could accommodate three hundred students.[29]

The work of the AMA teachers, however, was not without tremendous hardship. Teachers were beaten and tortured. One teacher wrote in 1866: "Twice I have been shot at in my room. Some of my night scholars have been shot but none were killed. The nearest military protection is two hundred miles away."[30]

Another in her Athens, Alabama, schoolhouse was repeatedly shot at by members of the Ku Klux Klan.[31] When she refused to move from her chair, the school was burned. Still refusing to leave, she taught members of the black community how to make bricks. The school was rebuilt, and the classes continued.

The attack was typical of the Klan. Formed in Pulaski, Tennessee, from a group of former Confederate soldiers, the Klan waged a war of terrorism. It became one of the most visible of a variety of secret societies that sought to purge the nation of all forms of racial and religious diversity. While the principal focus of the Klan and its Grand Wizard, General Nathan Bedford Forrest, was blacks, Catholics, and Jews, foreigners in general were also seen as subjects of attack. [32]

In 1868, another AMA missionary received a chilling threat from the Klan:

> 1st quarter, 8th Bloody Moon—Ere the next quarter be gone! Unholy teacher of the blacks, be gone, ere it is too late! Punishment awaits you, and such horrors as no man ever underwent and lived. The cusped moon is full of wrath, and as its horns fill, the deadly mixture will fall on your unhallowed head. Beware! When the Black Cat sleeps we that are dead and yet live are watching you. Fool! Adulterer and Cursed Hypocrite! The far-piercing eye of the grand Cyclops is upon you! Fly the wrath to come. [33]

Despite such warnings, schools continued to be initiated. The AMA not only brought teachers from the North to the South, it retained black teachers to work among the freedmen. In all, the organization initiated some five hundred schools. Of these, some continued and became such major educational institutions as Berea College, Fisk University, Hampton Institute, Atlanta University, Dillard University, Talledega College, Tougaloo College, and Howard University.

In all aspects of the religiously motivated abolitionist movement, the AMA was in the forefront. It maintained a firm position in the North, not only condemning the practice of slavery (as was common for religious organizations to do) but also actively seeking its end. It challenged organizations, denominations, and clergy who either sanctioned slavery or who preferred to turn the other way when their constituents remained slaveholders. The AMA urged emancipation, and when it finally came, it was in the vanguard of educational work with the freedmen. The AMA built schools and colleges and, with a cadre of black leaders in its midst, sought to aid black self-determination.

Ironically, if the vision of the AMA was culturally pluralist, its conception of religion was completely homogeneous. Here, there was room neither for diversity nor for any consideration of self-determination. These views were popularly expressed in the AMA's periodical, *The American Missionary*, whose masthead proclaimed, "I will be exalted among the heathen." [34]

In similar fashion, AMA missionaries in Siam (Thailand), India, Ceylon (Sri Lanka), and other Asian countries wrote of the perils of "Heathenism." Despite the fact that both the Hinduism and Buddhism they encountered had long, rich, ritualistic, scriptural, and theological traditions, they viewed these faiths as essentially rooted in ignorance.

It would be a tremendous fallacy, however, to conclude that the AMA stood alone in this position. The overwhelming majority of denominational organizations in the United States advocated conformity to Christian ideals and principles. This was for several reasons. First, the two Great Awakenings had produced a climate that welcomed both social reform and, when possible, conversion. In the second half of the nineteenth century, the cry for reform came on a number of fronts including temperance, the fair treatment of women, and the abolition of slavery. Second, and even more significant, was the notion of Christian civilization that had captured the churches. "America" was understood to have been given a divinely inspired destiny to bring not only Christianity but "Christian civilization" to the world. Also in common parlance was the ethnocentric notion that Christianity had reached the highest state of development in the United States, and even more specifically, in New England! Congregational leaders had written in 1846 "that the civilization which the gospel has conferred upon New England and other kindred communities, is the highest and best . . . the world has yet seen."[35] Such sentiments were popular in most mainstream Christian denominational groups. Together with the emphasis on reform, technological advancement, and military and colonial expansion, they produced a curious mindset that, while at times open to the notion of cultural diversity, had little patience with the concept of religious pluralism.

In keeping with the mindset of most North American Protestants on the issue of religious pluralism, the AMA condemned Asian religions and the rites and beliefs of African blacks and American Indians. All fell under the category of superstition. Buddhism was attacked with the zeal that came to typify the anti-Catholic rhetoric. An article in *The American Missionary* in 1849 thus concluded:

> This, then, is the great mystery of Boodhism [sic.]; every man who bows to this creed, is in league with the devil, contending for the throne of God. The devil, to urge on this contest and keep those hosts united, has invented a system that binds them into one mass as solid and impenetrable as a front of iron. It wears all the sanctity of, and is decked with as many charms as papal Rome. Its similitude to this last named religion, with the exception of names, is so striking that they must have had, unquestionably, the same origin; the same enemy of God must have molded them both.[36]

The author's remarks recognized many of the theological and scriptural similarities between Roman Catholicism and Buddhism that have been a particular focus of scholarship today. However, any objective observations were lost beneath a mantle of prejudice that assumed the superiority of the Christian faith and the depravity of anything else.

The intent of the AMA in supporting a vision of cultural pluralism (which was indeed ahead of its time) while yet accepting the popular image of religious conformity was illustrated by the final fate of the *Amistad* captives. After the former slaves were declared to be free by a federal court, it was their wish, and that of the AMA, to find a way to return them to Africa. In 1840 an agreement was reached with a shipping agent to transport them back to Sierra Leone. The event was viewed by the AMA as significant for two reasons. First, it was a symbol of their success in the courts, which, the association's leaders hoped, would fuel the abolitionist movement. Second, it was widely perceived that the return of the Mendis to Africa would be the beginnings of an African mission that would result in the conversion of countless Africans to Christianity.

The mission, which subsequently evolved out of the Mendis' return, became a focal point of the organization for many years. It was a popular destination for contributions from the United States. However, it ended largely in failure. Most of the returning Mendis, including the celebrated leader, Cinque, eventually abandoned their Christian practices and returned to African customs and tradition.[37]

The Anti-Catholic Reaction

The fury that surrounded the issue of slavery, which precipitated civil war, relegated another concern into dormancy—American nativism and anti-Catholicism. Only four years before the Civil War, the purge of Catholicism from the country was quickly becoming a national agendum.

A series of forces had fueled anti-Catholicism from the earliest colonial times. Old rivalries in Europe had given many of the colonies a strong antipapal bias.[38] Further, the Enlightenment emphasis on reason created a suspicion of both the Catholic hierarchy and the form of the faith practiced by European peasantry, which was equated with superstition. By 1776, seven of the original thirteen colonies had passed some form of anti-Catholic legislation.[39]

In most of the colonies, such laws were directed at a population that was clearly a minority. By the middle of the next century, that proportion had substantially changed. The steady flow of large numbers of Irish immigrants had made the Roman Catholic Church the largest denominational body in the United States.[40] With such a dramatic transition, those

Christians who were already convinced that Protestantism was the epitome of the civilized world found cause for concern. The vision of a
uniquely Protestant domain in North America was, many felt, quickly
being supplanted. This alarming development compelled them either to
change their vision of a Protestant America or to reinforce it. Most chose
the latter.

An example of the profoundly anti-Catholic mindset in the colonies was
a law passed in Massachusetts in 1700 entitled "An Act Against Jesuits and
Popish Priests."[41] The act was the result of the appointment of antipapist
Richard Coote, the Earl of Bellomont, as governor of New York, Massachusetts, and New Hampshire. The law boldly declared that by September 10, 1700, "all and every Jesuit, seminary priest, missionary, or other
spiritual or ecclesiastical person made or ordained by . . . the pope or see
of Rome . . . shall depart."[42] Moreover, it claimed that any priest was "an
enemy to the true Christian religion" and should be condemned to
"perpetual imprisonment."[43] An escape from prison was punishable by
death. With the provision that the act was not to cover the presence in the
colonies of priests who had suffered shipwreck or some other disaster,
rewards were offered for their capture.

Even in Maryland, established as a haven for Catholics, persecution
arose. Following the victory of Oliver Cromwell in England in 1649, the
government of the colony was overthrown and a rigidly anti-Catholic
policy instituted. Catholics were disenfranchised by act of the assembly.
Priests were attacked and had to be secretly transported out of the colony
to places of safety.

As the colonies began the process that would solidify them into a
nation, anti-Catholicism remained an active force. It drew the interest of
public figures such as John Adams. He wrote in a diary in 1761 about the
manner of the faith that he had observed in Europe:

> In the Countries of slavery, and Romish superstition, the Laity must not
> learn to read, least they should detect the gross Impostures of the
> Priesthood, and shake off the Yoke of Bondage. But in Protestant Coun-
> tries and especially in England and its Colonies, Freedom of Enquiry is
> allowed to be not only the Privilege but the Duty of every Individual.[44]

Adams irately concluded, "No Priest nor Pope has any Right to say what I
shall believe."[45]

While prominent leaders such as Adams had become nationally identified with abolition, they were staunch defenders of a homogeneous Protestant nation. For Adams, this was justified on the allegation that Catholicism itself was intolerant of other faiths.

With the birth of the republic and the beginning of the nineteenth
century, other public figures became significant voices in the call for

restrictions on the Catholic presence. The inventor Samuel Morse and the evangelist Lyman Beecher (who also condemned Unitarianism) were among those who called for reform.[46]

As these and other Protestant orators and national figures addressed the issue, so a variety of forms of anti-Catholic literature proliferated. Such popular tracts as *Six Months in a Convent*[47] and other hate literature helped congeal Protestant opinion against what was understood as the depravity of the Catholic faith.

By the middle of the nineteenth century, the voices for "reform" had solidified into an effective political force. The American Party was formed with, as its platform, a staunchly anti-Catholic mandate to return the nation to a pristine homogeneity.

Dubbed "Know-Nothings" because of its love for secrecy, the American Party quickly consolidated its political ambitions. Gathering strength in New York City, the party celebrated a number of victories in a very short period. By the fall of 1854, it had elected seventy-five persons to Congress:

> In Massachusetts they won every state contest except in the House of Representatives, where one Whig and one Free Soiler won the right to sit with 376 Know-Nothings. In 1855, they also did very well in Rhode Island, New Hampshire, Connecticut, Maryland, and Kentucky; not much worse in Tennessee, New York, and Pennsylvania; and they very nearly carried Virginia, Georgia, Alabama, Mississippi, and Louisiana. A presidential victory and control of the national Congress appeared to be in sight for 1856.[48]

The increasing agitation and political victories of the Know-Nothings during the 1850s caused Catholic leaders to consider ways of safeguarding their population. Bishops, priests, and editors of *The American Celt* and the Boston *Pilot*, for example, urged Catholic immigrants on the Eastern Seaboard to think of moving west.[49] In response to their concern, a convention to aid immigrants was organized in 1856 as a way of combating the inroads of Know-Nothingism. While the convention did not achieve its ends of large-scale resettlement, it was an important symbol of the trauma that the urbanized Catholic population was feeling.

Despite such mounting evidence of Know-Nothing victories, the beginning of the party's popularity was also its end. Nominating former President Millard Fillmore, the movement came to an abrupt halt when Fillmore lost. In reality, its platform was eclipsed by the growing concern over an even more divisive issue—slavery.[50]

The American Party had been an effective political force for only a few brief years. Yet, in achieving its victories, the movement had captured pieces of the nation's identity, including the value placed on religious conformity, the desire for a homogeneous Protestant nation, and a reveling in patriotism.

A frequently espoused sentiment of the party had attributed to George Washington the saying, "Put only Americans on guard tonight."[51] The movement had thus sought to define what an American was. Within this extraordinarily homogeneous view of the nation, there was little room for the Catholic, the Mason, or the Mormon, or for the Irish immigrant, who formed the core of cities such as New York. For the Know-Nothings, even the subsequent vision of the melting pot would not have made sense. There could be no melting, no fusion, and certainly no diversity.

The demise of the Know-Nothings as a political force, however, did not mean that anti-Catholicism had ceased to be a force in American life. Instead, it was submerged as the nation entered a period of civil war.

In the Reconstruction Period, the concern emerged again with a debate that had begun before the war but that now became a national controversy. The particular issue was parochial education.

As early as 1840, a Catholic bishop, John Hughes, had argued that public funds should be used for Catholic education.[52] In that same year, Francis P. Kenrick, bishop of Philadelphia, had petitioned the school board for redress, since Catholic children were required to use the King James Bible and to participate in Protestant religious exercises.[53] As a result of the bishop's protest, a group of ninety-four ministers had organized the American Protestant Association, a militant anti-Catholic organization. Two years later in May and July 1844, leaders of the association had helped incite bloody anti-Catholic riots in the city.

In 1875, Representative James G. Blaine introduced an amendment to the Constitution that would have cut off all public funds for Catholic education. It was touted by the President and hotly rebuked by Catholics, who saw it as an autocratic attempt to dictate religion. The amendment was eventually defeated in the Senate, but the debate continued. In 1890, Archbishop John Ireland wrote to Rome to defend his position: "My appeal for State Schools fit for Catholic children has been censured under the plea that a Protestant state should touch nothing Catholic. But America is not a 'Protestant State,' and if Catholics pay school taxes, they should receive benefit from them."[54] The focus of the discussion was more than the separation of church and state. Rather, at its heart, was the notion that America was first and foremost a Protestant nation, which was responsible for educating its children in a homogeneous manner. The opposing point of view, argued just as vehemently, looked at the manner in which Protestant values influenced public education, and vowed that Catholic ideals had the same right to be expressed in a religiously diversified society.

Archbishop Ireland's comments were also made at a time when the nation was experiencing a resurgence of anti-Catholicism. The American Protective Association, which was formed in 1887, held its first convention in 1890. It quickly became active in a wide variety of states and gathered popular appeal.[55]

The bitter reaction to Catholicism and parochial education was coupled with yet another nativist attack on religious diversity. Adams and other notables such as William Henry Seward spoke out against Masonry. Following the murder of William Morgan in Batavia, New York, in 1827 for failing to keep lodge secrets, public reaction escalated.[56]

The greatest outcry against nontraditional forms of religion was that levied against the Mormons. When Joseph Smith proclaimed that he had been visited by the angel Moroni and subsequently dictated the Book of Mormon, he became well outside the range of religious behavior that was generally deemed acceptable. In 1831, Smith, feeling public pressure, moved to Ohio. The Church of Jesus Christ of Latter Day Saints, which emerged from his revelations, gradually gathered strength. As it grew, so did the intensity of the reaction. The Mormons subsequently moved farther and farther west, settling in Illinois, Missouri, and ultimately in Utah.

The westward movement of the Mormon Church occurred for many of the same reasons that had led Roman Catholics to consider leaving Eastern Seaboard cities. Both groups were attempting to find solace and freedom in the frontier. For Catholics, the advent of civil war and the thrust into dormancy of the political movement against them, coupled with their relatively large numbers, made a mass migration to the frontier unrealistic. For the Mormons, a much smaller body, whose need to move came at a different time, the frontier was attractive. From New York to Illinois, Missouri, and Utah, the church sought freedom of expression in a frontier life. In the end, as the frontier continued to shrink, religious dissidents began to realize that often there was no escape.

The Mormon experience and the rise of nativism and anti-Catholicism in American politics were a clear expression of the escalation of the struggle with diversity. In the eighty-year period from the birth of the republic to the peak of the Know-Nothing movement in 1856, anti-Catholic sentiments had been transformed from divisive issues in the states to a national concern. The struggle had touched the heart of the nation's self-image—the sanctity of the one-room schoolhouse and public education. It had united opposition to a variety of religious movements, including Masonry, Unitarianism, and Mormonism. It had provoked an identification in the public eye between the Catholic Church and the immigrant population. Together, the combined image produced a virulent xenophobia coupled with a desire to translate into law a new self-portrait of an ideal American. Whether that image would be entirely homoge-

neous or would permit expression of ethnic and religious differences was a
question that the nation was to endure for a long time. It is a question that
is still unresolved.

The Churches and the American Indian in the
Reconstruction Period

Much as the AMA and other denominational organizations looked to
Africa as fruitful ground for proselytism, so they looked to the American
Indian. In addition to a source of converts, the churches also saw in the
Indian a strong issue of justice and human rights. This was particularly
true during the Reconstruction Period, when the westward movement
put Indians in a far more vulnerable position than before.

As the frontier became more and more accessible, and as the railroad
made travel faster, the quest for land accelerated. When Indian tribes got
in the way, they were either ignored by the outright claims of settlers for
their land, moved off the land by official United States government policy,
or in the countless acts of injustice and inhumanity in the "Indian Wars,"
exterminated.

In the early nineteenth century, attitudes nurtured during the colonial
period struggled over the problem of the Indian. Two sentiments prevailed. One was pluralistic and insisted in the spirit of the Enlightenment
that the Indian was inherently equal to the white man. The other was
entirely homogeneous and called for outright removal of the Indian population and the "legitimate" domination of whites. After 1830, this notion
became widespread and was understood to mean that all Indians, including those who had been assimilated into white society and those who had
not, were expendable.[57]

These sentiments led to a vociferous debate in the early 1830s. The
leading proponent of removal was no less a personage than Andrew
Jackson. Convinced that the Indian was an obstacle to the progress of the
nation and of society, Jackson argued for the divinely ordained right of
"Americans" to dominate the land.[58] Following the passage of a bitterly
debated removal bill, he worked hard to implement it.

The removal bill, which had been introduced to Congress in 1825, had
called for displacement of the Cherokee Indians to a region west of the
Mississippi River. The plan had all of the elements of what had become
the normative American solution to the problem of diversity—removal to
the frontier. It was a continuation of the dynamic that had led religious
dissidents to the unsettled regions of colonies such as Rhode Island or
Pennsylvania. It had much in common with the movement of the Mormon
Church west or in the desire of Catholics to leave the East Coast. The only
thing that distinguished this plan from earlier visions of the frontier was

that it was the product not of refugees seeking protection but of the continuing mindset of a white Protestant majority, whose solution to the issue of diversity was forcibly to remove it.

As the sentiments behind removal prevailed, the visions of those inspired by the Enlightenment were ultimately lost:

> As American hopes of creating a policy based on Enlightenment ideals of human equality failed, and as they relentlessly drove the Indians from all areas desired by the whites, Americans transferred their own failure to the Indians and condemned the Indians racially. By 1850 only a minority of Americans believed that transformed Indians would eventually assume a permanent, equal place within American society.[59]

By the late nineteenth century, two additional strains of thought greatly influenced public perception of the Indian. The first was expressed as a desire for "Manifest Destiny," the "rightful" claim of the United States to all of the land between the Atlantic and Pacific oceans. This sentiment was rooted in the popular belief that the expansion of "America" was God-given and biblically based. Much as kings in Europe were believed to rule by divine right, so it was believed that the moral obligation of the United States was to fill the land its people now occupied.

The other force was Social Darwinism. Following the publication of *Origin of the Species*[60] by Charles Darwin in 1859, the battle between evolutionists and biblical literalists occupied much popular attention. On the scientific side of the argument were such notables as the British philosopher Herbert Spencer. Outside of the scientific community, a number of national figures became enthralled with the new theory of evolution and its social and cultural ramifications. The most influential of these was the steel magnate Andrew Carnegie.[61] Carnegie became the spokesman of the elite—those who made fortunes and who controlled powerful corporate empires. He proposed that the process of natural selection was responsible for their success.

Driven by the increasingly intense desire to own land and compounded with the discovery of gold in Sutter's Creek in California in 1848, settlers had moved west at an incredible speed. Those who stood in their way were frequently dismissed with the pseudo-scientific arguments of the Social Darwinists, who proclaimed that their fate was simply a matter of the survival of the fittest. The ultimate effect of Social Darwinism was the legitimization of racial hatred of blacks and American Indians as innately inferior beings.

While the public often sought the removal or extermination of the Indian, the churches offered still another solution. Motivated by concerns for improvement of the management for Indian affairs, which had become corrupt, reformers such as the Quaker John Beeson[62] defended the rights of the Indians to their land and advocated humane treatment. Beeson was followed by an Episcopalian minister, Henry Whipple, who became an advocate of the process of assimilation of Indian tribes rather than their extermination. Whipple argued for the creation of a commission that would create a new and fairer system for the management of Indian affairs. Support for this position came also from Quakers. The two denominations united behind the cause, which eventually was adopted by President Ulysses S. Grant and became his "Peace Policy."[63]

The Peace Policy was an association between church and state around a common concern, the assimilation of the American Indian. It had the "purpose of preparing Indians to adopt Anglo-American culture."[64] For the government, which had run into one difficulty after another in attempting to manage Indian affairs, the presence of churches that were willing to take responsibility for this process was a blessing. Moreover, it was a way of avoiding a military policy, widely supported by the army, which suggested that there could be no peace with the Indian and that the only solution to the "problem" was the use of military force.

After a series of experiments with the Peace Policy, an assignment of tribes was finally made to the major Protestant denominations and to the Roman Catholic Church. Included in the agreements were Hicksite Friends, Orthodox Friends, Baptists, and Presbyterian, Christian, Methodist, Reformed Dutch, Congregational, Episcopalian, Unitarian, and Lutheran denominations.[65] Each was given charge of particular tribes in specific parts of the country.

Each denomination was responsible for oversight of the agencies under its authority. The governance was managed by executive committees from each church. As the system was put into place, the denominations were asked to name representatives to the Board of Indian Commissioners. This group, which persisted until 1934, proposed and created the reservation system in which thousands of Indian tribes were relocated.

The reservations were the tool of the assimilationists. They provided a closed arena, off limits to the general public and in theory to land-hungry settlers, where efforts to Christianize and "civilize" the Indian could continue unhampered. They also symbolized the value of the frontier, where diversity that was deemed unacceptable was removed from the mainstream of civilized society.

The reservation system succeeded in depriving countless tribes of large areas of land that they had occupied for centuries, moving them at times great distances to new and often desolate areas. To the military, they offered still another option; they legitimized the use of force on any Indians outside of the reservations or those who were openly hostile to the government.

The Peace Policy eventually succumbed, as did earlier attempts to manage Indian affairs. Ironically, the greatest threat to the plan came not from the government but from the churches, which divided over a variety of issues, including the value of a homogeneous or diversified Christian presence among the Indians. After reacting bitterly to the efforts of the Protestant denominations, who dominated the Peace Policy, the Catholic Church formed its own agency, the Catholic Bureau of Indian Missions.[66] The Catholic reaction was also heightened by the perception that the Protestants had been assigned an unjustly large number of tribes. In addition, such Catholics as Archbishop F. N. Blanchet felt that Protestant diversity in the Peace Policy meant a pluralistic approach to Indian affairs that prevented a meaningful, homogeneous Christian presence, which only Catholic missions could supply. He wrote:

> How can the government expect that a true civilization may be given our Indians by Sects, not Christian but infidel? No we are not of those who think . . . all . . . denominations are equally good, though teaching doctrines diametrically opposed to each other. Woe to the Indians to whome [sic] these contradictory doctrines are taught by dissenting sects.[67]

The Catholic Bureau of Indian Missions soon became competitive and successfully outbid the Protestant-dominated Board of Indian Commissions for government contracts on reservations. The result of this competition was a totally confused system that served the interests of its sponsors rather than the people it was supposed to protect.

The Peace Policy had set an unusual precedent. It established the marriage of public and private sectors in an attempt to remove objectionable elements of diversity from society. Similar policies were later to continue in efforts at refugee resettlement enacted through the Immigration and Naturalization Service following the Refugee Act of 1980.

Increasing Immigration From 1865 to 1924

As the United States entered the Reconstruction Period and began the arduous process of healing its wounds, it underwent a rapid diversification through dramatic increases in immigration.

The reasons for opening the United States to large numbers of immigrants were economic. Coal-mining and steel-producing companies in the East, railroads, gold- and silver-mining interests in the West, and textile mills in New England all sought a variety of ethnic groups as potential sources of inexpensive labor. Welsh, Slav, Irish, and Chinese immigrants, among others, in one dreary company town after another came to comprise this expanding population. Simultaneously, railroads and emigration companies sought to make substantial profits from the sale of land to immigrants. Through their efforts, Germans, Norwegians, British, Poles, and others made their homes in one bleak sod house after another.

At the same time that these various economic interests sought inexpensive sources of labor abroad, a widely appealing vision of the American Dream lured thousands of foreign-born persons to the United States. They came by ship and by rail, often experiencing the poorest of living conditions during transit. They came with the promise of employment and with the dream of owning land. Once arrived, they experienced the overcrowded squalor of urban ghettos and the stark, equally poor, isolation of the prairies. Yet, despite the differences between the visions of life in the United States that had attracted them and the far harsher realities they encountered, they continued to come.

The dream that lured them was given form and substance in 1903, when Emma Lazarus's poem "The New Colossus"[68] was affixed to the pedestal of the Statue of Liberty. A vision of "huddled masses yearning to be free" was quickly adopted as a symbol of the nation's self-image as a sanctuary and as an affirmation of cultural diversity. Together the statue's lighted torch and Lazarus's words have since been perceived as signs of a consensus of national opinion that has so valued individual liberty that it has welcomed a plurality of races, cultures, and religions.

In reality, the sentiments expressed in "The New Colossus"[69] did not reflect a national consensus at all but were instead one pole in a continuing debate focused on immigration. As the following pages show, the period from the end of the Civil War through World War I was both a high watermark in the number of immigrants and an escalation of hostility to diversity. By 1924, the reaction reached such a level of intensity that the Johnson Reed Act finally shut the nation's door to persons who represented the most extreme differences.

The sentiments that led to the act were captured by a popular writer in 1905. Doremus Scudder summed up the prevailing mood about diversity and the unwillingness of the nation to face it: "All the reforming forces of our civilization center upon those who strike us as most foreign, and as a result they change, not we."[70] Scudder's statement affirmed cultural uniformity as an inviolable principle and placed the burden of facing ethnic differences on the persons who had emigrated from Europe, Asia, and Latin America.

European Immigrants

The earliest mass movements of peoples to the United States had begun in the 1820s and 1830s. In Ireland, the combined forces of overpopulation and famine resulting from potato rot, as well as worsening economic and political conditions, drove a large number of peasant farmers to the United States. The number of immigrants steadily increased. "By 1850, there were almost one million Irish Catholics in the United States, especially clustered in New York and Massachusetts."[71]

As the flow of European immigrants to North America swelled, diversity became visible outside the cities. In the 1850s and 1860s in rural Trempealeau County, Wisconsin, for example, the population included a mix of American Indians, blacks, and immigrants from a wide variety of countries including Germany, Poland, Norway, Ireland, Scotland, Canada, England, and Bohemia.[72] In addition, the county included a number of persons from northern states such as Vermont, which people were leaving in large numbers.

As more and more immigrants came to Trempealeau County between 1850 and 1880, it became clear that, for the most part, there was an acceptance of diversity and even, to some degree, an attempt to welcome it. Newspapers frequently called attention to cultural activities among the immigrant groups. Some, like the Scots and the Norwegians, were singled out by the press as industrious and hard working. Other groups such as the Poles received less acclaim but were still welcomed. A U.S.-born observer of the period, Stephen Richmond, in observing Trempealeau County in 1870, commented on the differences in language, dress, and "the general inter-social manner of the people and their truly democratic manners and customs."[73] He concluded that "no notice appeared to be taken of difference(s) in nationality."[74]

While ethnic diversity was generally tolerated in Trempealeau County, there were also indications of social distinctions and of class formation. For example, newspapers referred to the immigrants frequently but usually with little or no reference to them by name.[75] Such patterns indicated that the immigrants were accepted as a part of the community but were not granted the privilege of intimate social interaction with the established native population. Moreover, Trempealeau County developed an elite gentrified class. References to the gentry, usually with Anglo-Saxon names, appeared in notices of public occasions, charitable affairs, celebrations, and anniversaries. The boundaries that defined the elite group were not rigid, however, nor did they reveal a strong element of social stratification. Rather, the principal dynamic that shaped the social relationships of ethnic groups was their common involvement in an agricultural society where both personal and occupational survival were the most important considerations.

In Trempealeau County, and in other comparable locations of the same period, differences in ethnicity were welcomed only to the extent that they were compatible with what was perceived as the norms of Christian civilization. Differences in language and dress were tolerated, and to some extent welcomed, as long as the ethnic groups in question valued the land and practiced "American" values of hard work and participation in community life. The vehicle for community participation was usually understood to be the church. There, differences in liturgy, polity, and ecclesiastical heritage were tolerated within limits; there was little doubt, however, about the attitude toward any practices that went beyond these limits:

> While there were differences among the various nativity groups in the manner and time and degree of adaptation to American ways of thought . . . acceptance was favored because in the new county there was an absence of any basic cleavages in the value systems of the various peoples. The native-born, even the old stock, were not a monolithic body themselves. Some were guzzlers, some gamblers. Most of them were Protestant but a few were Roman Catholic. In such deviations from the Puritan norm the Norwegians, Poles, and Germans were not essentially different from many native Americans. Had they embraced a different concept of religion (Mohammedanism, for example), or a different concept of marriage (as polygamy), the Yankees might very well have raised loud vocal objections to the immigrants. The Trempealeau papers contain many vituperous attacks on the Mormons. The essential thing was that Norwegians, Poles, Germans, the British-born, and the American-born all had common basic concepts as to the nature as well as the importance of honesty, proper deportment, and religion. The points at which differences occurred were those in which differences existed within the native culture. [76]

Immigrants came to the United States through a variety of arrangements. Many made agreements with the captains of vessels, who were repaid by their passengers' labor in the United States. Such contracts frequently resulted in cruelty by exploitative sea captains.

In 1817, an English traveler made the following observations about conditions on board the brig *Bubona* transporting immigrants from Amsterdam:

> The deck was filthy. The cooking, washing, and necessary departments were close together. Such is the mercenary barbarity of the Americans who are engaged in this trade, that they crammed into one of those vessels 500 passengers, 80 of whom died on the passage. [77]

Later, others were enticed by states who created immigration boards to publicize their attributes. This was the situation in Minnesota, which in 1871 named a board of five persons. [78] The committee advertised in newspapers in Germany and in Scandanavian papers in other states, which were also sent abroad. Pamphlets and maps were distributed in northern Europe. Local agents were also named to help immigrants on to their midwestern destinations.

The economic advantages to the immigrant were made clear. The Report of the Minnesota Board of Immigration in 1871 concluded:

> From Northern Europe a man, only capable of earning a bare subsist-
> ence there, can be transported to . . . a homestead in Minnesota for
> from $50 to $75. He locates on land, which, in its raw condition is not
> worth over $1.25 per acre, and at the end of five years he has subsisted
> his family and by his labor has advanced his quarter-section of land to an
> average value of $1,000, an advance of 300 per cent on the capital with
> which the settler commenced.[79]

While some undoubtedly did fare this well, others failed to realize the
promise of the American Dream to which the report alluded.

As large numbers of immigrants found new homes in the rural Midwest, so others continued to be lured to a variety of locations throughout
the United States by companies that found them to be a profitable
commodity. By the end of the nineteenth century, the movement of
European peoples had become so profitable that emigration societies
began to be formed.

Major European cities all had representatives of the emigration companies. Land was offered for sale, sight unseen, before ships ever left their
European harbors. Once in the United States, special emigrant trains
carried their passengers to specific areas of the West that the societies and
the railroads had deemed profitable for settlement. Emigrant trains carried the newcomers directly to the parts of the country where land had
been purchased. Much like steerage areas in the bowels of transatlantic
steamships, there were few comforts in transit.

The terms of such agreements were difficult. The railroads and emigration societies often gave new arrivals from six to eleven years to pay for
their land. They also charged from 7 to 10 percent interest—in those days,
a considerable sum. Default in payment meant forfeiture of the farm and
the loss of what had been previously paid. As a further indication of the
companies' power, no title was given to the property until it was paid for in
full.

While there were far more beneficial ways for purchasing land under
such federal programs as the Homestead Act, many European immigrants
never availed themselves of these opportunities. Instead, having been
sold a utopian vision of "America" by the emigration countries, they
encountered the worst possible conditions and frequently had few funds
to support the purchase of the land that they committed themselves to
buy.

Moreover, once deposited near their new "home," the travelers often
encountered living arrangements that were less than ideal. The isolation,
lack of community services, and primitive conditions frequently made
homesteading a far harsher reality than most immigrants had ever imagined.

Yet, despite incredible hardships, they continued to come. The lure of the new land was, in part, the result of the attraction of the frontier. America was in a very real sense the last frontier—a bastion of diverse peoples that even under the worst conditions maintained a way of life that permitted more freedom of belief and action than was held abroad. While this perception was certainly not entirely based in reality, it was the conviction that was often held in Europe and that became part of the ever-present American Dream. (See figure 2.1.)

As the Industrial Revolution progressed, immigrants were enticed to come to the United States through the mills and factories, who sent representatives overseas to secure cheap labor. An example was the Amoskeag Manufacturing Company, a veritable city in itself along the banks of the Merrimack River in Manchester, New Hampshire.[80] In the 1870s, the Amoskeag Company recruited women from Scotland who were expert gingham weavers. The recruitment was carefully negotiated. Once help was secured, a contractual agreement was made with the employee. Frequently, such agreements provided for a fixed period of time during which employees would guarantee to work for the company. They also agreed to reimburse the firm for the expenses of transit to the United States.

The ethnic environments in such large monolithic factories were often diversified. English was only one of many languages commonly spoken.

Courtesy: The Amistad Research Center, New Orleans,
The American Missionary Collection, ca. 1921.

Figure 2.1   Boarding the ferry from Ellis Island to New York in search of a new life

While at times friction developed between ethnic groups, often the commonalty of the company town produced a mood of tolerance and acceptance. Remembering this feeling of acceptance, one former employee of the Amoskeag Company wrote:

> At Chicopee, it was just one big, happy family. . . . For a place that big, for as many employees as they had, and for the ethnic groups that they had, the different people really got along beautifully. There were people . . . that couldn't speak English. They could only speak Greek, or they could only speak Puerto Rican Spanish or Colombian Spanish or French. But we always made out, and everybody always got along with everybody else.[81]

In the factories and on the farms, the European immigrants thus encountered a variety of conditions and responses to their presence. Some, if they were enterprising and inquisitive, secured farms and were, for the most part, seen as part of the community. Rarely becoming part of the inner circle of social elite, they nevertheless transported their religion and culture intact to a new land. Others, who came at the lure of emigration companies and railroads, were less fortunate. The land they farmed was often isolated, and at times, there were no established communities to welcome them. Still others, employed by the New England textile mills, were transported into large company towns where the diversity was mediated by the mill, which became common ground for all. In some regions where large numbers of immigrants were employed in industry, small towns developed along ethnic lines.

In Pennsylvania, for example, where steel companies and coal-mining interests were quickly becoming industrial giants, company towns became pockets of ethnicity, where language, religion, and cultural identity were all carefully maintained. In these instances ethnic groups were sharply demarcated. Conflict was frequent.

Many Europeans opted not for the farming communities of the Midwest, the isolated life of the prairies, or the New England mill towns, but instead chose an urban existence. Between 1830 and 1870, the cities were infused with burgeoning immigrant populations. Concentrations of Germans and Italians in New York and large numbers of Chinese and Japanese in San Francisco were common sights. Frequently, foreign-born persons were more often seen than "indigenous Americans" (see figure 1.6).

The growth of immigrant populations in large cities frequently followed a pattern. Poorer sections of the city became intake areas, where new arrivals found inexpensive housing in older, usually overcrowded tenements. Within these poorer core areas, concentrations of ethnic groups developed. Italians chose to live near other Italians, Germans near other Germans, Chinese near other Chinese. The operative factor that helped create strong ethnic neighborhoods were patterns of chain migration in which members of the extended family helped provide housing, employment, and socialization for other family members—even including distant cousins. In addition, neighborhoods were strengthened by the presence of ethnically oriented religious and cultural organizations. The church, temple, mosque, or synagogue and the voluntary association were important sources of identity.

As ethnic neighborhoods became established and as second- and third-generation families became acculturated, more persons moved to other strata of society. At times, this movement was aided by patterns of employment. This was true in New York City, where many Irish immigrants became household servants.[82] As a result, the Irish population moved to different sections of the city. By 1890, they had become a significant population in each of the city's wards, unlike other groups with different occupational patterns that were concentrated in only a few areas.

The geographic movement of early ethnic groups was accelerated by the arrival of other groups. New York City's history is filled with examples of Italian, Irish, and eastern European Jewish neighborhoods that changed their boundaries because of the arrival of new groups. This pattern was especially visible by the time of the 1890 census.[83] Some of the city's wards (in particular, the sixth, eighth, and fourteenth) were predominantly Italian. Others, reflecting the constant influx of new immigrant groups, included a mix of several kinds of people such as the eleventh ward, which was 50 percent Hungarian and 23 percent German. Still others included additional populations whose numbers were sizable. (See figure 2.2.)

One of the many different European ethnic groups that found the cities an attractive location for advancement were German Jews. Many who came to the United States in the early nineteenth century looked to the growing Reform movement in Judaism as a positive force. This liberalizing tradition was perceived as an affirmation of already existing patterns of acculturation. The mixture of identities that was claimed by Jews who had become assimilated was quite confusing. The testimony of Rabbi Bernard Felsenthal of Chicago provides an example:

> Racially I am a Jew, for I have been born among the Jewish nation. Politically I am an American as patriotic, as enthusiastic, as devoted an American citizen as it is possible to be. But spiritually I am a German, for my inner life has been profoundly influenced by Schiller, Goethe, Kant, and other intellectual giants of Germany.[84]

The statement revealed a hierarchical level of loyalties in which positive identification was made with life in the United States, German heritage, and Judaism. It also demonstrated the manner in which a large segment of

Courtesy: The Amistad Research Center, New Orleans,
Moore Collection, ca. 1921.

Figure 2.2   Some arrogant, others afraid

the American Jewish community affirmed the "melting" process as a
valuable asset.

A very different and often conflicting movement within Judaism was
Zionism. Following the teachings of Theodore Herzl, whose movement
led to the first Zionist Congress in Basel in 1897, the initial reaction
among Reform Jews in the United States was negative.[85] While leaders of

the Reform movement were eventually attracted to the Zionist cause, the early reaction represented a basic philosophical disagreement about the value of diversity. On the one hand, for those thousands of German Jews who had found life in the United States quite to their liking, and who had become acculturated, there was no contradiction between Judaism and the melting pot. The value of a homogeneous American culture was obvious—it rewarded those who became part of it with opportunity and at the same time permitted a certain freedom of belief. On the other hand, for the Zionist Jews, there could be no compromise in their faith. The Jewish state remained an ideal that was by definition to be placed over and above any other cultural, ethnic, or political loyalty.

Zionism was also a response to anti-Semitism, which first emerged in the 1870s, building on the foundations of the nativist movement.[86] Jews in the United States were also well aware of homogenizing attempts within domestic Christian missions whose primary interest was conversion. The American Society for Meliorating the Condition of the Jews, for example, had been formed in 1816 as a "benevolent" effort that sought ultimately to bring Christianity to the Jewish population. Anti-Semitism was a far more militant expression of the desire for a homogeneous white Protestant nation.[87] Much like the anti-Catholic movement, anti-Semitism became an active force in American life when the minority on which it focused its attention substantially increased in number. Zionism thus took the complementary stands of rejecting the lures of assimilation and bolstering the Jewish community in the face of increasing racism. It became especially important in later years, particularly in the 1930s and 1940s when anti-Semitism eventually culminated in the racist policies of the Third Reich.

As European immigrants agonized over the issue of assimilation, so the nation struggled with a dramatic increase in diversity. In the press, and even in scholarly publications of the day, the outcry against the immigrant population was verbose. Writing in 1909, I.N. Phelps Stokes, the author of a massive history of New York City, described the British, Irish, and Germans in Manhattan in stereotypical terms:

> Most of them were poor. In fact, it was often charged, and there seems to be no doubt of the truth of the claim, that many British parishes supplied their paupers with funds to enable them to reach America. Certain it is that a large proportion of the insane, the paupers, and the criminals, in the care of the New York Alms-House Department, were foreigners. . . . The social effect of the coming of these immigrants was to deluge the city with vice, crime, and misery.[88]

Similar sentiments had earlier led to the creation of the American Party. While the nativist movement and the anti-Catholic agenda of the party had been eclipsed by the Civil War, the sentiments that had fostered the

Know-Nothing movement remained deeply embedded in the American psyche. Between the turn of the century and 1924, when the nation voted into law the severest immigration restrictions of the century, the homogeneous view of "America" gradually succeeded in becoming public policy.

This is not to suggest, however, that the cry for an end to diversity went unopposed. In some instances, the plea for tolerance came from the churches. For example, in 1905, *The Home Missionary*, the publication of the Congregational Home Missionary Society, carried an article entitled "Why Despise the Immigrant" [sic.].[89] The article attempted to react to the prevailing stereotypes about Italian immigrants:

> There are two Italys in the popular mind of America. One is the Italy of Dante and Michelangelo; of Raphael and Leonardo da Vinci; of Verdi and Bellini; of D'Annunzio and Duse. A land of stately palaces, dripping with history; of ancient castles, whose stones reek with romance. . . .
>
> Then there is another Italy. The Italy that lies below Eighth Street in New York, and has a poor, struggling, darkskinned colony in every city of America; the Italy that stands behind the pushcart, and sprinkles an odor of garlic as it walks; the Italy that is hated by our workmen almost as much as the Chinese; the Italy that imports the Mafia, and pursues strange and terrible revenges in the slums of our great cities. . . .
>
> The average American makes no attempt to reconcile the two.[90]

The article continued to suggest that the two Italys are very much the same and that the use of separate standards to judge immigrants and Italian art and culture was both unfair and historically inaccurate.

Other articles of the same period wrote convincingly of the contributions that immigrants had made in the United States. They argued for fair treatment of the immigrant community and at times suggested that it was nothing less than divine intervention that had brought them here. Under the heading "What Shall We Do For the Immigrant" [sic] one observer wrote in *The Home Missionary*:

> What a matchless opportunity God's providences have opened to the people of the United States to do foreign missionary work at our own doors, at little cost, and under every advantage. God "hath made of one blood all nations of men"; but in the United States He is finishing the work and *making all nations of men into one blood.*[91]

The argument of the churches frequently took such a tack, welcoming ethnicity but only within a larger understanding of Americanization and conversion. This argument was a logical step, since it linked the concept of the manifest destiny of the nation with the acts of the Judeo-Christian God throughout history. (See figure 2.3.)

Figure 2.3   En route from Ellis Island to New York, pondering the future

Hispanic and Asian Immigrants

Beginning in the early Reconstruction Period, two very different groups
of people entered the United States in significant numbers. The first was
Oriental and included large numbers of Chinese, Japanese, and Asian
Indians. The second was Hispanic and was dominated by Mexicans.

Both populations came in response to the American Dream. The Chinese, the first to arrive, made the arduous journey of thousands of ocean
miles because they were convinced that life in America was unequaled.
The other Asian groups soon followed. The Mexicans immigrated because
there were opportunities across the border within easy reach. Once here,
both groups were exploited as cheap sources of labor.

The history of Spanish-speaking peoples in the United States includes a
wide variety of persons from Europe, Mexico, Central and South America, and the Caribbean. While all Hispanics have experienced exclusionary national attitudes, the Mexican American, or Chicano, population,
which has been in the United States for a longer time than many other
Hispanic groups, has encountered them most visibly.

Large numbers of Mexicans have entered the United States in different
periods for a number of reasons, including the incorporation of whole

populations through the acquisition of territory and the movement of individuals as immigrants, refugees, and undocumented workers. Annexation of Mexican territory began in 1845, when the acquisition of Texas incorporated a Spanish-speaking population within U.S. borders. Three years later the treaty of Guadalupe Hidalgo added a far larger territory and an increasing proportion of Mexicans. Immigration from Mexico began in 1894, although numbers did not substantially increase until after 1903.[92] Revolution in Mexico in 1913 caused large numbers of refugees to emigrate to United States.

As the Mexican American population increased, it was subjected to greater exploitation. This process accelerated when, following the passage of the first Chinese exclusion law in 1882, employers sought a fresh, unrestricted source of cheap labor.[93] Mexican Americans were perceived as a pool of both expendable and exploitable workers that were close at hand. Mexican Americans were particularly attractive to employers who needed short-term labor, such as farmers, who relied on the seasonal use of migrant workers. Mexican Americans were also employed during labor disputes as strike breakers.

The exploitation of Mexican Americans in this period set the tone for further exploitation later in the twentieth century. For example, following the establishment of the bracero agreement (initiated in 1942, legalized in 1951), thousands of temporary workers were brought into the United States to do farm work.[94] When the population of both documented and undocumented workers dramatically increased, the Immigration and Naturalization Service led a drive to rid the nation of what it described as the "wetback menace."[95] "Operation Wetback" in 1954, which deported thousands of Mexican Americans, was directed by Commissioner of Immigration Joseph M. Swing. He had served with General John Pershing against Pancho Villa in 1916, had been accused of being a Mexican hater, and was a strong advocate of deportation.[96] This push and pull between cries for cheap labor and calls for its expulsion was also characteristic of U.S. treatment of Asian populations in the country in the nineteenth and early twentieth centuries.

After the discovery of gold in Sutter's Creek in California in 1848, the vision of new wealth attracted not only persons from all over the nation but from overseas as well. As the mining camps boomed, companies looked for cheap, exploitable forms of labor. This they found in the Chinese, who worked long hours, prepared their own food, and accepted low pay.

As the railroads helped open the West to settlement, so the industry also looked to the Chinese as a source of labor. Chinese railroad gangs became common sights in the West as the country was united by rail.

Because of barriers of language, culture, and the isolated conditions in the mines and railroads, the Chinese resisted assimilation (see figure 2.4).

Figure 2.4   Chinese retention of traditional ways

Religious practices continued much as in the Orient. Buddhist, Taoist, and Confucian traditions were practiced in family settings. In time, a few temples and shrines were built, but the faiths remained, for the most part, home centered.

As the first Asian group to emigrate in large numbers to the United States, the Chinese encountered discrimination on a wide scale. They were exploited in the mines and the railroads and forced to look elsewhere for livelihoods where they could exercise self-determination. The ubiquitous Chinese laundry and restaurant were a natural outgrowth of this process. These businesses provided a way through which families could become self-sufficient and a source of employment for members of the extended family. As these businesses prospered and as more Chinese came to North America, Chinatowns emerged in cities on both the East and the West coasts. The continued movement of Chinese people to the United States was formally recognized in 1868 in the Burlingame Treaty negotiated between the two nations.

North Americans and Chinese looked at one another through a bewildering maze of first impressions. When the Chinese were observed in railroad and mining camps or in the numerous Chinatowns, they were perceived as pagan. Rituals associated with Buddhism, Confucianism, Taoism, and Chinese folk religion were all dubbed equally superstition. Ironically, North Americans were at times viewed in much the same way by the Chinese. A Chinese tourist in the United States wrote:

> A charming American woman, whom I met at the _____ Embassy at dinner, told me with seriousness that our people may be intelligent, but the fact that in San Francisco and Los Angeles they at certain times drag through the streets a dragon five hundred feet long to exorcise the evil spirits, showed that the Chinese were grossly superstitious. If I had told my companion that she was the victim of a thousand superstitions, she would have taken it as an affront. . . . The Americans are the most superstitious people in the world.[97]

The Chinese visitor went on to describe beliefs surrounding the number thirteen, walking through graveyards, breaking mirrors, spirits, and a variety of other common superstitions in North America, amply making his point.

He also encountered a wide variety of cultural differences. Not the least of these was the question of the relative age of the two societies: "when a woman in New York told him she knew her ancestral line as far back as 1200 A.D., he replied that he himself had 'a tree without a break for thirty-two hundred years.'"[98]

The conversation showed that most Americans had little conception of the age or rich cultural traditions of the Chinese. In the same way, the Chinese immigrant was frequently at odds to understand cultural conventions in the United States. The same Chinese traveler, for example, was particularly puzzled by the practice of chewing gum. It elicited a host of questions regarding its purpose, origin, and even its scientific value.

Also a source of confusion were social practices often taken for granted as matters of etiquette. To treat a friend to dinner or to offer a cigarette or cigar are such common parts of life in the United States that most people never think of them as having anything to do with cultural differences. Yet, to the Chinese, who had never witnessed such conventions before, they were very strange.

The encounter of the Chinese and American populations is particularly revealing for the study of pluralism. China had been the recipient both of Western imperialism and of sustained missionary activity. As objects of conversion, Chinese were popularly perceived as largely uneducated and as entirely in need of the benefits of Christian civilization.

In reality, education had always been an important part of Chinese culture. The combination of the importance placed on learning, the role of a tightly defined family structure, and, especially among the immigrant population, the desire for advancement enhanced the ability of the Chinese to prosper. Similar values in other Asian populations, including most notably the Indian and Korean, also the subject of numerous missionary activities, aided their adaptation in the United States, often at a faster rate than other immigrant groups.

As the numbers and visibility of the Chinese in the United States increased, the public became increasingly intolerant. Journalists wrote of the "Yellow Peril" and the dangers of a "backward" class of people whose values were alien to those of the society at large. In 1872, the legislature of California asked for federal restrictions on Chinese immigration. An initial law was passed in 1875. National legislation was realized in 1882 when President Chester Arthur signed into law the first Chinese Exclusion Act. It prevented Chinese laborers from entering the United States for a ten-year period.

It is important to realize that such stringent, racist laws were also in keeping with the earliest understanding of naturalization in the United States. Benjamin B. Ringer has aptly pointed out that the first naturalization law, as voted by Congress in 1790, at the urging of President Washington, was defined in racial terms.[99] A successive law passed five years later cemented similar language into place concluding, "any alien, being a free white person, may be admitted to become a citizen of the United States."[100] Ringer concludes that the words "free white person" remained in effect for 157 years until the McCarran-Walter Act in 1952. The phrase became a principle of racial interpretation that was in full support of the Chinese Exclusion Act, which sought to prevent Chinese from entering the country, let alone seeking naturalization.

Following further treaty negotiations with China, a second exclusion law was passed in 1884, a third in 1888 (with other supporting legislation), a fourth in 1892, and a fifth in 1893. The laws sought not only to end immigration from China but attempted to place strict regulations on those Chinese who remained in the United States. The Geary Act of 1892, for example, required all such Chinese to secure certificates of residence.

After another treaty was negotiated with China in 1894 prohibiting the admission of Chinese laborers for a ten-year period, Congress accelerated its drive for total exclusion. Between 1895 and 1901, it passed a number of laws to strengthen its policy.

The principle of exclusion was given further backing by a Supreme Court decision in 1889.[101] Identified as the Chinese Exclusion case, the decision rejected the attempt of a Chinese immigrant to reenter the United States after visiting his homeland. Chae Chan Ping had lived in the United States from 1875 to 1887 and had then journeyed to China. He arrived back in San Francisco a year later holding a valid return certificate as required by law. Citing the exclusion act of 1888, which had become law in his absence, the authorities refused to allow him to reenter and placed him in detention. The case was reviewed by the Supreme Court, which reaffirmed the constitutional right of the federal government to exclude whatever group of foreign-born persons it saw fit. Later decisions (such as that involving Fong Yue Ting in 1893) continued the Court's affirmation of exclusionary legislation. Exclusion laws were passed in subsequent years beginning in 1902 and 1904.[102] They were not repealed until 1943.

The same Chinese tourist that had so humorously commented on life in the United States was outraged by the new restrictions. In a letter to his brother he wrote:

> Millions are spent yearly in keeping . . . [the Chinese] out after he had been invited to come. He built many American railroads; he opened the door between the Atlantic and the Pacific; he worked in the mines; he did work that no one else would or could do, and when it was completed the American laborer . . . demanded that the Chinaman be "thrown out" and kept out.[103]

Citing a statement by then ex-Congressman Thomas J. Geary, who had complained of the "limitless" wants of Chinese immigrants, who did damage to the American labor market because of their ability to undercut it, the author rebutted:

> Mr. Geary forgets that when Chinamen go to America they adapt themselves to prevailing conditions. . . . In China, where there is an enormous population, prices are lower, people are not wasteful, and the necessities of life do not cost so much. The Chinaman goes to America to obtain the benefit of *high* wages, not to *reduce* wages. . . . Mr. Geary scorns the treaties between his country and China, and laughs at our commercial relations. . . .
>
> In answer to this I would suggest that China take him at his word, and I assure you that if every Chinaman could be recalled, if in six months or less we could take the eighty or one hundred thousand Chinamen out of the country, the region where they now live would be demoralized.[104]

Public reaction to the exclusion legislation neither understood nor was sympathetic to the Chinese position. Instead, concern more often focused on the popular fear that the Chinese population posed a threat to the nation and that their presence in large numbers would ultimately be corrupting. These sentiments had led to mob violence against the Chinese in a number of cities, to the destruction of Chinese homes and property, and to the creation of organizations such as the Asiatic Exclusion League in California. Measures had also been taken by a number of state legislatures to prevent Chinese immigrants from owning land—a tactic that would also be applied to the Japanese.

This profoundly antipluralist position was also heard in the churches. It was nurtured by a growing sentiment that sought a unified global Christian civilization. This attitude often found expression in the denominational gatherings. In 1900, for example, an assembly of the Methodist Church decried the racial and cultural differences in U.S. cities:

> The American city is a conglomerate of all races, nations, tongues, faiths, customs, and political ideas; and by this fact, and that of an easily attainable citizenship, it is the menace of the American State and Church. To penetrate this alien mass by an evangelical religion is as difficult as it is imperative. The question of the city has become the question of the race. How to reach the heart of the city and to change its life is, indeed, the question of questions.[105]

In some instances, opponents of exclusion argued that it would be more fruitful to assimilate the Oriental population than to exclude them. While this position was certainly more liberal than that of the exclusionists, it still denied ethnic diversity as a desirable part of life.

This tenant also found strong support in the church. In 1876, for example, the General Assembly of the Presbyterian Church in the United States of America wholeheartedly recommended that the mission activities of the church on the West Coast be intensified to prevent harm to "American society, morals, and civil institutions"[106] and to convert Chinese to the Christian faith both in the United States and in China.

In a few instances, the reaction in the churches rebelled against the political process that had led to exclusion. A missionary who had been stationed in China referred to the forthcoming presidential election:

> Another Olympiad came round—a term which we might very well apply to the periodical game of electing a president—and on the high tide of another presidential contest a new exclusion law, surpassing its predecessors in the severity of its enactments, was successfully floated.
>
> Could such a course have any other effect than that of exciting in the mind of China profound contempt for our republication institutions, and an abiding hostility towards our people?[107]

The statement expressed the view of the unique audience to whom it was addressed, the Parliament of Religions held in Chicago in 1893 as part of the World's Columbian Exposition. In the increasing national concern for racial and religious uniformity, the parliament was a brief but important interlude.

Tolerance and the Parliament of Religions

The United States was caught up in the gay nineties. The temperament of the nation had turned inward and was captivated with the quest for wealth and prestige. Newspapers extolled the activities of the rich and famous, men such as J.P. Morgan, John D. Rockefeller, and Cornelius Vanderbilt, who had made fortunes many times over and enjoyed a style of life that had never before been equaled in the nation's history. While the middle classes tried to emulate them, everyone else simply tried to survive.

The 1890s was also a time of adventure. The United States saw itself on the edge of a new age of technological discovery. Mass communication and industrialization were increasing and the automobile, telephone, and electric light were coming of age. It was the time of great inventions and great inventors, such as Thomas Alva Edison, the wizard of Menlo Park, who continued to impress upon the public the magnitude of the possibilities that lay ahead.

Discovery applied not only to inventions but also to the human spirit. Leaders of the women's rights movement, such as the suffragettes Susan B. Anthony and Antoinette Brown Blackwell fought for equality in every area. Leaders in the sciences and the arts sought to test the outer limits of the possibilities of human nature.

In the midst of these pursuits, the World's Fair in Chicago (dubbed the Columbian Exposition) was conceived as a monument to the age (see figure 2.5). With Columbus's spirit of discovery as its focal point, the exhibition focused on the industrial, commercial, and spiritual advances of the day in a way that captured the public's imagination and curiosity. Plans for the exhibition had all of the characteristics of the design of a great amusement park, including a subterranean theater, which presented viewers with the illusions of a coal mine, the Arctic, a cave, and the bottom of the sea.[108] Other exhibits broadened awareness of cultural diversity. An entire Javanese village and a street from Cairo were recreated in the exposition. In addition, the planners of the fair recreated a Turkish mosque, which was utilized both as an attraction and as a place of worship at those times when it was closed to the public.

> In the Turkish village, in the Midway Plaisance, is a beautiful Mosque.
> . . . Visitors are allowed to enter only when the hour of prayer is over, as
> the Mosque is not considered a show-place in the general sense. This

From *Glimpses of the World's Fair: A Selection of Gems of the White City Seen Through a Camera* (Chicago: Laird & Lee Publishers, 1893).

Figure 2.5   Parade on opening day of the Columbian Exposition, Chicago, 1893

building is a reproduction of one erected by the Sultan Selim, in Constantinople, and is a great comfort to the three hundred Mussulmans who attend its services.[109]

The attention to detail in the mosque and the priority given to worshipers over tourists demonstrated the exposition's sensitivity to cultural and religious differences.

The fair received public attention around the globe. London newspapers announced in 1892 that lists of pickpockets were being sent to Chicago in anticipation of the great crowds.[110] In Washington, D.C., the Columbian half dollar was minted in honor of the event. In 1893, the Bohemian composer Antonin Dvořák conducted a new symphony at the Columbian Exposition and a year later completed his *New World Symphony*, whose sweeping dramatic themes expressed the excitement of a land just coming of age.

Developing the Parliament of Religions

The pervading sense of discovery included religion, and the West began to hear and appreciate the spiritual insights of the East. The Parliament of

Religions, conceived as an addition to the fair, became the arena for this new appreciation. A *New York Times* article in September 1893[111] talked of dignitaries who bore the image of Eastern spirituality and mysticism as they arrived in New York aboard the steamship *Paris* in transit to the parliament.

Among the passengers was an Englishwoman, Annie Besant, who was a disciple of the founders of theosophy, Russian-born Madame Helene Blavatsky and the North American Colonel Henry Olcott. The theosophists looked to India and Tibet as their primary source of inspiration and often spoke of the authority of mysterious seers who communicated their thoughts to the leaders telepathically. In time, the Theosophical Society established its roots in the United States and enjoyed great intellectual appeal.

Other passengers aboard the *Paris* included several East Indians, who were to take part in the parliament. The *New York Times* noted that as vegetarians they had difficulty securing acceptable food on the ship and had almost starved. Among them was a Jain, Virchaud A. Gandhi, who was described as "a young man with a heavy black mustache. . . . He wore a London-made suit of ordinary clothes and a dickey and white tie."[112] To a reporter for the *New York Times*, he explained that the Jain faith was the oldest in the world and that he had had great difficulty in leaving Bombay.

> "It's the first time a priest of your sect has ever left his country, is it not?" asked Mr. Pipe.
> "Oh, no," replied the teacher.
> "Why, when did ever that happen before?" asked Mr. Pipe.
> "About 2,000 years ago," replied Gandhi in a matter-of-fact tone. "No one has made a pilgrimage since then."[113]

The reporter's assumption that it was virtually impossible for a member of such an esoteric religion ever to have left India was based on his own sense of wonder at someone so very different from himself. The response, equally surprising, that "only" 2,000 years ago a pilgrimage outside of the subcontinent had been made, showed the antiquity of the faith in which two millennia were seen as inconsequential. To a reporter in a nation a little more than 100 years old, the response must have seemed incredible.

The task of developing the parliament was formidable. Its organizers worked for two years, creating a large, broad-based advisory board and obtaining the support of prominent religious leaders. Their strategy was effective. After voluminous correspondence in which more than 10,000 letters were mailed and 40,000 documents sent out, an advisory body was formed that exceeded 3,000 persons.[114] As consultants, the members had an investment in the project, and thus the organizers were assured of wide support. Moreover, they ensured that the success of the parliament would not depend on the votes of ecclesiastical organizations, which, given the subject matter, were extremely unpredictable. Instead, they appealed to their consultants and other individuals for both financial support and personal endorsements.

The schedule of events called for seventeen days of presentations. Included in the plan were times for questions, discussions, and social gatherings, as well as major addresses so that the representatives of Asian religions could meet with smaller groups of participants. In addition, a plan for denominational caucuses was initiated. Representatives of many major denominational bodies secured an important place in the proceedings.

Despite the careful planning, the organizers of the parliament encountered formidable obstacles. For example, in 1892, the General Assembly of the Presbyterian Church in the United States meeting in Portland, Oregon, passed a resolution disapproving of the parliament.[115] Debate soon followed. Subsequently, a number of Presbyterian journals approved of the event in opposition to the General Assembly.

The severest criticism of the project, however, was voiced by the archbishop of Canterbury. Proclaiming the importance of understanding Christianity as the only true faith, he wrote as follows:

> The difficulties which I myself feel are not questions of distance and convenience, but rest on the fact that the Christian religion is the one religion. I do not understand how that religion can be regarded as a member of a Parliament of Religions without assuming the equality of the other intended members and the parity of their position and claims.[116]

The archbishop's attitude reflected the popular sentiment that Christianity was the only source of revelation and truth and all other faiths were erroneous. This position was supported by missionaries from a variety of denominations. It was not, however, universal.

Interest in Asian Religions

A number of missionaries went to great lengths to appreciate and document the religions they observed. An example is Abbé J. A. Dubois, who spent many years in India early in the century, collecting perhaps the most complete record in English of his day of Hindu ceremonial practices.[117]

Sustained interest in the religions of Asia emerged from two other sources. The first was the great literature of the day, in particular, the work of Ralph Waldo Emerson and Henry David Thoreau, who lifted up pieces of Asian wisdom that hitherto had been unknown in the West outside of academic circles. The monistic philosophy of the Vedanta school of Hinduism was attractive to both authors, as they explored avenues of mysticism.

The second source of interest in non-Christian religions was Orientalists. A variety of scholars had compiled an exhaustive array of translations and commentaries on Hindu, Buddhist, and Jain scriptures and for the first time made them available in the West. Undoubtedly, the greatest of these scholars was Max Müller, whose multivolume *The Sacred Books of the East*[118] became the standard for such works.

Interest in the East grew to such a point that the Indian poet Rabindranath Tagore made several speaking tours in the United States. Tagore later won the Nobel Prize in 1913, which further increased the demand for his presence and at the same time called more attention to the East Indian religious experience.

The vision of the Orientalists was perhaps most eloquently captured by the British poet Sir Edwin Arnold, whose epic *The Light of Asia*[119] first appeared in 1879. The poem described the life of Siddhartha Gautama, the Buddha, whom Arnold revered as a savior. The epic is a sweeping interpretation of the Buddha story, embodying many of the scriptural legends that came to surround the birth, life, and death of the "Enlightened One."

The planners of the Parliament of Religions understood the power of Arnold's work and soon persuaded him to become a member of the advisory committee. Other notables followed, including scholars in a variety of disciplines.

European and North American Participants

By the time it opened on September 11, 1893, the parliament had attracted a large and impressive list of Western religious leaders, scholars, and social reformers. Denominational gatherings represented a wide variety of Christian doctrines, polities, and outlooks.

Doctrines ranged from the pronouncements of Mary Baker Eddy, founder of Christian Science (who could not be present but sent a paper to be read), to the evangelical zeal of the Rev. Josiah Strong, who later became an executive of the Congregationalist Home Missionary Society. Polities represented included on the one hand the local-church-centered government of the Free Will Baptists and Congregationalists and on the other the hierarchical structures of the Orthodox and Roman Catholic churches. Extremely conservative and doctrinally orthodox views were represented along with the concepts of the new Social Gospel movement.

A courier of this dynamic movement was a University of Wisconsin professor, Richard T. Ely. He pointed out the inconsistency between individualism, as embodied in the movement toward individual salvation, stressed by such popular evangelical leaders as Josiah Strong, and Christianity, as interpreted by the Social Gospel. Ely proclaimed:

> Individualism, as ordinarily understood, is anti-Christian, because it means social isolation and disintegration. Individual liberty, as frequently proclaimed, means the right of one man to injure others to the full extent of his capacity and resources. The claim to this liberty (which is not liberty at all in the true sense of the word) is anti-Christian. Individual salvation, in the strictest sense of the word, is an impossibility, because it implies a denial of that which is fundamental in Christianity.[120]

Scholars attracted to the parliament included Williston Walker of Hartford Theological Seminary, who became known as an authority in church history, and Philip Schaff, a leader in the Mercersberg movement within the Reformed Church, who talked of the ecumenism related to that movement. Another scholar was Robert Hume, who became noted for his translation of the Upanishads.

Among the social reformers were two prominent women—Jane Addams, the pioneer of Hull House, in Chicago, and the Rev. Antoinette Brown Blackwell, the first woman to be ordained in the United States and also a suffragette. She talked of the need for women in the pulpit in a way that could well be seen as present-day feminism. She said,

> Women are needed in the pulpit as imperatively and for the same reason that they are needed in the world—because they are women. Women have become—or when the ingrained habit of unconscious imitation has been superseded, they will become—indispensable to the religious evolution of the human race.[121]

The parliament also attracted a variety of missionaries. Among them was W.A.P. Martin, president of the Imperial Tungwen College in Peking. Earlier in his career, Martin had been a Presbyterian missionary in China and had assisted in the negotiation of the Treaty of Tientsin. He addressed the parliament about U.S.-Chinese relations, expressing his anger at the exclusion of more and more Chinese from the United States, implemented by legislation beginning in 1882 and renewed as late as 1904.

As the parliament gave missionaries a voice, so it also became a forum for people engaged in a unique kind of adventure. From time to time, individuals from Europe and the United States, captured by the mystique of the Orient, sought to live as Asians. In the same vein as Kim in Rudyard Kipling's novel *Kim*, some Westerners sought to identify completely with the cultures of the Orient. One such individual, Alexander Russell Webb, who had become Mohammed Alexander Russell Webb, told the parliament of his conversion to Islam:

> I am an American of the Americans. I carried with me for years the same errors that thousands of Americans carry with them to-day. Those errors

have grown into history, false history has influenced your opinion of Islâm. It influenced my opinion of Islâm and when I began, ten years ago, to study the Oriental religions, I threw Islâm aside as altogether too corrupt for consideration.

But when I came to go beneath the surface, to know what Islâm really is, to know who and what the prophet of Arabia was, I changed my belief very materially, and I am proud to say that I am now a Mussulman [sic.].[122]

Such a statement, delivered in a period of conservatism, national self-indulgence, and backlash against Oriental immigration, was radical, to say the least. Yet at the same time, it represented the spirit of the parliament. The assembly promoted an openness to other faiths and to those who lived them. While Webb's enthusiasm for Islam ultimately led him to adopt the faith (conversion to or from any faith was not part of the intention of the event), his sense of openness toward other religions was part of the vision that motivated the gathering.

Asian Participants

As if this level of Western diversity was not enough, the interfaith dimension of the gathering included a variety of representatives from the Jewish, Hindu, Muslim, Buddhist, Shinto, Confucian, Jain, and Parsi traditions. Within this potpourri of perspectives, speeches ranged from pleas for tolerance to statements of extreme doctrinal authority. (See figure 2.6.)

From the Western point of view, perhaps the most startling figures at the parliament were the leaders of these Eastern traditions. Undoubtedly, the most charismatic of them was Narendranath Datta, or Swami Vivekananda.

Vivekananda was a disciple of the Hindu mystic Ramakrishna, a leader of the nineteenth-century Hindu renaissance movement in India. Having arrived in Boston virtually penniless, months before the parliament, Vivekananda made his way to Chicago intent on addressing the gathering. Young, energetic, eloquent, and filled with an understanding both of his own faith and of the audience that he addressed, he spoke not only of his guru, but of the Vedanta school of Hinduism. As a monistic philosophical tradition, Vedanta posited the existence of one reality, Brahman, clouded by *maya*, the illusion of separateness.

Vivekananda met with both enthusiasm and suspicion at the parliament. But his presence at that event and his subsequent appearances in the United States had a great effect. Through his efforts, the Ramakrishna mission established a firm U.S. presence, which has continued to this day.

Vivekananda saw the parliament as an opportunity to break down the stereotypes that most Westerners held about Hinduism. Missionaries,

From John Henry Barrows, ed., *The World Parliament of Religions*,
2 vols. (Chicago: Parliament Publishing Co., 1983) 1:ii

Figure 2.6   Western and Eastern leaders in session at the Parliament of
Religions, Chicago, 1893

British civil servants, and others had frequently brought back to Europe
and America the impression that icon worship was idolatry. The Great
Tradition of Hinduism, inspired by the large body of Vedic and post-Vedic
scriptures, was not known or was dismissed as superstition. The Little
Tradition, those village-centered beliefs and rituals so integral to the heart
of Hinduism, was seen as evidence of paganism.

Speaking little of the esoteric mysticism of Ramakrishna, Vivekananda
sought first to help the parliament alter these basic misimpressions. He
did this by drawing on Christian imagery that was understandable to the
audience he addressed.

> As we find that somehow or other, by the laws of our constitution, we
> have got to associate our ideas of infinity with the ideal of a blue sky, or a
> sea; the omnipresence covering the idea of holiness with an idol of a
> church or a mosque, or a cross; so the Hindus have associated the ideas
> of holiness, purity, truth, omnipresence, and all other ideas with dif-
> ferent images and forms. But with this difference: upon certain actions
> some are drawn their whole lives to their idol of a church and never rise
> higher, because with them religion means an intellectual assent to
> certain doctrines and doing good to their fellows. The whole religion of
> the Hindu is centered in realization. Man is to become divine, realizing
> the divine, and, therefore, idol or temple or church or books, are only
> the supports, the helps of his spiritual childhood, but on and on he must
> progress. [123]

Vivekananda also sought something else from the parliament. He
worked to put interfaith dialogue into a single ideational framework in

which different mystical experiences were seen as pointing to the same end. He openly rejected any uncompromising claim to truth. He advocated balance between perspectives and, to this end, looked for harmony between divergent beliefs. While Vivekananda's remarks were not always enthusiastically received, they carried a conviction and a logic that were remembered long after the parliament had ended.

As Vivekananda sought a confluence of religions moving toward the same end, other Asian dignitaries brought equal challenges to the West. Such claims were frequently couched in a stereotypical language about Western materialism and Eastern spirituality. Nevertheless they spoke to a harmonic viewpoint of seeking unity in diversity rather than the imposition of one set of beliefs and values on another. Vivekananda concluded:

> In the East we have a number of systems of philosophy, a deep insight into the spiritual nature of man, but you have at the same time to make an earnest and deep research to choose what is accidental and what is essential in Indian philosophy. Catch hold very firmly of what is permanent of the eastern philosophy. Lay it down very strongly to heart and try to assimilate it with your noble western thoughts. You western nations represent all the material civilization. You who have gone deep into the outward world and tried to discover the forces of outward nature, you have to teach to the East the glory of man's intellect, his logical accuracy, his rational nature . . . you will have the harmony of the East and the West, a union between faith and reason, a wedding between the Orient and the Occident.[124]

The seventeen days of the parliament were characterized by an atmosphere of tolerance combined with a willingness to debate. The transcripts of the event (which fill two thick volumes written in the politest Victorian language) conveyed both the mutual respect of the participants and at the same time the strongest disagreement and conflict. One participant observed, for example:

> The Parliament was not a place for the suppression of opinions but for their frankest utterance, and what made it so supremely successful was mutual tolerance, extraordinary courtesy, and unabated good will. Christians who entered the Hall of Columbus with timidity and misgivings found themselves entirely at home in an atmosphere charged with religious enthusiasm. They felt that the spirit and principles involved in summoning the non-Christian religions to a conference in that great hall were precisely the spirit and principles with which a Christian missionary invites a Moslem and a Brahman into his own house—the spirit of love, inquiry, a desire for mutual understanding, a desire to learn as well as to teach.[125]

Other observers suggested that simply because there was tolerance it did not mean there was no conflict. "It must not be imagined," wrote one reviewer, "that all the speakers piped low and soft. Not at all. There were clouds big with thunder, and there were thunders with lightnings in them that smote as with strokes from God's own right hand."[126]

That was the spirit of the parliament—a willingness to stand up for beliefs and convictions even to the point of conflict, yet conflict all the while mitigated by a pervading sense of tolerance and respect. To be sure, there were exceptions to this premise. There were those who came to the event to demonstrate the superiority of their faith. There were those who came not to listen but to argue. There were those who would have preferred to convert rather than to enter into conversation and dialogue. But the overall spirit of the event nevertheless remained one of un-paralleled tolerance at a time when the nation was gradually closing its door.

The Door Is Shut

Until 1882, the authority to regulate the flow of immigrants to the United States was held by the states. It was also on the state level that the most vociferous opposition to diversity arose.

The struggle within the states is best exemplified by California, which had attracted large numbers of Orientals. In the years following the discovery of gold in 1848, the Chinese population of the state dramatically increased. The influx further accelerated following the Burlingame Treaty in 1868, which encouraged Chinese immigration to the United States.

As the numbers of Chinese increased in California, pressure mounted to prevent further immigration. Many white Californians feared that large numbers of low-paid Chinese laborers would be unfair competition for jobs and, moreover, as an inferior people, would be a corrupting drain on society.

In 1859, the state superintendent of public instruction rebelled against the possibility that Asians would be treated on equal footing with Caucasians in public education. He argued that if the attempt were made to integrate the schools they would be ruined, suggesting that "The great mass of our citizens will not associate on terms of equality with these inferior races, nor will they consent that their children should do so."[127]

In 1860 Chinese fishermen were taxed. In addition, restrictive legislation regulated the size of the small-mesh fishing nets that they traditionally used. Chinese were forced into a limited market that would not be competitive with the rest of the industry. The scenario had noticeable similarities to the efforts to restrict Vietnamese fishermen in the same state more than a century later. A variety of options were tried to limit entry. Head taxes were levied on ships bringing Chinese immigrants to the coast. Provisions were also made to tax foreign miners. A police tax in 1862 assessed all "Mongolians over eighteen years of age who were not engaged in the production of rice, sugar, tea or coffee, or who had not already paid the Miner's License Tax."[128]

Other attempts at exclusion tried to identify different minorities as a homogeneous whole. A California supreme court justice thus attempted to justify discrimination against Chinese, Indians, and Negroes, all of whom, the court decided, were properly forbidden to testify against white persons:[129]

> The question was finally settled for a generation by the decision of Chief Justice Murray of the California Supreme Court, that the word "Indian" included Mongolian. Judge Murray's opinion began with an attempt at ethnological discussion of the colored races and finally arrived at the theory that although the word "Indian" as commonly used, referred only to the North American Indians, yet as in the days of Columbus all shores washed by Chinese waters were called the Indies, therefore all Asiatics were Indians. In the second place the word "white" necessarily excluded all other races than the Caucasian; and in the third place, even if this were not so, he would decide against admitting the testimony of the Chinese on grounds of public policy.[130]

Legislation also sought to prevent Chinese from owning real estate. Changes in the state constitution (and additional legislation)[131] sought to restrict the influx of Chinese laborers. Many Chinese were attacked and some were forcibly removed from their communities.

In succeeding years, other groups encountered similar pressures. By 1910, the public became alarmed about the continued ownership of land by Japanese. Many Japanese immigrants were farmers, who purchased land in California to continue their traditional occupation. Beginning in April 1913, the state of California introduced legislation to prevent Japanese farmers from buying property. Other laws were passed in the states of Arizona, Washington, and Wisconsin.

Figure 2.7 shows the degree of fear that led to laws such as these. Appearing in a voluminous text of scholarly repute of the period, the map gives the impression that a great deal of land in California was controlled by Oriental people. In reality, according to actual population figures included with the map, only 16 percent of irrigated land in California's valleys was owned by Asians.

Moreover, the map also demonstrates two popular misconceptions of the time. The first was the impression that all Indians were Hindus. In reality, the majority of Asian Indians in the United States before 1924 were Sikhs. In the eyes of the press, Hindus and Sikhs alike were dubbed

From W. Jenks and W. Kett Lauch, *The Immigrant Problem: A
Study of American Immigration Conditions and Needs* (New
York: Funk & Wagnalls Co., 1922), 248.

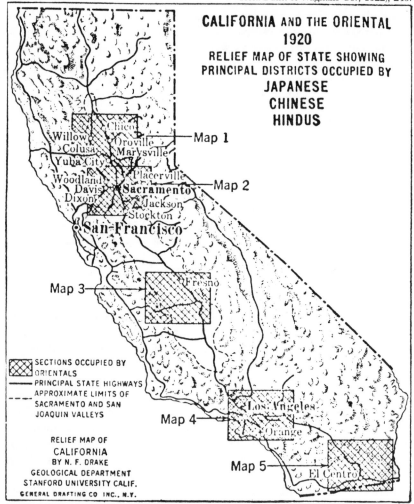

Figure 2.7   Map published by the State of California (1920)
            showing Oriental population

"ragheads"—a derogatory term that made no distinction between religious traditions. The second was the confusion of the term Hindu with
ethnic identifications. The map thus refers to Japanese, Chinese, and
"Hindu" populations, ignoring the fact that Hinduism is a religious rather
than an ethnic distinction.

The intention of states to exclude Japanese from owning land was
eventually reaffirmed by the United States Supreme Court. In three

cases, *Porterfield v. Webb*, *Terrace v. Thompson*, and *Webb v. O'Brien*, the Court supported the right of states to prevent Japanese immigrants from owning property or of laborers from working for other Japanese who did.

Beginning in 1917 Congress passed several laws restricting immigration based on race. The Immigration Act of 1917 had created a barred zone from which persons were not permitted entry into the United States. The zone included India, China, and Japan. The Immigration Act of 1921 established the principle of an exclusion system based on national origin. In the case of the *United States v. Bhagat Singh Thind*, a Sikh immigrant contended that as a descendant of the original Aryan settlers of India, he was Caucasian and therefore should not be subject to the restrictions based on race embodied in these two laws but should be allowed to remain in the United States. The court overruled his claim, thus paving the way for the severest of immigration statutes, the Johnson Reed Act of 1924. The act cemented into place a quota system based on national origins, which excluded persons by virtue of race.

Although there were attempts to redress the imbalance created by the exclusion of Asians, and other important immigration statutes such as the McCarran-Walter Act in 1952, no significant change in the flow of Asian immigrants was realized until 1965. At that time, President Lyndon Johnson signed into law an act that abolished the national-origins quota system. In its place was a revisionist system that instituted quotas by hemisphere and by country of origin rather than by race.

A Postscript

This chapter has shown that the issues of cultural and religious diversity were powerful social forces from the earliest colonial times to the beginning of this century. The periods and issues discussed are only a portion of a wide variety of times in which pluralism profoundly affected life in the United States.

The same issues continue to shape our history. In the 1960s, for example, civil rights developed into a national struggle. Equality became an important issue in public life. The struggle was so pervasive that it left important legacies in the courts, in education, and in the cities.

Similarly, but with less fervor, immigration became a national issue. As a result of the 1965 reforms in immigration law, thousands of Asians entered the United States. In time, as numbers increased, a backlash became evident both among the white majority and among other competing minority groups.

The 1960s were also a time of religious discontent. More than any other period in this century they saw the formation of a wide variety of new religions, which were popularly termed cults. From the International Society for Krishna Consciousness (Hare Krishna) to the preaching of Rev. Sun Myung Moon, to the activism of the Black Muslims, to numerous other movements, the 1960s were a period of intense religious struggle. What was at issue was the ability of minorities to practice alternate forms of faith in an environment where conformity to the status quo was expected and genuine diversity rarely encouraged.

The significance of the 1960s was that the historical issues relating to pluralism, civil rights, immigration, and religious diversity discussed in this chapter were all simultaneously the subject of debate and national struggle. The legacy of this struggle affected three areas. First, there has been a continuing challenge to both government and the private sector to be more responsive to the needs of racial minorities. Second, with the vast increase in ethnic groups after 1965, pluralism emerged as not just an urban issue but rather as a concern of suburbs and even rural areas. Third, religiously, the nation entered a period of conservatism. This was seen in both a backlash to the proliferation of new religions (or "cults") and in the rapid growth of conservative Christian movements.

In each of these three areas, the tension between pluralism and homogeneity has been far from resolved. Civil rights, immigration, and alternative modes of religious life remain important, much-discussed issues. The prolonged debate in the Congress in 1984 concerning the Simpson-Mazzoli Bill and immigration reform and the popularity of Jesse Jackson as the first black presidential candidate all attest to their relevance. Moreover, as history has repeatedly shown, the ability of the nation to deal with the question of diversity has rarely been quiet, totally contained, or one sided. Because the struggle about pluralism and homogeneity remains an unresolved part of our national identity, it periodically reemerges, in different forms with new and more powerful symbols of American life as its objects of discussion.

This chapter has suggested that the national struggle about identity and diversity is best interpreted as part of a historical continuum. The same dynamics that welcomed the tired, the poor, and the oppressed and simultaneously cried out for immigration reform remain an important part of American life.

Symptoms of the continuing struggle are reflected, for instance, in the long history of debate about the role of refugees in American society. They are also easily identified in the way that alternative forms of religion are perceived. Religious dissidents, including Guru Rajneesh and Rev. Sun Myung Moon, remain as unwelcomed visitors who have been expelled from the mainstream of American life. While in both instances the issues that have led to their ouster have been arguments of corruption, the dynamics of their expulsion have had important historical parallels. The forces that propelled dissidents away from other colonies to seek refuge in

Rhode Island, the plan for Catholic exodus from the Eastern Seaboard following the stinging attacks of the Know-Nothings, and the movement of the Mormons to Utah all were scenarios in which there was a profound struggle with the notion of diversity seen through a veneer of accusations of unacceptable behavior. Whether the question was one of polygamy, "popery," or the acquisition of power by religious groups on the fringes of society, the result has often been a public thrust to remove the offending group. The safety valve in the face of the threat of removal has been the frontier. Whether this came in the form of unsettled land in Pennsylvania or Rhode Island or the rough terrain of Utah, the perception has been much the same.

In its schizophrenic reaction to diversity, the United States continued to find meaning in the notion of an expansive wilderness. It has been seen as a safety valve and quite conversely as a place in which the expendable and the unmeltable elements of society could be housed. It has been freeing and confining, the subject of theological debate (in the notion of manifest destiny) and at the same time a highly politicized concept associated with the manipulation of power. Now that the frontier can no longer be defined geographically, its functions must be performed in other ways. The development of strong idealogies has been one way of filling the vacuum left by the absence of a physical frontier. As the following pages will show, these idealogies have created ways of helping the nation both to justify and deny diversity as a seminal ingredient in American life.

CHAPTER **3**

Melting Pot and Mosaic

In the preceding two chapters this text has explored two contradictory visions of American society—conformity or homogeneity and pluralism or diversity. These visions are not based merely on sketchy beliefs but on developed ideologies that have each been claimed as an important part of our national identity. Because there has been no single dominant vision or interpretation of that identity, diversity has been a puzzle and often an obstacle. Communities that have become greatly diversified have been caught in a quandry between the competing visions. And certain aspects of American history, as discussed, have particularly reflected the contradiction.

This chapter examines the ideological arguments and social theories that have formed these visions. It suggests that each has been influenced by patterns of thought with long histories and large popular followings.

The new opportunities and the new frontier offered by this continent to persons from a wide number of lands has been an important part of the American experience. Idealogical currents long dormant, persecuted, and brewing in Europe found new expression to shape and test images of homogeneity and diversity. America was everyone's dream—a nation with a fresh beginning that could retain the old and accept the new at the same time—a New Holland, a New Amsterdam, and a New Hope.

In some instances, experience gave rise to conformist and pluralist ideologies. The period of the largest influx of immigrants into the United States, between 1890 and 1924, saw an incredible diversification of cities, towns, and farms. Many who came clung desperately to existing values, languages, and ways of life. Others sought acceptance as Americans. The vision that arose out of their experience, combined with the fear of what would result if they continued to express their differences, became the melting pot. The melting pot found support in the American Dream and found expression in short stories, novels, and plays. It became a justification for both the forced amalgamation of immigrants and for racism. The concept of the melting pot attracted countless thousands to the United States and, once they were here, compelled them to forget from whence they had come.

At other times, visions of homogeneity and diversity, in addition to becoming ideologies, also became sophisticated social theories. For example, the study of the "new ethnicity" in the late 1960s and early 1970s has been both ideological and theoretical. Scholars have fostered a different vision of pluralism from that of half a century before, sustaining strident voices of contention.

The following pages will first examine the American Dream as a composite of the conflicting visions of conformity and diversity. They will then consider these visions as reflected in the concepts of the melting pot and the mosaic. Finally they will deal with the outgrowth of these visions as put forth by assimilationists and the new pluralists.

The American Dream

In the nineteenth century, the American Dream was a catalyst that attracted thousands of immigrants from Asia, Europe, and the Americas to the United States. It lured the Chinese to California after the discovery of gold at Sutter's Creek in 1848. It drew the Irish to New York City as a result of famine and worsening political conditions in Ireland. It caused thousands of others of every ethnic identity to leave their family, friends, and homes behind to seek a better life.

They traveled across the oceans cramped in the steerage of passenger liners to Angel Island in San Francisco and Ellis Island in New York. They came not because there was no place else to go but because the vision of life in the United States was so alluring that they left behind everything that they had previously known in order to pursue it. (See figure 3.1.)

As a powerful, utopian ideology, the American dream was the product of two streams of philosophy that converged in the infant nation. These two streams, flowing from different values, were not always compatible. One avowed individualism (which implied the right to be different), and the other avowed conformity. Together they became the foundation of an ambiguous national self-image.

It should be noted parenthetically that while the American Dream had a powerful attraction abroad, it rarely was an incentive to minorities with long histories of subjugation in the United States. For blacks and Amer-

Courtesy: The Amistad Research Center, New Orleans, Moore Collection, ca. 1922.

Figure 3.1   Immigrants for whom the American dream was never realized

ican Indians, the dream was an empty one. For them America was not a utopia at all but rather the fruit of broken covenants and forgotten promises. Indeed, it was frequently a nightmare (see figure 3.2).

The Influence of the Enlightenment and the Frontier

In tracing the origins of the American Dream, Howard F. Stein and Robert F. Hill have identified several important influences. [1] The first was

the emphasis placed on the individual during the eighteenth-century
Enlightenment.[2] Europe had sought conformity during the feudal period.
It had emphasized the role and weight of tradition and the place of an
obedient citizenry in an ordered society. The Enlightenment was a depar-
ture from these concerns. Through the work of Descartes and others,
there was a new emphasis—the role of the individual and the significance
of reason. Enlightenment thinkers proclaimed the prerogative of the
individual to question not only his or her own existence but the very
foundations of society and even God.[3]

Rationalism and individualism, as basic foundations of the American
Dream, implied that as an expression of individuality, diversity should be
positively received. The individual could, through the process of reason,
survive quite apart from the constraints of traditional society. Moreover,
reason and intelligence were held to be the foundations of a new social
order in a new land. If God was removed from the daily workings of the
universe, then surely he was replaced by humankind.

In colonial America, the Enlightenment had an important impact on
the way diversity was understood. Thomas Jefferson used the philosophy
actively to promote disestablishment and religious pluralism.[4] Others,
including Southern Anglicans, defended established linkages between
church and state.[5]

The American Dream was shaped by still another force. The Age of

Courtesy: The Amistad Research Center, New Orleans.

Figure 3.2   On Indian reservations, the hollow promise of the American dream

Exploration and the colonization of the North American continent promised a future laden with riches:

> America became the new Eden. Explorer Ponce de León sought the ancient orphic "fountain of youth" in Florida. A host of explorers expected to find gold everywhere, and those who did became the first great despoilers in the name of God, king and avarice. Gold was the universal standard of wealth and was symbolically not unrelated to the cult of youth that lies at the foundation of American mythology, a mythology that, although ancient, seemed *realizable* on American soil. America itself became the alchemist's magic catalyst.[6]

The imagery of the new Eden infused a creation narrative with a lust for youth and for wealth. In so doing, it made a lasting association between biblical symbolism and the accretions of mythology that surrounded the developing nation. America became quickly identified as a new Israel. The promised land became the frontier.

In its ideology and in its geography, the American frontier was popularly understood as a realm of individual opportunity.[7] The great expanse of the North American continent and the raw wilderness that comprised it were a natural symbol of openness, tolerance, and freedom of expression. The frontier was equally identified as a shelter for religious groups that crossed the boundaries of social acceptance.

A case in point was the Church of Latter-day Saints. The Mormon followers of Joseph Smith sought the frontier as a place of refuge away from public scrutiny of their unconventional beliefs. Not the least of these was the provision in the faith for polygamy. The argument over the issue was so strong that polygamy was outlawed by the federal government in 1890. Utah was only admitted into statehood on the condition of the legal abolition of the practice.

As Jews, Baptists, Quakers, and Roman Catholics in the colonial period found refuge in the frontier of their day—Pennsylvania, Rhode Island, and other tolerant colonies—so the Mormons looked westward in their time. The same ideology that led them to Utah has also continued in the modern period. Such publicly scorned religions as that of the followers of Guru Rajneesh, who fled from suburban New Jersey to Oregon, or the Krishna Consciousness movement isolated in the mountainous, sparsely populated terrain of West Virginia have both relied on a sense of security in the "frontier."

As the frontier held promise for individualists who sought freedom of self-expression, so it also was the locus of a quest for a utopian, homogeneous Christian society. Horace Bushnell was perhaps the most eloquent spokesman of this position:

> The wilderness shall bud and blossom as the rose before us; and we will not cease, till a christian [sic] nation throws up its temples of worship on

every hill and plain; till knowledge, virtue and religion, blending their
dignity and their healthful power, have filled our great country with a
manly and happy race of people, and the bands of a complete christian
[sic] commonwealth are seen to span the continent.[8]

Using the same imagery of a budding and blossoming wilderness that led
others to the frontier as a refuge from conformity, Bushnell spoke of a
Christian commonwealth, suggesting a level of uniformity that was in
keeping with the nation's manifest destiny. In this context, the individual,
much like the citizen of Bellah's Virtuous Republic, worked for the common good. For Bushnell, the vision was so uniform and without diversity
that he excluded women, restricting his imagery to that of a "manly" and
(with an added note of Darwinian superiority) a "happy race."

A concurrent mindset that influenced the American Dream also sought
uniformity and establishment. Beginning in 1720, the first Great Awakening bolstered New England Congregationalism and Calvinism, which
looked to the revival of popular piety as an opportunity for conversion.
The First Awakening was followed in short order by the second, which
began in New England in 1790s.[9] Both movements emphasized the role of
America as the epitome of the potential that was inherent in a Christian
civilization. Together the Awakenings were a significant attempt to move
the pendulum of change away from the threat of diversity toward a
homogeneous social order.

The American Dream thus grew from a confluence of ideologies. Para-
doxically, it became equally identified by an image of conformity and by
symbols of freedom of expression and diversity. The skeleton of the dream
was given flesh by Enlightenment individualism. Yet, individualism had
also found expression in the model of an informed citizenry who served
the needs of a virtuous republic. To work for the common good was the
highest individual honor. Both forms of individualism found expression in
the mythology of the frontier.

In a historical context, the dream was pushed in the direction of
rationalism and religious pluralism, profoundly symbolized by such expressions of enlightenment philosophy as the Virginia Bill for Establishing
Religious Freedom.[10] At the same time, it was pulled by the fiery oratory
of Jonathan Edwards and other leaders of the Awakenings to the acknowledgment that America was properly the pinnacle of Christian civilization.

The Influence of Horatio Alger

As the nation matured, so did the dream. Retaining its inherent ambi-
guities, the dream became a symbol of the Protestant ethic as a key to
success. As the stepchild of philosophers and orators, so it also drew
momentum from literature. In particular, the literary image of the indus-

trial giants of the late nineteenth century, enhancing the role of the individual and the quest for prosperity, became attached to the dream. Perhaps the greatest popular influence in this process was the work of Horatio Alger.

The name was virtually a household word in the late nineteenth and early twentieth centuries. As the author of 135 books,[11] many of which first appeared as serials, Alger wrote of a new type of hero. Ragged Dick, Phil the Fiddler, Paul the Peddler, and a host of other characters became the mainstay of his success. Each story fit a rigidly defined scenario of a poor, struggling worker who captured a vision of success and worked hard to realize it. This rags-to-riches model of achievement was also the stuff of the American Dream. Alger's books tapped the dream and gave it flesh and personality. At the same time, they magnified the level of escapism that was associated with it. Ragged Dick became an ideal that most persons could aspire to but, despite Alger's contention otherwise, few could realize.

There was little doubt that the author's ability to speak for the mythos of America was the reason for his popularity. Success certainly did not come about because of his literary style. He did not pen a great American novel. His characters did not possess the depth that is usually found in fine literature. The playwright Russell Crouse, in an introduction to a compendium of Alger's stories, perhaps best expressed these sentiments:

> Horatio Alger wrote 135 books. They sold close to 200,000,000 copies, I am told. I am not, however, told why. I don't think anyone knows the complete answer. They are completely devoid of literary style. They reflect truth no more accurately than a Coney Island mirror. They contain about as much humor as the Greek Orthodox funeral service. They have neither sound construction nor true characterization.[12]

Crouse also concluded that the heroes of Alger's novels were not the Ragged Dicks or the innumerable other young men (there were virtually no heroines) who miraculously rose from rags to riches. Rather, the real heroes of his books were those persons the youths sought to emulate.[13] The "opulent bankers," the "successful lawyers," the millionaires—these were the pivotal characters of his work. The struggling young men who tried to imitate these barons did not always meet with success through hard work and struggle. The chance reward of a wealthy stranger, a stroke of good fortune, or even blind luck itself frequently propelled them to succeed. The qualities that made them successful reflected their willingness, like the baronial figures who were their models, to use any opportunity to climb farther up the ladder.

But that was the nature of the American Dream. Foremost, it proclaimed that through hard work and perseverance one could rise from rags to riches. Nelson, the newsboy, or Ragged Dick improved their lot through personal sacrifice and hardship. But Alger added yet another layer to his interpretation of the dream—the prevalence of compassionate benefactors who would reward struggle and hardship with almost a divine blessing.

For example, in *Street Life in New York*, fourteen-year-old Ragged Dick makes his living as a bootblack.[14] Alger presents Dick as unabashedly poor but also as honest. He does not want to be like his other friends, who think nothing of stealing. To the author, morality is always rewarded, and so in this story, Dick's life takes an important turn when he returns fifteen cents to an industrialist named Greyson, who soon takes him in and becomes his benefactor. The "hero" (Alger's term) is clearly Dick. Yet the real focus of the story is the kindly benefactor who makes Dick's rise to success possible.

That Horatio Alger was caught up in his times is unmistakable. Born in 1832, he was the son of a Unitarian minister.[15] Ordained in the same tradition in 1864, he witnessed the beginning of the Industrial Revolution. Before he died in 1899, the giants of his day, including J. P. Morgan, Cornelius Vanderbilt, and Henry Ford, were popularly identified as pinnacles of the American Dream. They were self-made entrepreneurs who had amassed great fortunes in rapid succession. They controlled vast numbers of lives and rewarded those who had won their approval.

The Influence of the Lincoln Legend

Alger's portrayal of the American Dream was influenced by yet another image that reinforced the emphasis on individualism, the life of Abraham Lincoln. The Lincoln legends had become part and parcel of the nation's vision of itself. While the dream was formed before the birth of the republic, it found its greatest personal identification in the legends of the backwoods lawyer who, through hard work and achievement, became President. Alger was drawn to this mythology and ultimately used it in a novel.

The legends, apart from the reality of Lincoln, emphasized several characteristics that supported the American Dream. On the one hand, they emphasized honesty and the ability of the individual who worked hard to achieve success. As a folk hero, Lincoln was virtually uneducated (having attended but one year of school). In spite of his lack of formal education, he acquired enough knowledge to become licensed as a lawyer and to maintain a well-reputed practice. Further, in the legends Lincoln was popularly identified as the champion of the poor. This image was enhanced by his leading the war that ended slavery and his evolution as an emancipator. It placed Lincoln solidly on the side of the oppressed. However, in so doing, it ignored another dimension of his background—

that of the shrewd corporate lawyer who comfortably and intentionally acquired power.

On the other hand, the legends present a picture (which was perhaps more grounded in truth) of the rise of the backwoods laborer[16] to power through association with the rich and powerful, the same scenario that dominates Alger's books. Lincoln's marriage to Mary Todd, who came from a prominent southern family, was a significant turning point in his career. Her father had been an officer in the War of 1812, a state senator, and a bank president. Lincoln's continued association with persons of position and power ultimately was responsible for gaining him the support of such people as Attorney Edwin M. Stanton.[17] This support served to furnish opportunities for debate. It was a debate with Stephen A. Douglas that ultimately catapulted Lincoln to seek the nomination for President. His marriage, friends in high places, and his ambition and drive had put Lincoln in a position to run for office. Thus a helping hand from an entrepreneur and an opportunity provided by a kindly benefactor were important parts of the Lincoln legend. The United States was viewed as a land of opportunity where perseverance could pay off not only by direct compensation but by providing additional opportunities for patronage.

Alger's extension of the American Dream, like the dream itself, drew its momentum from a variety of sources. Enlightenment philosophy, nurtured by images of a land whose streets were paved with gold, gave the narratives a firm hold on the importance of the individual. Accretions of legend about Abraham Lincoln provided a mold into which these earlier idealogies were cast. The fusion of philosophical currents was completed by the addition of a passion and a pietism whose origins were religious. As filtered through Alger's books and stories, the American Dream gained its spirit from the Great Awakenings. It was not an accident that Alger had begun his literary career as a divinity student. The dream thus became a utopia, emphasizing the natural role of America as a land of fulfillment and hope.

Yet, it was in this part of Alger's work that the dream crystallized a contradictory image. It came to affirm both the potential of the individual to find success and at the same time a larger homogeneous view of the society in which that achievement could take place. To this end, it found support in yet another ideology—the melting pot.

The Melting Pot: Israel Zangwill

In 1756, the French-born essayist J. Hector St. John de Crèvecoeur talked of a new "race."[18] He saw America as a cauldron, a crucible, in which all of the races, ideologies, belief systems, customs, and cultures of other countries were melted down into a superethnic amalgam. It was this "new" American that became the fruit of the American Dream. Unhampered by any of the old idealogies or ways of life, the new American would achieve all that other races and cultures could not accomplish. After he had visited the colonies, he described this new American in 1782:

> I could point out to you a family . . . whose grandfather was an Englishman, whose wife was Dutch, whose son married a French woman, and whose present four sons have now four wives of different nations. *He* is an American, who leaving behind him all his ancient prejudices and manners, receives new ones from the new mode of life he has embraced.˙. . . Here individuals of all nations are melted into a new race of men.[19]

Later, this vision would find compatability with the theories of the Social Darwinists. The image of an evolutionary superior race was quite compatible with the notion of an amalgam, purified in the refiner's fire.

Although the melting pot imagery had long existed in the public consciousness, it was catapulted into the forefront of the nation's attention shortly after the turn of the nineteenth century. The impetus was a play first produced at the Columbia Theatre in Washington, D.C., in 1908. Israel Zangwill's *The Melting Pot*[20] illumined the struggles of a Jewish family in New York City. In a variety of encounters with their Irish maid and Gentile friends, the family experienced life in a new land with constant reminders of the difficulty of maintaining their religious heritage and Russian identity.

Zangwill's melting pot imagery was an example of what sociologists now term an amalgamation theory.[21] Unlike assimilation theories in which minority groups become consumed by a dominant culture or majority, in amalgamation theories, there is no assimilative process. Rather, each minority becomes part of a continual process of fusion. While there may be traces of the earlier groups in language or in religion, the new amalgam bears little resemblance to its component parts. Zangwill wrote:

> The process of American amalgamation is not assimilation or simple surrender to the dominant type, as is popularly supposed, but an all-round give-and-take by which the final type may be enriched or impoverished. Thus the intelligent reader will have remarked how the somewhat anti-Semitic Irish servant of the first act talks Yiddish herself in the fourth. Even as to the ultimate language of the United States, it is unreasonable to suppose that American, though fortunately protected by English literature, will not bear traces of the fifty languages now being spoken side by side with it, and of which this play alone presents scraps in German, French, Russian, Yiddish, Irish, Hebrew, and Italian.[22]

The central character of *The Melting Pot*[23] and the vehicle for its symbolism is David. A young boy with a Nordic appearance and a zest for

composing, David represents the immigrant experiences in glowing, utopian imagery. He cherishes the discovery of the new land as the fulfillment of a dream. Even the ordeal of Ellis Island, the disembarkation
point for thousands of immigrants, is depicted with a sense of fulfillment.
Despite its overcrowded conditions, it is a symbol of hope. That hope is
conceptualized by the image of the crucible:

> Now understand that America is God's Crucible, the great Melting-Pot
> where all the races of Europe are melting and re-forming! Here you
> stand, good folk, think I, when I see them at Ellis Island, here you stand
> in your fifty groups, with your fifty languages and histories, and your fifty
> blood hatreds and rivalries. But you won't be long like that, brothers, for
> these are the fires of God you've come to—these are the fires of God. A
> fig for your feuds and vendettas! Germans and Frenchmen, Irishmen
> and Englishmen, Jews and Russians—into the Crucible with you all!
> God is making the American.[24]

As the play continues and as David completes the symphony that he is
composing, the reader is aware that the symphony is itself a symbol of
amalgamation. The variety of sounds of the instruments, each of which is
unique, produces an even greater sound in the orchestra.

The heart of *The Melting Pot*[25] as a play and as an ideology was the
assumption that all vestiges of race and religion would be boiled down in
the crucible and remade. Thus, when queried about his identity as a Jew,
David was quick to reply that, while in the older traditional civilizations
race and religion had to stand out, in the United States, it was just the
opposite and the process of amalgamation was more important.

Zangwill's understanding of the melting pot is also given theological
significance. The creation of the crucible is seen as an act of God—a
manifest destiny—in which America becomes a savior. The play concludes
with David's benediction to America—a land in which he now finds great
peace:

> There she lies, the great Melting Pot—listen! . . .—the harbour where a
> thousand mammoth feeders come from the ends of the world to pour in
> their human freight. Ah, what a stirring and a seething! Celt and Latin,
> Slav and Teuton, Greek and Syrian,—black and yellow—. . .
>
> Yes, East and West, and North and South, the palm and the pine, the
> pole and the equator, the crescent and the cross—how the great Al-
> chemist melts and fuses them with his purging flame! Here they shall all
> unite to build the Republic of Man and the Kingdom of God.[26]

It was no accident that *The Melting Pot*[27] utilized religious imagery in
making its point. Long before Robert Bellah developed the concept of
American civil religion, *The Melting Pot* had hinted at it. What the play

depicted in its description of the amalgam was not just a secular image. The symbolism also spoke to the issue of homogeneity in religion. In so doing, it lifted up a combined image of God and country that merged the two so completely that they were often difficult to separate. The grace of God was the salvation of America. Both offered a new identity, which was equally linked to the concept of a beneficent creator and the fruit of the creation—America.

The current regeneration of civil religion by members of the conservative right has drawn on the same affirmations that *The Melting Pot*[28] identified. Again, there is a blurring of lines between allegiance to God and allegiance to country, each of which is given equal priority. This has been coupled with an emphasis on conformity that is the actualization of the melting process that Zangwill envisioned. Differences are melded into a homogeneous whole where distinctions in race or ethnicity are understood as secondary to the divine order. In other words, the crucible, the "refiner's fire," is of greater importance than the components that are melted together.

Ironically, while Zangwill's imagery became popular, the play met with mixed reviews when it was first performed. Some called it an idyllic, utopian vision of little substance. Others praised its vision. The greatest criticism, however, came not from the general public but from Jewish organizations and congregations.[29]

Equally ironic was the fact that Israel Zangwill had been instrumental in the resettlement of thousands of Russian-born Jews in the United States.[30] For him the significance of this work and of the play was the promise of a utopian world in which there was both racial and religious homogeneity. While surmising that Jews would "melt" more slowly than other groups, Zangwill nevertheless posited, and even hoped, that they would be fused into the larger fabric of American life. He boldly asserted that "There will be neither Jew nor Greek."[31]

It is no wonder that *The Melting Pot*[32] became controversial. While it was performed countless times both in formal theaters and on college campuses across the nation and in Europe, it managed both to excite a vision of a utopian America and at the same time to raise the ire of those who sought a very different ideal. One of these was Horace Kallen, who first popularized the term cultural pluralism.[33]

The Mosaic, or Cultural Pluralism: Horace M. Kallen

If the melting pot imagery was born on a stage, so the response—a vision of cultural pluralism—was the product of a classroom. In 1915, Harvard-educated Horace M. Kallen began a series of articles in *The Nation*.[34] For the next nine years in a variety of journals, the author's arguments continued, culminating in a book, *Culture and Democracy in the United States*.[35]

Kallen was a philosopher who wrote from the point of view of history and psychology. He sought to counter three sources of contention about race: the racist teachings of the Ku Klux Klan, the popular understanding of assimilation as a means of neutralizing the perceived threat of immigration, and the appeal of the amalgamationist vision of the melting pot as promulgated by Israel Zangwill. Kallen argued that neither the process of imposing the characteristics of the majority on minorities (assimilation) nor the combined "melting" of groups to produce a "new" American race (amalgamation) was compatible with democracy.

It is hardly surprising, given the tenor of the times, that Kallen came forward. Between 1910 and 1924 more immigrants than ever before entered the United States. As their numbers swelled, a backlash steadily increased, generating more hate literature and a renewed cry for restrictive legislation. The result of this continued agitation was the series of immigration statutes previously mentioned (focused particularly on Asians) that sought to curb the flow.

The nation had entered a period of extreme conservatism. It was marked by a resurgence of the Ku Klux Klan and by a tremendous Red scare in the United States at the time of the Russian Revolution. But more than that, following the end of World War I, there was a pervasive general malaise. The uneasiness and despondency were, in part, due to a realization that the war had made unavoidable, the realization that the vision of racial superiority, born of colonial imperialism and nurtured by accretions of Social Darwinism, was not without substantial challenge in a world that was more interdependent than most Americans had wanted to believe. Kallen surmised:

> What this war did was to turn the anxiety about the independence of American culture into a despair about its existence. . . .
>
> A widespread hysterical taking of stock began. Immigration, formerly more than welcomed as an economic boon, was now scrutinized as a eugenic menace. The stuff and form of the American being were reëxamined, not by visitors from abroad any longer, but by scared lodgers at home. Racial theories were promulgated descanting variously upon the magical superiority of the Nordic Stock.[36]

The malaise helped accelerate public acceptance of both assimilation and amalgamation as national emphases. Accordingly, legislation in 1917, 1921, and 1924 reduced the numbers of the most diverse of the immigrant groups and the most difficult to assimilate—the Asians.[37] Racially motivated, this powerful series of laws supported the views of those who sought to end immigration as a major force in American life.

The argument over the wisdom of assimilation as a national policy was both a scholarly debate and a significant public movement. The movement was dubbed Americanization and gathered a wide base of support. It became official policy in a number of states including Nebraska, Iowa, and Minnesota with more liberal versions in Delaware and California.[38] The Americanization movement demanded deference to the dominant Anglo-Saxon culture and called on immigrant groups to assimilate.

The movement was so broadly based that it spawned an occupation, that of the "Americanizer."[39] These professionally trained persons worked with the immigrant population in a variety of places, from shops and factories to night schools and settlement houses, teaching English and basic American values. The movement was so strong that even private industry was caught up in it and proudly contributed to the effort.

The Americanization movement was supported by a number of prestigious studies, some of which were backed by industry. One such effort was the Carnegie Study. Like other analyses, it was based on the premise that cultural assimilation was inevitable. It was identified as a homogenizing process that melted cultural differences into a new form.

Another study, Emory S. Bogardus' *Essentials of Americanization* (1919), suggested, "Americanization is a phase of assimilation—a process which transforms unlike attitudes and behavior into like attitudes and behavior."[40]

However, as "unlike" became "like," a number of other concerns entered the process. Bogardus concluded:

> Americanization is teaching foreigners to be satisfied with their jobs.
>
> Americanization is the suppression by vigorous means of all radical elements in our country.
>
> Americanization is the reducing of the foreign-born to a uniformity of opinions and beliefs in harmony with Americanism.
>
> Americanization means teaching English and civics to foreigners in order to enable them to secure naturalization papers.
>
> Americanization is a paternalistic program for helping ignorant foreigners by utilizing the superior ability of the native-born.[41]

Bogardus's conclusions about the Americanization process were related to the mood of the country. The prevailing fear of Communist intrusion provided incentive for the deportation of persons suspected of being radicals. Also expelled were religious dissenters such as Seventh Day Adventists.[42]

Kallen was convinced that despite attempts at Americanization, racial differences could not be reduced. Again, with a strong note of sarcasm, he concluded, "Different races responding to the same stimuli are still different, and no environmental influence subtle as thought and overwhelming as a tank can ever remold them into an indifferent sameness."[43]

Kallen saw the Americanization movement as the ideological tool of the monied, Anglo-Saxon upper classes, supported by complacent industry. Its objective was to assimilate members of diverse ethnic groups into a pliable mass whose identity and values were compatible with those of the majority. As public policy, the Americanization effort was industry serving its own ends, providing an available, cheap source of labor that would not question the values of the system within which it was employed. Kallen later chided that the euphemism "one for all and all for one" had been replaced by a new concern, "all for one and all in one."[44]

Such a public policy, Kallen theorized, was not in the best interests of a democratic social order. To counter the popular appeal of both the Americanization and the melting pot imagery, he coined a new term and a new ideology—cultural pluralism. He suggested:

> Cultural growth is founded upon Cultural Pluralism. Cultural Pluralism is possible only in a democratic society whose institutions encourage individuality in groups, in persons, in temperaments, whose program liberates these individualities and guides them into a fellowship of freedom and cooperation.[45]

Kallen envisioned unity in diversity. He contended, in perhaps his most remembered symbol, that like the instruments of an orchestra, each producing a distinctive sound, racial differences are unique and cannot be diluted.[46] While they may work together in a harmonious relationship, they can also work against one another in dissonance. But like the sounds of a symphony, they retain an individuality. Ironically, the same metaphor had also been used by Israel Zangwill as an image of the melting pot, as has been noted. In the eyes of David, the symphony and the orchestra that produced it were analogous to the creation of a new, vibrant sound that differed from any of its component parts.

Kallen presented the image of the orchestra not as a utopia as much as a process. He reasoned that while an orchestra may perform a symphony in which elements of harmony or dissonance are part of a score, a civilization of differing ethnic groups does not predetermine its course. There is no utopia, no goal toward which every group and the nation itself must move. Rather, there is a process in which cultural identity is a creative tool capable of shaping the advancement of civilization.

The Americanization effort and the melting pot each produced powerful ideologies that gripped the country. In conjunction with the American Dream, they lured countless thousands of immigrants to the nation's shores, and once they had arrived, proclaimed that their only legitimate identity was that of Americans. Names were shortened upon entry at Ellis and Angel islands, efforts at Americanization were vehemently pursued, and ethnicity was denied as being beneficial in any way. As Tatha in E. L.

Dockterow's novel *Ragtime*[47] demonstrated, for many immigrants the route to "success" was accomplished by a combination of ingenuity, resourcefulness, and above all, prompt attention to the matter of Americanization.

The vision of cultural pluralism was much less powerful. Where the melting pot was a popular image, the idea of cultural pluralism appealed to a smaller cadre of intellectuals. Perhaps the greatest legacy of this approach, however, was the influence that it had on a variety of subsequent studies.

A Renewed Vision: Louis Adamic

Between the wane of the Depression and the beginning of World War II, Louis Adamic wrote that America had lost its vision and its dream.[48] His concern was born from the earlier work of Horace Kallen, who had opposed the melting pot ideology. Adamic wrote:

> But somewhere in the roar of our industrialism, somewhere in the tension of our commercialism, that dream was all but lost. . . . we are a rootless, bewildered, uncertain people. Life on a mere economic plane, we have come to realize, has proved as impermanent, shallow, and sterile as the lands of the Dust Bowl, and we fume and blow fruitlessly in the winds of Depression. We have no deep tap roots in a cultural past to give us continuity, stability.
>
> Now here we are . . . our thoughts and actions touched by hysteria; the strands of our complicated ethnic past not yet interlaced into anything that gives pattern and texture to our life as individuals and as a people. Here and there the stuff in the "Melting Pot" has melted the pot.[49]

Adamic rejected the wisdom of the melting pot, doubting if such an amalgamation process could occur. On another level, he rejected the concept altogether. The "stuff in the pot," he theorized, could melt the pot because ethnic values could not be suppressed and in fact were to be celebrated.

Adamic wrote against the tenor of his times. The nation had passed laws severely limiting immigration. The Depression and the slow tortuous recovery had focused the nation's energy and attention at home. There was very little concern for ethnicity or cultural pluralism.

In a number of books, Adamic addressed the concerns of ethnic groups that had been forced to "melt," suppressing their identity. Nowhere were his sentiments more clearly expressed than in a description of an anonymous Japanese émigré.[50]

Arriving in California's Angel Island with thousands of other Japanese, he had been immediately aware of the prevalence of anti-Oriental feelings. There were those who called for the assimilation of all Asians. More frightening sentiments came from yellow journalism—hate literature in newspapers and journals that were aggressively racist. Such odious pieces as the *Anti-Japanese Hymn of Hate*[51] appeared in newspapers on the East and West coasts in 1916.

Under these strained conditions, Japanese immigrants were often tempted to forego any association with their national origins. Adamic's Japanese émigré chose a small California town in which to live, away from the larger Japanese community. There, the family ignored Japanese customs as they tried to assimilate. They gradually drifted away from eating traditional Japanese foods or from doing anything that might be seen as Oriental. Yet, they were not ready to suppress their identity entirely:

> As for clothing, we all wore Western clothes. The only Japanese articles were the house slippers. None of us has any Japanese costumes, except Mother—her wedding dress, a lovely, if a little faded, kimono decorated with Japanese designs or symbols. My father had a Japanese wedding costume, too, but he threw it into the sea on the trip from Japan, just before reaching San Francisco. . . .
>
> There are no other pictures in our home, no Japanese prints or mottoes, and definitely no picture of the Emperor or of the sacred, snow-capped Fujiyama. In his shop, on the shelf above the stack of towels, behind the gas water heater, my father has a little statue of Buddha.[52]

The icon of Buddha was symbolic of a level of ethnicity that refused to melt. After all of the American patterns of dress, diet, and cultural conventions had been peeled away, there was still a kernel of Japanese identity that, hidden behind the towels and the gas water heaters, could not be suppressed. It was this of which Adamic wrote. To the Japanese émigré, it was symbolized by a small icon. To an Austrian, whom Adamic gingerly characterized as "The Old Alien by the Kitchen Window,"[53] it was an understanding that he was both Austrian and American. He was American by virtue of twenty-five years of work in the mills, and because of the fact that despite his failure to obtain naturalization papers, he was here. He was Austrian because of his language, his refusal to change his name, and more important, simply because that was who he was. To these persons and to others, Adamic lifted up a vision of unity in diversity, of the need to take ethnicity out of the attic and to celebrate it, all the while building ties with other ethnic groups and with the "Old Stock" Americans.

The Triple Melting Pot: Will Herberg

Perhaps the most significant advance in theory following Horace Kallen's introduction of cultural pluralism was Will Herberg's triple melting pot. The theory was promulgated in 1955 as part of a text entitled *Protestant, Catholic and Jew*.[54] Acknowledging the influence of H. Richard Niebuhr (*The Social Sources of Denominationalism*)[55] and Oscar Handlin (*The Uprooted*),[56] Herberg offered an observation based on earlier theories.

His assumption was that among immigrants the third generation was particularly significant. The first generation still retained the language and customs of the parent country. While many first-generation immigrants were caught up in Americanization movements and wanted to adopt the prevailing way of life in the United States, their allegiance was nevertheless to the culture from which they had come. Thus, as Kallen had correctly understood, among these persons the prevalence of Norwegian on Sunday morning in Norwegian churches in states such as Minnesota might well be more concentrated than in Norway itself.

Members of the second generation, Herberg theorized, were often caught up in an attempt to ignore their cultural origins. They had been raised not as the "uprooted" but as persons whose homeland was the United States. Pressures in public education frequently persuaded many second-generation immigrants to forego their cultural origins and the language of their forebearers.

The third generation, Herberg further hypothesized, was marked by a return to a search for identity. By the time that most immigrant families had reached the third generation, they had also moved away from the center of the ethnic community. Frequently they had become suburbanized and were part of the evolving middle class that grew so dramatically after World War II.

For members of this generation, identity was not found in the ethnic enclaves that they had left behind but was discovered in religion. For them, their identification as Protestant, Catholic, or Jew became paramount and was a way of marking an identity that the second generation had lost.

The triple melting pot was a unique synthesis of earlier theories. First, it suggested that for third-generation immigrant groups, religion frequently replaced ethnicity as a primary means of self-identification. Second, it affirmed a relationship among the three dominant religious groups—Protestant, Catholic, and Jew—that had many of the same dynamics as Kallen's vision of cultural pluralism. Third, Herberg theorized that while a "melting" process was not evident among Protestants, Catholics, and Jews, it was visible within each community.

Herberg's theory was also a product of its times. In the 1950s the United States was in the midst of an accelerated return to religion. Across denominational lines, church membership had increased. Writing from a perspective that saw accelerated growth in the three religious communities, Herberg sought to explain the vibrance of the traditions.

Again, conditioned by his times, Herberg saw Protestantism, Catholi-

cism, and Judaism as the only real options for religious identification of
any substance:

> A convinced atheist, or an eccentric American who adopts Buddhism or
> Yoga, may identify himself to himself and find his stance in life in terms
> of his anti-religious idealogy or exotic cult, although it is more than likely
> that a Yankee turned Buddhist would still be regarded as a "Protestant,"
> albeit admittedly a queer one. But such people are few and far between
> in this country and are not even remotely significant in determining the
> American's understanding of himself.[57]

Writing in the early 1950s, Herberg was undoubtedly correct. Other
religious groups were small. The growth of the new religions, which
escalated later during the Vietnam War period, and of the mainstream
Asian religions, which increased after the liberalization of immigration
laws in 1965, had not yet taken place.

He could hardly have imagined that the characteristics of religion in the
United States would have changed so much. Thirty years later, the mainstream Christian denominations he saw growing have declined, and the
religions that he described as esoteric and remote have become increasingly familiar. While Protestantism, Catholicism, and Judaism are
still the dominant forms of religion in the nation, the experience of
diversity has moved out of the periphery into the mainstream of American
life.

The New Ethnicity

After the difficult and often tumultuous decade of the 1960s, sociologists began to take a new and increasingly sophisticated look at the
consideration of ethnicity. What they found was a substantial lack of any
scholarly study of the field since Herberg's work.

The students of the new ethnicity included Andrew M. Greeley (*Eth-
nicity in the United States*,[58] *The Denominational Society,* [59] and numer-
ous other papers and articles); Nathan Glazer and Daniel P. Moynihan
(*Beyond the Melting Pot*[60] and *Ethnicity, Theory and Experience*);[61]
William Newman (*American Pluralism: A Study of Minority Groups and
Social Theory*);[62] Michael Novak (*The Rise of the Unmeltable Ethnic*);[63]
Milton Gordon (*Assimilation in American Life*);[64] Harold Issacs (*Scratches
on our Minds: American Images of China and India*);[65] and others.

These authors had come to the conclusion that the dynamics of ethnicity in the 1960s and 1970s had changed. In *Beyond the Melting Pot*[66]
and *Ethnicity: Theory and Experience*,[67] Glazer and Moynihan hypothesized that the "new" ethnicity is not simply a continuation of cultural
identity as understood in the past. Instead, they suggested that like the

word ethnicity, which appeared first in English dictionaries in the United
States in 1953, the concept is new:

> We are suggesting that a new word reflects a new reality and a new usage
> reflects a change in that reality. The new word is "ethnicity," and the new
> usage is the steady expansion of the term "ethnic groups" from minority
> and marginal subgroups at the edges of society—groups expected to
> assimilate, to disappear, to continue as survivals, exotic or trou-
> blesome—to major elements of a society.[68]

The authors also emphasized a seemingly contradictory experience.
They suggested that on the one hand the nation is deemphasizing ethnicity as the designation "American" is more broadly defined in the
society.[69] Yet, on the other hand, there is also a tendency for ethnic
groups to emphasize their racial and cultural heritage.

In making this claim, the authors pointed to the experience of black
Americans in the 1960s. The tenor of the civil-rights movement was an
effort for blacks to be included in the society and to enjoy the same
opportunities as all other citizens. Blacks did not choose to separate from
the society at large. Yet, at the same time, the adjective "black" rather
than Negro American was adopted, and it was accompanied by a fresh
concern for ethnic history, cultural values, and African heritage. There
was a tendency to become more ethnic and to increase the level of ethnic
identification while seeking a greater level of participation and ownership
in the society.

In a revision of their text in 1970 Glazer and Moynihan described what
they saw:

> When we wrote *Beyond the Melting Pot*, the alternatives seemed to lie
> between assimilation and ethnic group status; they now seem to lie
> somewhere between ethnic group status and separatism. Earlier assim-
> ilation seemed to us the unreal alternative, today it is separatism that
> holds that status.[70]

By far the most comprehensive of approaches to the "new ethnicity"
were those that understand assimilation and cultural pluralism as interrelated processes.[71] This tack has been advanced by Glazer and Moynihan,
who also suggest that minority groups assimilate at different rates, generating social identification and developing entry into the political process.[72]

Related positions have been maintained by both Greeley and Newman.
Greeley concludes:

> William Newman makes the point that the assimilation and pluralist
> model can coexist in complex societies. The assumption that they are

mutually exclusive concepts for understanding American society cannot be accepted.[73]

Gordon argues that not only are pluralism and assimilation interrelated, but they interface through the association of two sets of variables.[74] These include race, religion, and ethnicity as well as class, urban-rural residence, and sectional patterns of residence. In making these observations, he assumes that the study of minority groups is related to the social context in which they occur.

Gordon's major study, *Assimilation in American Life*,[75] discusses the process of adaptation from cultural assimilation—the way minorities adopt patterns of dress, customs, or languages of a dominant culture[76]—to structural assimilation—the acceptance of minorities by the mainstream. Various aspects of that process include, on the part of the minorities, intermarriage with the mainstream and a tendency to identify themselves as American, and on the part of the mainstream, the elimination of prejudice, discrimination, and conflict.

The Irish in New York in the nineteenth century are an example. Unlike other ethnic immigrant groups, the Irish moved throughout the city as domestic servants. As this process continued, and as the waves of anti-Catholicism subsided, the Irish were able to enter a number of societal institutions, achieving a greater degree of structural assimilation than other groups.

Gordon theorized that if structural assimilation occurred, a number of other stages often followed.[77] The first stage of this continuing process of adaptation and adjustment was the large-scale intermarriage of members of minority groups with persons in the societal mainstream. Intermarriage was often followed by the tendency of minorities to identify themselves as American. As greater identification with the dominant society took place, prejudice and then discrimination were eliminated. The final stage in the process, civic assimilation, was the absence of conflict between the minority and the dominant society over values or power.

While the study of pluralism and assimilation included important advances in theory such as the contributions of Gordon, it also encompassed visions that were overtly ideological. At the forefront of this genre was Michael Novak, author of *The Rise of the Unmeltable Ethnics*[78] and a leader of the white ethnic movement.

Incorporating the approach of his predecessor Louis Adamic, Novak argued that the European ethnic groups had been forced to abandon their ethnic and cultural heritages. The offending ideology was the melting pot, which, he argued, had insisted that the only identity of value was American. For many first-generation immigrants who sacrificed their names and their ethnic identities, the promise of the melting pot was the hope that their children and their grandchildren would have a different life. Of this, Novak, a third-generation Slovak, writes:

> What has happened to my people since they came to this land nearly a century ago? Where are they now, that long-awaited fully Americanized third generation? Are we living the dream our grandparents dreamed when on creaking decks they stood silent, afraid, hopeful at the sight of the Statue of Liberty? Will we ever find that secret relief, that door, that hidden entrance? Did our grandparents choose for us, and our posterity, what they should have chosen?[79]
>
> Now the dice lie cold in our uncertain hands.

In the midst of his pessimism, Novak captured a fresh vision of ethnic identity. He became an outspoken leader of the new pluralists, who touted cultural pluralism as an ideology and who supported their position with refinements of established theory.

Novak suggested that it was the immigrant experience that frequently imparted an understanding of what ethnicity actually meant. Thus, immigrants from Italy did not think of themselves as Italians but as Calabresi or Siciliani. With a high level of humor, he later concluded that the State of Czechoslovakia "was chartered in Pittsburgh."[80] These and other observations led Novak to assume that the melting pot simply hadn't worked. Moreover, it had quite an opposite effect. It had actually increased a sense of ethnic awareness among persons who found that while the new nation in which they lived did not value their ethnicity, they did. This was a reaffirmation of Kallen's suggestion that Norwegians in churches in Minnesota often spoke more Norwegian than in Norway. Adamic would have certainly agreed.

Novak concluded that the white ethnic movement, the empowerment of predominantly blue-collar workers who had long been forced to forego their ethnic identities, was changing. What was replacing an artificial identity imposed in the melting process was a new vision, born on the foundations of theory and nourished by a powerful, long-dormant ideological force. This was America coming of age—a phoenix rising from the ashes of a giant cauldron in which groups did not melt but only remained hidden beneath the surface. Novak suggested:

> In any case, millions of Americans, who for a long time tried desperately even if unconsciously to become "Americanized," are delighted to discover that they no longer have to pay that price; are grateful that they were born among the people destiny placed them in; are pleased to discover the possibilities and the limits inherent in being who they are; and are openly happy about what heretofore they had disguised in

silence. There is a creativity and new release, there is liberation, and there is hope.

America is becoming America.[81]

Assimilation Versus Pluralism: Opposing Points of View

From the debate between the followers of Israel Zangwill and Horace Kallen to the supporters and detractors of Louis Adamic, the discussion on assimilation and pluralism has always been dialectical. Whenever theories have been recognized publicly, they have been challenged.

The arguments of the new pluralists in the 1970s were not an exception. Perhaps the strongest criticism of their position came from two scholars, Howard F. Stein and Robert F. Hill.[82] They questioned the initial premise of the new ethnic movement, namely, that it is new at all. In so doing, they correctly suggested that the emphasis on ethnicity and plurality has had ample historical precedent—and by implication, has been both lauded and berated before. Weston La Barre in the foreward to *The Ethnic Imperative* thus concluded, "In the hands of most writers the 'new ethnicity' has seemed to many anthropologists no more than the old and familiar 'ethnocentrism' dressed up with a modish new cant title."[83] Similarly, Stein and Hill questioned the "mystification" of the ethnic studies movement and the manner in which ethnic identity had been glorified by it. They suggested that the new ethnic movement spent too much time lifting up the value of cultural differences:

> The impulse to create culture anew arises from a crisis in the existing culture. The New Ethnicity is one among many diverse expressions or symptoms of the contemporary American malaise and of attempts to resolve it. . . .
>
> In contemporary America pluralism prevails, legitimating every conceivable kind of difference. Difference itself is glorified. . . . The New Ethnicity emphasizes that to be ethnic, as opposed to being 100 percent American, is not to be a deviant, a cultural oddity, or even un-American. On the contrary, to be ethnic is to possess "soul," to have an authentic identity, and to be mentally healthy. Thus the New Ethnics are far superior to the rootless Americans.[84]

Stein and Hill did not deny the existence of a plural society. Rather, it was with pluralism as an ideology that they quarreled.

The debate has been more than academic. It has been the passionate conflict of diametrically opposed ideological forces. This is nowhere more clearly evident than in the dialogue with Michael Novak. Each of the three authors uses terms that are thickly laden with ideology. In critiquing Novak, for example, Stein and Hill characterize him as a prophet, albeit of a movement that, to them is misguided. The "prophet," they contend, is a herald of the creed of plurality, who, with a cluster of "disciples" and supporters, holds that "American culture is especially culpable because of its insistence on homogeneity and homogenization."[85]

Stein, Hill, and Novak have each built their arguments on the foundations of earlier ideologies. Thus, in rebutting the pluralist imagery, Stein and Hill tout the value of the original melting pot theory:

> The mosaic mythos . . . is static and expresses a yearning for completeness, finality. While the principle of *fusion* describes the dynamic of the Melting Pot, the principle of *fission* describes the process underlying the mosaic. Whereas the Melting Pot mythos suggests an open-ended process both in spatial and temporal representation, the mosaic mythos suggests spatial closure and a time-frozen, stagnant quality. . . . While the Melting Pot was exclusively American, the mosaic is both ethnic and American. The new whole is thus by design fragmented. "Unity in diversity" is a motto which expresses the pluralist ethos.[86]

For Stein and Hill, the melting pot remains a dynamic process while cultural pluralism becomes a static vision, devoid of any process at all. Pluralism is instead, they suggest, a pattern—a mosaic—whose principal characteristic is fragmentation. In advancing this argument, the authors seek to discredit a newer ideology advocating a return to an older vision, which they suggest holds the essence of the American experience at its heart.

In Conclusion

Each of the ideologies briefly described in this chapter has developed in concert with the American experience. De Crèvecoeur's notion of a unique American amalgam was based on his experience of life in the American colonies. Later, Zangwill, the Russian-born Jew, put forth the idea of a giant cauldron, a melting pot, in which the new American conceived by De Crèvecoeur was given substance and identity.

As the vision of the melting pot was born of French mothers and Dutch wives, so it claimed the American Dream for its support. The dream was given new life by the transformation of an infant nation from a colonial empire to an industrial giant. Horatio Alger popularized this vision in his novels on the theme of the ability of even the poorest of poor persons to rise to success through honesty, preseverance, and above all, the aid of a kindly benefactor.

Ironically, the ambiguity of the dream gave equal support to the very different emphasis on freedom of expression and unity in diversity. Kallen conceived of a model that was more like an orchestra than the crucible of the melting pot. The power of the American experience, he argued, was not in a process that reduced cultural differences to obscurity but rather one in which they would remain as symbols of a freely expressed identity.

It was not until the 1960s that racial criteria for immigration were eliminated and the vision of the new ethnicity arose. Glazer and Moynihan wrote of a new sense of ethnicity that they observed in New York City, where large populations of blacks, Puerto Ricans, Jews, Italians, and Irish did not "melt." They suggested that now race and ethnicity rather than religion had become decisive forces. The new ethnicity was carried even further by Novak, who talked of the growing sense of cultural identification among white ethnics, and William Newman, who probed the relationship between pluralism and conflict.

Since these works have been written, the 1980s have been characterized by a high incidence of intergroup conflict. For instance, in 1985 violence erupted when a black family moved into a white neighborhood in a highly segregated part of Philadelphia. In the midst of the race riots of the 1960s, such an incident would have drawn little attention. However, in a period that is often perceived to be beyond such intense racial conflict, the event rapidly became national news, suggesting that ethnicity has not ceased to be an important source of identification—or of prejudice.

Similarly, examples of conflict over the introduction of non-Christian traditions into community life are not difficult to find. Whether the group is a mainstream Asian religion or a new religion with its origin in the counterculture, the unfavorable reaction has been the same. The groups are stereotyped as cults and rejected much as the nation has historically singled out varient forms of non-Protestant religions as beyond the best interests of public life.

As ethnic and religious groups continue not to melt, so the 1980s have also included a significant backlash to racial and religious diversity. There has been an increased tendency to segregate communities that are already ethnically polarized. Minorities with long histories in the United States have often reacted strongly and sometimes violently to the continued presence of newer groups. There has been a further call for immigration "reform."

These developments suggest that the national struggle with questions of homogeneity and diversity has far from subsided. The struggle has produced conflict both in acts and in ideas. The debate has been ideological and theoretical and has been intertwined with events in different historical periods. During peak periods of immigration before 1924, theories of amalgamation and Americanization flourished. As the nation's doors were finally shut, an argument for cultural pluralism arose. As ethnic diversity increased in a climate that emphasized freedom of expression and identity, as well as civil rights reforms, the debate about pluralism continued in the form of new argument over the new ethnicity.

The next stage in the polemics over racial and religious diversity and homogeneity is uncertain. Whatever the focus, the same ideologies of assimilation, amalgamation, and cultural pluralism will influence the form of the discussions. They continue to be supported by an ambiguous and equally divided national self-image—the American Dream. In light of the nation's new diversity and the strong conservative appeal for conformity, it is doubtful that the issues will soon be resolved.

CHAPTER **4**

Pluralism and Denominationalism

This chapter examines the ways in which the two contradictory views of a homogeneous or a diversified society have been manifested in the American denominational system. The most obvious manifestation is the historical tension between levels of establishment and disestablishment, between those who have defended orthodoxy and those who have dissented from it.

This tension is well known and is intrinsic to the denominational system and its tendency toward schism, division, and increasing amounts of diversity. Dissenters and advocates of alternatives to orthodoxy have created a panoply of denominational forms such as the southern Old School Presbyterians, who differed with the northern New School Presbyterians over the issue of slavery, and the Unitarians, who were convinced that New England Congregationalists were too dogmatic.

The following pages focus on other expressions of the contradiction, which are less visible. Following an introduction to the characteristics of American denominationalism, the chapter examines a variety of the most diverse religious bodies, some of which are popularly looked upon as cults. A cult, or "new religion," is an alternative pattern of faith to mainstream patterns.[1] Cults are often publicly stereotyped as corrupted forms of religion that exhibit behavior that is contrary to accepted American values. Despite this perception, this chapter demonstrates the manner in which these "new religions" have begun to conform to the mainstream American denominational model and, as a result, the struggle that many have had to retain their identity.

The chapter concludes with a discussion of systemic movements that

126

have been influenced by the two ideologies. They include the rush toward uniformity in civil religion and Christian ecumenism and the affirmation of a unity in diversity (analogous to Horace Kallen's perception of cultural pluralism) in interfaith dialogue.

Characteristics of a Denominational Society

Religion in the United States is active, not passive; outgoing rather than contemplative. It is generally accepting of the social order, although it has periodically sought reform. It is pluralistic, congregationally ordered, and highly susceptible to schism and division. At the same time, in its pragmatism, it has a tendency to be highly individualistic, a tendency that has been understood in the context of denominational and congregational autonomy. Much in keeping with the values of the nation in which it is practiced, religious values in the United States are understood to be a matter for profoundly individual decision.

Originally the product of seventeenth-century Calvinists and Independents in Holland and England, the concept of denomination as a voluntary association quickly was adapted to the United States.[2] It was a natural vehicle for a developing society that was increasingly pluralistic and that sought a way both to comprehend and, in many instances, to contain diversity. As more and more churches competed for members, even those religious groups that held a vision of an established state church soon accepted the principle of disestablishment and diversity, with the denominational form as its most logical expression.

Voluntarism

Unlike Europe, where established churches had a long history of governing religious life, the voluntary association became dominant in the United States.[3] It received momentum from the Second Great Awakening, at the close of the eighteenth century. When church and state became entirely separate and religion became innately associated with voluntarism, the denominational model gathered strength.[4] Voluntarism was that understanding of religion that saw the denomination as dependent on actively securing its means of support (and the basis of its organization) from gifts of time, talent, and treasure from members. The chief characteristic of voluntarism as the *modus operandi* for the denominational movement was the gathering of people of similar ethnic backgrounds and social rank to worship and congregate together. Thus, the historian Sidney E. Mead defined the denomination as "a voluntary association of like-hearted and like-minded individuals, who are united on the basis of common beliefs for the purpose of accomplishing tangible and defined objectives."[5]

Voluntarism differs from the type of behavior in what sociologists have called *Gemeinschaft* societies.[6] In such traditional cultures, religion is not defined in terms of membership. Instead, persons are born into their faith and assume a role in it in the same way that they do in the larger society about them. While religious organizations may exist, they are not responsible for fund raising or for evangelizing new members. Rather, these avenues of support come about because of the nature of society itself.

In a denominational society, voluntarism is based on the principle of religious freedom. Mead concludes, "Voluntaryism is the necessary coralary of religious freedom which, resting on the principle of free, un-coerced consent made the several religious groups voluntary associations, equal before but independent of the civil power and of each other."[7] Ross Scherer also surmises that denominations exist within an environment whose premise is toleration in the midst of a competive, pluralistic system. He suggests that "when the term denomination is used, it refers not simply to the kind of internal form but to a kind of sociopolitical environment—that of pluralism, competition, church-state detachment and agree-to-disagree toleration."[8]

Another characteristic of denominations as voluntary associations is their relative decentralization and congregational orientation. Even the most seemingly bureaucratic denomination relies on a decision-making process that may be spread out over a wide geographical area involving large numbers of congregations.

David A. Roozen, William McKinney, and Jackson W. Carroll suggest that congregations perform a number of functions. They are social and economic institutions. They provide people with a sense of meaning in their lives and "the opportunity to see their own existence in relation to a source and purpose that transcends everyday life."[9] They are agents of socialization for children; status-giving agencies that are avenues of location in community life; and sources of social solidarity, control, and reform, as well as being important symbols of continuity.[10] While congregations may reflect the values of the community around them, this is not always true, particularly for groups that see themselves in a prophetic role. Finally, congregations are frequently homogeneous organizations containing "like-hearted, like-minded," people.[11] Yet, this principle also has exceptions widely known and easily identified.

Problems of Transplanted Asian Religions

Because American denominations stress congregational worship and voluntarism, faiths that do not may have difficulty adapting to life in the United States. A congregational and voluntarist emphasis is foreign to most traditional Asian religions. Hinduism, for instance, is centered in the family and in private acts of devotion. The home, not the temple or church, is the locus of worship. Temples do not contain space for congregational gatherings.

When Asian religions are transplanted and begin to become denominations, they become voluntary, emphasizing defined membership patterns and a communal or congregational emphasis, which is integral to their survival. Like the European Christians who established churches in the United States in the colonial period, Asian devotees have been drawn to congregational life because of the common need of strangers who share the same ethnic and religious backgrounds to find avenues of emotional support.[12]

The European churches, already congregational in worship, readily adapted to American denominationalism. Unlike the churches, the Hindu temple, the Buddhist *vihara,* and other Asian institutions often experienced difficulty with this emphasis. As a result, the process of denominationalization has been more threatening and the risk of the loss of tradition greater.

As European transplants, the churches also had little difficulty integrating diverse numbers of immigrant peoples into common fellowships. Although regionalism in Europe produced differences that were often hard to overcome in the United States, there was no natural barrier that prevented a church from integrating a diverse membership and from retaining a standard of orthodoxy.

For a tradition such as Hinduism, however, the same integrative function is not as easily assumed. In India the Hindu temple functions within a defined level of ritualistic purity, or caste, that attracts only a particular range of believers. The temple cannot integrate devotees of differing ritualistic status through worship. It may, however, perform this function economically through the villages and lands that it controls.

When Hinduism has become a denomination in the United States, it has been faced with a contradictory role. Since Hindu temple societies are frequently sources of solidarity for the Asian Indian minority, they must integrate their membership. Through social events, in worship, and in the organization's structure, members often form a tightly knit community. Yet, in the majority of U.S. Asian-Indian communities, persons originate from a variety of locations in South Asia and therefore exhibit different levels of ritualistic purity. Since the temple is cut off from its traditional economic role, worship becomes one of the few contexts within which integration can occur. Persons exhibiting different levels of purity are brought together in the same sanctuary, a practice that would cause great distress in India. As a result, the loss of caste is inevitable.

Another characteristic of American denominationalism is its relationship to ethnicity. A strong case for this correlation has been made by both Martin Marty and Andrew Greeley.[13] Greeley concludes that American denominations tend to support rather than deny bonds of ethnicity:

> . . . religion will come to play a quasi-ethnic role under two sets of circumstances: (1) a deprivation of intimate community as a result of the collapse of the *Gemeinschaft* village; and (2) the absence of an established church (official or unofficial), membership in which is almost coextensive with membership in society. Where these two conditions emerge, as in the United States, Canada, Switzerland, and Holland, religion will provide self-definition, social location, and a pool of preferred role opposites and will flourish in its organizational forms.[14]

Even when religious traditions are not dominated by particular ethnic groups, they come to play a quasi-ethnic role by helping members maintain a common allegiance.

American denominationalism, then, is a voluntary system characterized by its relative decentralization. Denominations have important associations with ethnicity and are congregationally ordered. They also rely on a certain homogeneity of form and function and frequently have affirmed and supported the status quo. As H. Richard Niebuhr authoritatively expressed it, "Denominations, churches, [and] sects are sociological groups whose principle of differentiation is to be sought in their conformity to the order of social classes and castes."[15]

An interesting example of the tendency of denominations to conform to the expectations of society is the effort of churches to increase membership. Corresponding to accepted marketing and management practices, some advocates of church growth have rejected diversity altogether, suggesting that is a hindrance to growth. Instead, they emphasize single-cell organizations in which churches can maximize their potential for membership and expansion.[16]

Four Types of Ecclesiastical Organization

The drive for church growth illustrates one way that the denominational system exercises its expectations of conformity and homogeneity. Other ways denominationalism encourages uniformity are common elements of structure from one denomination to another. Gary Burkart has developed a helpful typology of ecclesiastical organizations that shows some of these characteristics.[17] Within the typology, there are two types of organization, coalitions and federations. A coalition is defined by cooperation between relating organizations in a denomination, while a federation depends on a more formal structural association.[18] There are also two styles of decision making, authoritative and democratic. Four combinations of types of denominational organization are therefore possible: the authoritarian coalition, the authoritarian federation, the democratic coalition, and the democratic federation.

In Burkart's typology, the **authoritarian coalition** is described as a "small, autonomous, homogeneous, undifferentiated and a non-formalized group headed by a charismatic leader."[19] This kind of structure is often found in many new religions, or cults. The new religions have relatively small memberships in which theological and behavioral conformity is expected. Members may wear similar clothes (often in keeping with the country of origin of the tradition), and they may pay allegiance to a single, charismatic figure who, in many instances, founded the faith.

The **democratic coalition** is much like the authoritarian coalition with the difference that it has not fully legitimized power into authority.[20] There is no basis in this kind of structure for a single, charismatic leader with total authority. Therefore, authority is often invested democratically in a variety of strong leaders. Burkart describes the structure of the Churches of Christ as an example of this kind of organization. As a coalition, the organization claims to maintain no denominational framework that goes beyond the local church (although a variety of "agencies" do exist). Instead, complete authority rests in each local church. Projects are funded cooperatively among congregations, with the money usually staying on a local level.

The next type of denominational structure in the typology is the **authoritarian federation,** in which power is fully institutionalized.[21] Burkart uses a corporate analogy in describing this kind of organization but carefully distinguishes it from its secular counterpart. The difference lies in the fact that denominations are voluntary organizations. Decisions made in the hierarchy are thus always subject to the ability of each level of structure in the denomination to be persuasive and to motivate the membership to support it. Unlike the democratic federation, the authoritarian federation is often confessional. In each instance, power is fully legitimized into authority. The bishop, the district superintendent, the archbishop, and other ecclesiastical offices are all understood as legitimate parts of faith and have theological as well as organizational support. The United Presbyterian Church, the United Methodist Church, and the Episcopal Church are examples of authoritarian federations.

These offices find no counterpart in the **democratic federation,** where authority is less rigidly defined and consequently where there is greater difficulty in legitimizing it. The democratic federation "structurally resembles the authoritative federation but has not sufficiently institutionalized power into authority."[22] As a federation, it includes an organizational structure that goes above and beyond the local church or religious institution, and hence, there is a variety of levels in which authority exists. Because of its democratic nature, however, where power exists, it may not necessarily be seen as legitimate authority. There is no system of rules or confessional structure that gives unhesitating support to, or legitimizes, all forms of power. Therefore, when differing agencies, instrumentalities, or parts of the total denominational structure attempt to exercise power, there is always a need to legitimate their authority. The United Church of Christ is an example of a democratic federation. Each of this denomination's agencies or instrumentalities, therefore, must legitimize power each time that it acts. The distinction within the denomination of established and recognized instrumentalities reflects this same concern.

Asian Religions in the United States: Identity, Diversity, and Assimilation

This section examines Hinduism, Buddhism, and Islam as practiced in the United States by persons born into the faith and by converts. Each religion has experienced some form of societal reaction to its degree of diversity. Each has also experienced a tension between its ability to retain its identity intact and the pull of a denominational society to assimilate and adapt to that society. Together they represent a cross section of the struggle for religious freedom and the functional reality of a voluntary society in which that freedom has specific limitations that govern an organization's ability to survive.

Most traditional Asian societies are *Gemeinschaft* societies built on the premise that religion and the social order are much the same thing. The majority of persons are born into a faith and perceive religious obligations as an important duty within the context of their family, village, or larger community. Religion is closely linked with law, art, science, and a host of other facets of civilization. This close relation between religion and the social order is in contrast to the situation in the United States, where religion plays a less important part in everyday activities and denominations are voluntary associations whose ties are easily switched or broken. Many Americans will go "church shopping" when moving to a new community, often cutting across denominational lines to choose a congregation in which they feel at home. Americans join a church in the same way they join a fraternal or benevolent association or social club. If membership is not satisfactory, they can easily withdraw.

The following pages will demonstrate the manner in which transplanted Asian religions as practiced by converts and those born into the faith have adapted to this denominational milieu.

Hinduism in the United States

Among converts to Hinduism, denominationalism is an important dynamic. It exists in the great variety of religious centers, ashrams, and communes that are currently found across the United States. One of the more important movements of Hindu derivation that has become profoundly denominational is the International Society for Krishna Consciousness (ISKCON), also known as Hare Krishna.

Converts: The International Society for Krishna Consciousness. The ISKCON was founded in 1966 when a devotee of the deity Krishna, Srila Prabhupada, visited the United States.[23] Prabhupada (born Abhay Charan De) came from Calcutta and had turned to a religious vocation late in life. A disciple of the spiritual master Srila Shakti Siddhanta Saraswati (1874–1936), Prabhupada became convinced that it was his master's wish that he bring Krishna Consciousness to the West. In 1965 he left India aboard a steamship with only seven dollars in his pocket, convinced of the importance of his mission. Arriving in the United States, he began his missionary work among members of the counterculture, eventually forming the International Society for Krishna Consciousness.

Prabhupada and the organization that he developed had their roots in the bhakti, or devotional, movement, which flourished in North India in the fifteenth through the seventeenth century and continues to the present day. It stressed intense devotion to a single god and was highly pluralistic with numerous sectarian forms. Among the Vaishnava forms, dedicated to the worship of the god Vishnu, was the Chaitanya Sampradaya (sect), devoted to Krishna, an incarnation of Vishnu. The chief inspiration of the sect was Chaitanya, a sixteenth-century religious leader who preached the importance of worship of Krishna and the *kirtan*, or repeated singing of Krishna's name. This practice, in keeping with the tenets of the bhakti movement, was egalitarian and available to all. It marked a change that was perceived as a reform of classical Hinduism, which limited access to scripture and to direct service of the gods to the upper strata of the caste system.

The ISKCON has adopted not only the theological stance of the Chaitanya form of Vaishnavism but it has also patterned a life-style built on stereotypical assumptions about Indian culture. In this process, it has imposed a higher level of conformity than the environment in which its parent tradition formed. For these devotees, the ideal life is patterned after a utopian interpretation of classical Indian civilization. The desire to replicate this pattern of life has progressed to the extent that the ISKCON's leadership now speaks of their intent to replicate the *varnashramadharma* system, which, in Vedic literature, is identified as the fabric of the social order. *Varnashramadharma* is that system of social stratification in which there are four caste groups (priests, soldiers, merchants, and laborers) and four stations of life (those of student, householder, retiree, and ascetic). The system is based more on scriptural images of life than on the historical reality of Hindu society.

The ideal life that the ISKCON seeks to reproduce is that of a *Gemeinschaft* society in which religious obligations are central to the life of the individual and the community. The organization believes that the best way to continue this interaction in a secular society is to form a monastic community. Members live in complete isolation from the rest of the world, away from any influence that would distract their attention from

Krishna. Everything is oriented to his service. Children learn of him in school and also learn Sanskrit, along with the same fundamental literacy and mathematical skills that most American children learn. Adults symbolize their complete absorption in the deity by the shaven heads of men and the covered heads of women. Their dress in the fashion of the Brahmin, or priestly, caste symbolizes their renunciation of the world. They are expected to participate in daily devotions at 4:30 A.M., in which chanting is the chief practice. This community worship reinforces believers' values.

As the community has specific expectations of its members, it also provides for their needs. Some receive stipends. Others may have an outside income. Still others receive food, clothing, or supplies from a free store in the commune. Even vehicles may be provided.

While the intent of the community's organization and its life-style is not denominational, its structure is, although its leaders would deny it. As the community has increased in size, it has evolved from an authoritarian coalition in the 1960s (which was governed by the directives of founder Srila Prabhupada) to an authoritarian federation in the 1970s and 1980s. In that time, the ISKCON has developed a structure akin to that of mainline Protestant denominations. Its use of management techniques, public-relations tactics, membership-growth principles, fund-raising tools, and building programs clearly demonstrates that it has accepted the denominational milieu in which it exists.

In New Vrindaban, near Moundsville, West Virginia, a center of the Krishna Consciousness movement in the United States, there are a variety of indications of the increasing tendency toward denominational structure and organization (see figure 4.1). The community has created a management board that meets weekly. The board makes administrative decisions for the commune that were formerly made by the resident spiritual master. The weekly meetings include the heads of departments in the organization and persons responsible for public relations, planning, and other functions common to denominational life.

Beyond the accretions of structure, the strongest evidence of denominationalism in the New Vrindaban community is its increasing concern for voluntary support. The primary manifestation of this trend has been the creation of an additional level of organization for the purpose of raising funds. New Vrindaban now claims 20,000 "congregational" members.[24] The term is used to refer to persons who contribute to the work of the New Vrindaban community but who are usually not residents. Many of the congregational members are Asian Indians, who contribute to the programs of ISKCON as links with their heritage and background. For many of them, contributions replicate the patterns of giving within established denominational groups in the United States. The desire to contribute in similar fashion to an evangelical effort of Hindu derivation, but not

Figure 4.1   Palace of Prabhupada, a center of the Krishna Consciousness
movement in the United States, New Vindraban, West Virginia

necessarily to participate directly in it, has given the Krishna Consciousness movement a natural appeal.

The strongest denominational thrust of the New Vrindaban center is a
pledging program for the construction of a new temple. The temple is
conceived as the largest effort of its type. Congregational members are
urged to contribute to it through a dollar-a-day program, which offers
incentives, including a pledging bank, two photographs of an artist's
conception of a new temple, and a free three-day stay at a motel in New
Vrindaban, as well as sectarian publications and discounts on meals. In
addition, contributors' names are placed on plaques in front of the current
temple, and each benefactor is supplied with a membership card. The
donor's list and the membership card are clear indications of the successful adaptation of a voluntary system of support commonly found in
most Protestant churches in which membership is clearly associated with
an ability to contribute.

As an international organization, the ISKCON has created denominational structure. One such body is the Governing Board Commission,
created to oversee policy for the international organization to regulate its
spiritual affairs. The commission meets annually to discuss a range of
matters. Included in the organization are leaders, temple presidents, and
spiritual masters. Spiritual masters, or gurus, are highly respected
sources of authority in the faith. In the history of the total organization,

they have been in charge of different parts of the global movement, which has been organized in zones. There has been a recent tendency to define the zones less rigidly than during the ISKCON's early history, giving the spiritual masters more latitude in their control.

The current structure of the ISKCON is a decentralized authoritarian federation in which each temple is considered to be autonomous, owning its own property and maintaining its organization as it sees fit. The spiritual masters and the zone system help give the total organization a sense of unity but are also avenues of authority. Because the total system functions according to rigidly defined rules and because the spiritual masters are legitimated sources of authority, the authoritarian federation prevails. Control of the community, however, has not been acquired without challenge and conflict.

Conflict in the New Vrindaban community has been frequent. The most widely reported violence has been the murder of a disaffected member of the commune, Steven Bryant, and an attack on Kirtanananda Swami Bhaktipada, its spiritual head.[25] Before his death, Bryant, who the sect claims had been excommunicated, alleged that the eleven gurus of the faith (who have now been increased to thirty) had used power for their own gain.[26] The murder of another former associate of the sect and the charging of two others with the crime and a two-million-dollar lawsuit have all been part of the movement's continuing difficulties. The suit charges a former guru with corruption and suggests that he attempted to gain control of a California foundation for personal gain and for the benefit of the New Vrindaban community.[27]

Following the murders and the discovery of a body on the New Vrindaban property, a number of criminal investigations began. As part of these inquiries, Bhaktipada was ultimately tried on arson charges and acquitted. Concerns were also raised within ISKCON's governing body about activities in the commune. The Governing Body Commission finally alleged that Bhaktipada had violated the wishes of founder Prabhupada by allowing himself to become an object of worship.[28] As a result of this concern the fifty-year-old guru was expelled from the organization. However, due to the decentralized nature of the federation, he has retained his leadership position in New Vrindaban.[29]

The conflicts suggest a pattern of dispute revolving around the gurus, who are the primary sources of power. Because authority is focused on these individuals, and because the overall organization is decentralized, rivalry is common. While the incidents have been sensationalized in the media, and are frequently touted as part of the ills of the cult experience, in reality they suggest a level of competition that is not unusual in a denominational society.

Immigrants: Hindu Temples.   Among immigrant Hindu communities in the United States, the denominational model is a sharp contrast to the experience of religion in India.[30] In South Asia, denominationalism as identified in the United States does not exist. While in India, Hinduism is defined in terms of a broad-based sectarian affiliation (Vaishnava, Shaiva, or Shakti), there is no organizational, pan-India form of each belief system. Instead, persons who worship Vishnu, Shiva, the mother goddess Kali, or their incarnations are connected by a series of interrelationships that are more cultural than institutional and are directly related to the predominantly rural environment within which they are found. There is no overt denominational structure and no concept of membership in a national organization.

As indicated earlier, the focus of the Hindu tradition in India is usually centered in the home. There the family worships its tutelary god or gods and provides for the services of the priest, or *acharya*, who officiates at marriages, funerals, and ceremonies of coming of age (*Upanayana*). Religion is understood as a societal obligation that has strong cultural associations, the most pervasive of which is caste. The caste system and Hinduism itself are related to a complex system of purity and pollution that not only determines an individual's relationship to society but to the very god or gods that are worshiped. For Hindus who have been born into the faith and who have immigrated to the United States, the home remains the center of the religious tradition. Prayers may be conducted there daily. A family priest may even be flown to North America from India to conduct particularly important services.

In India, the temple is a traditional center of Hindu culture. It is the abode of the gods. In most villages where it appears, it provides an important economic, cultural, and religious function. Temples often control large amounts of property, provide opportunities for the sale of numerous goods and services, and are important avenues of power in the village. While temples have acquired great economic power, however, it is not understood in the same philanthropic sense as in a denominational society.

Beginning in the 1970s, Hindu temples were transplanted to the United States as more Indians emigrated to North America. Large temples were constructed in residential sections of New York City. A prime example of a South Indian Hindu temple was erected in a suburban area outside of Pittsburgh, Pennsylvania. In other localities across the United States from Allentown, Pennsylvania, to northern California, the Hindu temple tradition began to become a noticeable part of religion in North America (see figure 4.2).

As the temples were erected, there was a curious addition to the tradition rarely encountered in India—the Hindu temple society. In a clear denominational presence, temple societies were established as voluntary (nonprofit) organizations. They maintained an elected body of leaders and devised ways to raise revenue including large festivals and

Figure 4.2   Shiva Vishnu Temple, Livermore, California, a replication of
         classical Hindu architecture in a North American setting

dinners in which the worshiping public was invited to make donations. In
every respect, they began to carve out an existence that was in complete
harmony with the denominational model.

The need to adapt was obvious. While some temples were built with
money supplied from parent religious institutions in India, this effort
could not continue indefinitely. Further, for smaller groups of devotees,
ties with prestigious Hindu temples in India were more difficult to obtain.
For most, the only alternative was to become a voluntary organization and
to raise the funds necessary for the operation of temples, locally and
regionally.

Because temples are religious institutions, they have been accepted as
nonprofit institutions. This designation has posed difficulties for sectarian
leaders, who have had to respond to queries from agencies such as the
Internal Revenue Service concerning the number of members who belong to their "church." It has also come to symbolize the pressure on
Hindu temple societies to maintain a congregational organization.

The denominational model was also perceived as a way of gaining
acceptance by the general public, which frequently has misunderstood
Hinduism. It afforded shelter from public scrutiny and means of self-
sufficiency with no obligations to relate to other religious institutions.

As already suggested, however, denominationalism brought about significant changes in the operation of temples. In India, the cycle of daily

worship in the majority of temples is conducted for the benefit of the deity. The god is awakened, given a showerbath, and offered food and entertainment as an honored and regal guest each day in established routines. At some of these times, worship, or *puja*, is open to the public, providing opportunity for the temple to receive offerings.

In the United States, while the regimen of the god may be equally important, there is a considerable difference in the life-style of his or her supplicants. Many leave home in the morning and commute to work in another location. There is no village tradition to support the temple and no regular offering for its maintenance and support. In these instances, many temples have adapted *pujas* to fit the schedule of commuters and have advertised the sponsorship of *pujas* by mail. In such instances, *prasad*, or food offered to the deity, may be mailed to the faithful. This practice assures devotees that the merit they receive from regular worship can still be secured from major temples, even at a distance.

Throughout India, Hindu temples own vast quantities of land and frequently lease it to entire villages. The system provides for an income for the temple and also for the laborers who serve it. There are a great variety of these, including sweepers, washers, cooks, attendants of the deity, and priests. They belong to caste groups, that is, levels of purity or pollution associated with occupation, and are part of a complicated social system called *jajmani*. In a reciprocal arrangement, members of these caste groups perform services for one another as well as for the temple. In return, the temple servants may be provided a place to live in a temple-owned village. Such arrangements, inherited within families, are maintained over many generations. Thus, through the social network that it controls the temple integrates different strata of society.

In the United States, such a complex social system does not exist. Temples are not economically connected to villages as they are in India. There is no caste system to provide caste-related services, and few persons are able to serve the temples in the same manner as in India. The only alternative for the temple is to seek the services of volunteers. However, because volunteers usually include a broad spectrum of the Indian community, they represent a wider variety of caste than in an Indian village. When U.S. temples integrate such a diverse body of volunteers in functions associated with worship, there is an inevitable loss of tradition.

In summary, both converts to Hinduism in the United States and immigrants who have been born into the faith have been denominationalized. Each group has perceived the need to participate in the voluntary system, recruiting membership (through conversion and invitation), raising financial support, and securing both professional and lay leadership.

As a result of this activity, American Hindu groups have formed a wide variety of denominational forms whose focus has been the individual temple. Small local groups of converts, under the leadership of a guru figure, have tended to form authoritarian coalitions. Larger federations such as the ISKCON tend to move toward increased decentralization but still retain their authoritarian control.

Among immigrants, there has been a tendency to form democratic coalitions and federations. This has often occurred because Hindu temple societies have formed without the kind of guru figure common to that form of the faith practiced by converts. Instead, the principal dynamic within the immigrant community has been that of lay leaders, who have banded together to form coalitions. Significantly, this has been a locally based movement in which permanent national bodies have not yet been created. The organizational activity has been almost entirely democratic with the Hindu temple society or association as its most prolific form. Like its Christian counterparts, each organization supports itself through fund raisers and appeals. It may solicit support from a region that is wider than the area in which its primary membership lives. In a few instances, support may also come from temples in India.

Larger coalitions and federations have, as a rule, not been organized religiously. Instead, they have been formed around linguistic and cultural lines. India clubs and Telagu, Gujarati, or Bengali associations have attracted strong followings.[31] In turn, large federations such as the Federation of Indian Associations in North America have become increasingly important. They have entered the political process, forming grass roots networks that are sensitive to national issues affecting the Asian Indian community.

Buddhism in the United States

Buddhism as practiced in the United States covers a vast array of traditions and movements. Included are Chinese forms (T'ien T'ai, Ch'an, and Pure Land), Japanese forms (Pure Land, Nichiren, and Zen), and forms from Tibet, Thailand, Sri Lanka, (Theravada Buddhism), Korea, Laos, Cambodia, and Burma.[32] Denominationalism has become an important ingredient in many of these forms, among both converts and persons born into the faith. This has been true to such an extent that in 1987 a number of U.S. Buddhist groups initiated a national organization not unlike the National Council of Churches.

Converts: The Nichiren Shoshu Academy.   Of all the new religions of Buddhist derivation in the United States, one of the most overtly denominational is the Nichiren Shoshu Academy (NSA). The organization was formed in 1960 with an initial chapter in California and another in South America. It began as a missionary endeavor of a popular Japanese movement called Soka Gakkai.[33]

Soka Gakkai has been identified as one of Japan's new religions. The new religions flourished after the end of World War II and represented both a reform movement and a popularization of older traditions. Soka Gakkai, founded in 1937, was based on the teachings of Nichiren (1222–1282), a monk from the Tendai Buddhist school. Nichiren emphasized the teachings of the Lotus Sutra, which he saw as superior to all other Buddhist scriptures. Further, he considered all other Buddhist schools, especially the popular Pure Land tradition, heretical.

From the time of its inception, Soka Gakkai has been highly denominational and has relied on layers of structure. Its counterpart in the United States, the Nichiren Shoshu Academy, has continued to embellish this pattern, which has easily adapted to the West. The academy has been concerned with membership trends and, like many of its Christian counterparts, has developed programs to increase its growth. At the end of 1970, the organization claimed a membership of approximately 200,000 and a growth rate of 1,000 new members per month.

Yet, like other new religions in the United States, the NSA has resisted attempts to be seen as part of the denominational system. It shunned identification as a church, undoubtedly fearing any assimilation or change in its basic Buddhist doctrines. For this reason, the movement has retained the designation "Academy."

The Nichiren Shoshu Academy has advanced in the United States by continuing the existing concerns of Soka Gakkai for membership growth, doctrinal conformity, and conversion. North America provided a natural environment for the academy's rapid growth, since each of these elements is already a significant part of the denominational system. In many ways the academy's rapid acquisition of new members has been similar to the growth of some conservative Christian churches. Like its Christian Fundamentalist counterparts, the NSA maintains strict doctrinal exclusiveness. All other forms of Buddhism are dismissed as irrelevant, as are other non-Buddhist religions.

The NSA's appeal has been particularly strong among persons who converted to the faith from Protestantism and Catholicism and who were already receptive to participating in a voluntary organization through the gift of their time and financial support. This appeal was augmented even further by the academy's emphasis on nationalism. This emphasis derives from Soka Gakkai, which has historically been exceedingly patriotic.[34] American flags commonly fly from NSA temples. Discussions that include American values are common. Its publication, the *World Tribune*,[35] often includes an emphasis on United States history.

As a result of its patriotic flare, the growth of the academy is not surprising. It has had a natural appeal for persons who are dissatisfied with their own faith, who may hold strong patriotic values, and who seek an uncomplicated expression of truth. This emphasis has also made con-

version to the faith easier for persons from other denominational backgrounds and at the same time has facilitated the movement's autonomy
and isolation.

The basis of the Nichiren Shoshu Academy's structure is rooted in a
defined membership process. The membership system is based on a
model of personal advancement and reward, determined through a series
of examinations eventually leading to a bachelor's or master's degree in the
faith.

The academy's organizational structure is hierarchical.[36] At the top is a
general headquarters located in Santa Monica, California. A general
director is assisted by three executive directors, each responsible for a
territory (Eastern, Western, and Pacific). Within the territories are area
headquarters, each with its director. In 1974, there were sixteen such
areas within the United States.[37] Every area, in turn, is divided into four
or five communities, each of which is organized in chapters. A chapter
includes five to ten districts, and each district consists of five to ten groups
(han). At every level of the total structure there is a chief or supervisor.

This highly vertical organization is quite aptly characterized as an
authoritarian federation, a description that also applies to Soka Gakkai in
Japan. Although in the United States the Nichiren Shoshu Academy is
considered to be fully independent from Soka Gakkai, control is retained
by communication with the Japanese leadership, which monitors the
academy's progress.

In the United States, the NSA's concern for homogeneity and hierarchical control is so strong that it begins as soon as a convert is identified.
Converts are treated as the disciples of the persons who brought them into
the organization. Several converts with their spiritual leaders form
groups. Groups are in turn organized into peer groups, which are also
established in a strict hierarchical order. The assignment of individuals to
groups and their upward movement in them are strictly supervised.

The vertical structure is repeated within the successive layers of peer
groups. Each level sponsors meetings as well as group activities. In
addition, the peer groups are often used competitively to help promote
the greatest possible level of participation.

Thus, the total structure is vertical, hierarchical, and fully denominational. Not only is membership an important concept, but it is directly
associated with achievement, which is rewarded. The academy's system of
awards is designed as an integral part of its understanding of voluntarism
and is an asset in recruiting and retaining members.

Immigrants: The Buddhist Association of the United States.   Examples
of Buddhist denominationalism are not difficult to find among persons
who have been born into the faith and who have emigrated to North
America. This trend is illustrated by an article about the twentieth anniversary of the Buddhist Association of the United States, which appeared
in a publication of a Chinese Buddhist monastery in New York State in

1984.[38] Printed in Chinese, the publication is directed at the predominantly immigrant community in the metropolitan New York area. The article describes the progress of the Buddhist Association in gaining new members.[39] To illustrate its success, a graph of membership gain is used, identifying the percentage of increase of both Chinese and Caucasians. The use of charts of this type has become popular in church-growth efforts in mainline Protestant churches. Efforts are based on the principle of net membership gain as the necessary ingredient for denominational viability locally, regionally, and nationally.

The emphasis on numerical growth has several different implications that are usually taken for granted in Christian denominations but that may be outside the experience of Asian Buddhists. The emphasis infers, for instance, that the tradition is one that can be joined and that membership has certain obligations such as attendance and financial support. In addition, there is also the implication that competition among denominations is basically healthy and that net gain in membership is the highest possible attainment. Moreover, growth is understood as a congregational endeavor in which membership can be calculated on the bases of attendance or formal affiliation.

None of these assumptions is part of Buddhism as practiced in China or elsewhere in Asia. Ch'an (the precursor in China of Zen Buddhism in Japan), T'ien T'ai, and the Chinese Pure Land schools are each highly ritualistic traditions. They emphasize the role of the individual in achieving enlightenment in the context of the larger Mahayana Buddhist community as defined by the temple, the family, and Chinese culture. There is little understanding of membership, nor is religious obligation seen in the context of joining an association or organization. Rather, what is more commonplace is religious syncretism and the understanding that one can practice more than one form of the faith (or different faiths) simultaneously, depending on individual need and circumstance. This view is so prevalent that it is often difficult to separate elements of popular religion as belonging completely to the Buddhist, Taoist, or Confucian tradition. Finally, while religion may at times be congregational, there is no understanding that it must be so.

The use of a membership chart by the Chinese temple tradition has still another implication. Since the graph demonstrated the growth of both Chinese and Caucasian populations, there is the clear implication that both groups are welcomed. Unlike other Chinese Buddhist organizations, which often prefer to keep their membership almost exclusively Chinese, this association actively seeks converts. The tradition is also assimilative. By welcoming Caucasian devotees and by adopting a denominational model, the association seeks social acceptance and additional support.

Immigrants: The Buddhist Churches of America. In this and other instances, denominationalism becomes a valuable tool for the assimilation of members of the faith who may be foreign born. It is intentionally adopted as a way of achieving institutional survival and continuing the faith in a pluralistic society. It was also true for a Japanese Buddhist denomination in the United States, the Buddhist Churches of America (BCA).

This Pure Land tradition was brought by two Japanese Jodo Shinshu missionaries to San Francisco in 1898.[40] They had been appointed to nurture the Jodo Shinshu faith in the United States by Myonyo Shonin, the twenty-first abbot of the Hompa Hongwanji in Kyoto, Japan.

The Pure Land schools in China and Japan stress the importance of Amida Buddha. This popular bodhisattva (a divine being who postpones enlightenment) is understood as the guardian of a heaven identified as the Western Paradise. Symbolically, the Western Paradise represents enlightenment and release from the cycle of birth and rebirth. The path to enlightenment for the Jodo Shinshu school in Japan, which had been popularized by Shinran Shonin (1173–1262), is the repetition of the *nembutsu*, a sequence of holy words much like a mantra, or sacred formula, in Hinduism. The *nembutsu* consists of the words *Nama Amida Butsu*, or "Praise to Amida Buddha."

As more Japanese emigrated to the United States, the Jodo Shinshu faith grew rapidly. By 1931, the missionary arm of the Hompa Hongwanji in Japan, the North American Buddhist Mission (NABM), had established thirty-three temples with many branches.[41] Tetsuden Kashima suggests that the NABM (which later became the Buddhist Churches of America) adopted a similar structure to that of its parent tradition in Japan.[42] Both were denominational traditions that shared a concept of a hierarchical ecclesiastical organization.

Although the structure remained much the same and approximated that of a democratic federation, the BCA experienced a variety of changes, which were precipitated by an upheaval in the Japanese American community. For most members of the faith, World War II was a traumatic experience. In 1942, persons of Japanese descent were ordered to report to "relocation" centers in the western United States for detention.[43] They remained in these compounds until the end of the war, deprived of property and possessions and separated from the communities in which they had lived.

The effect of the experience was profound. Upon release, many Japanese still felt an intensified pressure to prove their loyalty to the United States and to assimilate rapidly. This pressure was also felt by religious organizations. After the war, Jodo Shinshu leaders voted to change the name of the movement to the Buddhist Churches of America, emphasizing both an identification as churches and as North Americans. Emphasis was placed on the role of the religious leaders as ministers. Temples could either retain the designation common to the faith in Japan or adopt the term church, which many did.

Before World War II, ties between temples in the United States and the Hompa Hongwanji were carefully maintained. All national programs of the BCA were first approved in Kyoto. Structurally and theologically, the movement remained a missionary effort. After the war these ties were gradually redefined as the denomination sought to be more closely identified as North American.[44] Buddhist clergy, who previously had been selected in Japan, were secured by a ministerial association in the United States. Further, the office of bishop underwent dramatic change. In 1968, Bishop Kenryu Tsuji became the first Japanese American to hold such an office, ending the restriction that bishops be born in Japan and affirming the identity of the faith as that of a North American denomination.

In 1973, leaders of the BCA and the Hompa Hongwanji met in an unprecedented session to negotiate their future relationship. The meeting produced agreements on a variety of subjects, including the recognition of the autonomy of the movement in the United States and the right of the BCA to charter its own churches.

Other changes came about with a greater decentralization of the faith in the United States. This was indicated by a transition in the understanding of the designation *betsuin*. In Japan, *betsuin* temples had had a special relationship with the Hompa Hongwanji and were understood to be sources of authority. In the United States, the term was used simply to refer to large temples or churches, often in the center of a district. No special linkage to the Hompa Hongwanji was implied. As part of this change, the BCA created seven districts in the United States to facilitate its organization. Each temple or church was incorporated in its own right and a member of the corporate body of churches.

It was a natural development for a tradition that had denominationalized in Japan to continue on the same track in the United States. The process has not, however, gone unchallenged. The greater decentralization of the churches, the emphasis on the ability of clergy to receive a seminary education in the United States (through the Institute of Buddhist Studies), and the BCA's adaptation of many of the same techniques in education, organization, and church extension as its Protestant Christian counterparts have been important changes. Yet, they have also precipitated a conflict between the desire of the faith to accommodate to its environment and to retain a level of orthodoxy and authority.

Islam in the United States

As a major world religion, including persons from widely divergent cultures, Islam is a complex tradition with a variety of forms. Where it exists in its idealized Qur'anic form—the Islamic state—denominationalism (in the North American model) is usually foreign. Within the Islamic state, emphasis is on the unity of the faith and the oneness of God, or Allah. This pervasive association between praxis and theology is so strong that it makes any identification of religions as a separate domain both untenable and unnecessary. Muslims, like other members of *Gemeinschaft* societies, have had to face the challenge of adapting to the denominational pattern in the United States.

Converts: The Nation of Islam. The movement of Islam among converts in the United States began in 1930, when W. D. Fard, an itinerant preacher, suddenly appeared in black neighborhoods of Detroit.[45] His identity, reason for coming to Detroit, and source of authority were all equally mysterious. Fard was perceived almost immediately as a prophet. Some thought that he was an Arab, but there was little confirmation of his ethnic identity.

Attracting a following, Fard began to preach from the Bible, with which his adherents were familiar. He soon shifted their attention to Islam, however, and to the revelations of the Qur'an. A temple was built, and the mysterious prophet began to build associations between himself and the teachings of the prophet Muhammad. He inferred that he held a special position within the faith.

> My name is W. D. Fard, and I come from the Holy City of Mecca. More about myself I will not tell you yet, for the time has not yet come. I am your brother. You have not yet seen me in my royal robes.[46]

As the infant movement gained support over a three-year period, Fard recruited active leaders from the black community. The foremost of these was Elijah Poole, who later became known as Elijah Muhammad. By the time of Fard's disappearance in 1934, Elijah Muhammad had become the organization's head and had gained full authority. With this change in leadership also came a transition in theological understandings of the role of Fard. The prophet became closely identified with Allah and Elijah Muhammad with the role of prophet. The organization became denominationalized and initiated a building program in which a variety of temples were constructed as well as schools, businesses, and even residences for members.

The denominational thrust of the Nation of Islam (the formal name for the tradition as it evolved under Elijah Muhammad) is best illustrated by the way in which the organization raised funds. A visitor to a temple in the early 1960s recorded a change from previous practices:

> While the minister lectures, money receptacles are in continuous circulation, and the challenge to "support your own" is insistently urged by young ushers moving among the audience. The receptacles are not inconspicuous: they are plastic wastebaskets or large brown paper bags. Such collections are a recent innovation. The Muslim brothers formerly took no public offerings and announced proudly: "Islam takes care of its

own." Now they explain that, since Muhammad has become well-known and "his aims and integrity are established," the public can be permitted to contribute toward his work, "especially the proposed building of an Islamic Center in Chicago."[47]

Under the leadership of Elijah Muhammad, the Nation of Islam became fully denominational, functioning as an authoritarian coalition. Muhammad, who was identified with the prophet, became the sole source of recognized power within the faith.

After Elijah Muhammad's death in 1975, the movement again went through a transition. The change was intentional and assimilative as the tradition sought acceptance by other denominational bodies in the United States. As the faith evolved, it decentralized and was increasingly transformed into a democratic federation of local institutions, or *masjids*.

An effort was also made to place the organization in the mainstream of the global Islamic community. A publication concluded:

> Imam Warith Deen Muhammad, the son of the late Elijah Muhammad, took leadership of the Nation of Islam at the death of his father in February, 1975. He immediately, boldly, insisted on the end of materialistic, racist teaching! . . .
>
> He began to teach Muslims, Christians, and Jews—as People of the Book—that there is but one God, Allah, that we must all serve. Under his leadership, the Nation of Islam grew out of narrow Black Nationalism into Islamic universality.[48]

In addition to these changes, the business activities of the organization were turned back to private ownership. Its name was changed from "The Nation of Islam" to "The World Community of Islam in the West." Linkages were made with public officials in major cities in an attempt to establish better rapport, and ties with other religious organizations in the West were intentionally pursued. Later, still another name was adopted, "The American Muslim Mission," in an attempt to secure the movement within the context of the global community of Islam.

In 1985, the American Muslim Mission announced that its national organization was being dismantled. Individual mosques would continue to exist but without the structure that had formerly coordinated their activities. At the same time, a faction within the movement rose to power. Under the leadership of Louis Farrakkahn, a new organization gathered authority, adopting the original name of the faith, "The Nation of Islam." The faith was once again identified with strict racial policies and with the teachings of Elijah Muhammad. The Nation of Islam became less interested in placing itself in the mainstream of American religion; but within its newly found autonomy and isolation, it remained equally denominational.

Immigrants: The Federation of Islamic Associations and the Islamic Society of North America. When a Muslim soldier, in the United States Army in World War II, Abdallah Igram, encountered frequent prejudice because of his religion, he vowed to find a way to save other members of his faith from similar experiences.[49] Igram's concern was deepened by the failure of the army to recognize Islam as a "legitimate" religion and to identify it on his dog tags. As a result of these experiences, which limited religious identification to Protestant, Catholic, or Jew and denied the option for further plurality, Igram conceived of an organization that might protect the interest of all Muslims in the United States. The result of this vision was a denominational organization, the International Muslim Society, formed in 1952. The society sought to unite Islamic associations in a representative, democratic federation. By 1954, the organization had grown and had adopted a new name, the Federation of Islamic Associations in the United States and Canada (FIA).

For many Muslims, the federation came to symbolize their cohesiveness as a broadly based religious organization that included numerous ethnic groups. While frequently stereotyped as a faith unique unto the Middle East, Islam is in reality a global religious tradition with adherents in such widespread places as Indonesia, northern Africa, Pakistan and India, China, Indonesia, France, Germany, and the United States. It is a highly diversified religion in which the two major sectarian divisions, Shi'i and Sunni, both support the primary tenet held by all Muslims—there is one God, Allah, and Muhammad is his prophet. Although they differ in the perception of authority within the faith, the two divisions are both considered to be Muslim (figure 4.3).

Prior to Igram's bold initiative in 1952, Islamic associations had existed in relative isolation from one another across the United States. Many were formed in cities with large concentrations of Muslim peoples. In Detroit, Michigan; Dearborn, Michigan; Cedar Rapids, Iowa; and other places throughout the East and Midwest, Islamic associations had developed slowly. Staffed by imams, or religious leaders, these institutions were frequently the focal point of the Islamic community. Through classes in Arabic taught in the mosques, children born in the United States were acculturated into the faith.

With the formation of the FIA in 1954, the Islamic associations had an even stronger voice. Large conventions annually provided a forum or seminars on issues affecting many Muslims. Annual contact with representatives from Islamic associations from all over the nation provided an important means of interaction.

This model of organization, governed by elected leaders, was strongly denominational. Its form was a democratic federation, which was national in scope. Much like a synod or national conference, the annual conventions both gave a representative voice to members of individual associations and helped strengthen the cohesiveness of the total organization.

Chester Higgins, Jr., *The New York Times*. By permission.

Figure 4.3 Muslims praying toward Mecca in festival ending Ramadan, in Prospect Park, Brooklyn, New York

In 1982, still another broadly based national Islamic organization, the Islamic Society of North America (ISNA), was formed. The ISNA was organized through initiatives of the Muslim Students' Association (MSA). The Muslim Students' Association is a coordinating body in both the United States and Canada for an Islamic presence on college campuses. As a result of this work, it has established mosques in many communities and schools. The ISNA includes the Muslim Students' Association; the Muslim Communities Association; and three professional bodies: the Islamic Medical Association, the Association of Muslim Social Scientists, and the Association of Muslim Scientists and Engineers.

Both the Muslim Students' Association and the ISNA are democratic federations and are compatible in organization and means of support with other nationwide denominational bodies. As an example of this movement toward democratization, the Muslim Students' Association has traditionally been divided into regions through which it is administered. These zones include the Western, Central, and Eastern parts of the United States, as well as two zones in Canada. Each zone is divided into regions, which are in turn under the authority of regional representatives. Zones are administered through regular council meetings.

Because the denominational model of religious organization adopted by Islam in the United States is so different from Islamic tradition, it has often been a significant source of difficulty in the area of financial support.

For example, the question of contributing to religious organizations in the United States is usually understood as the most private of concerns. Churches go to great lengths to protect the confidentiality of members' contributions. The number of persons with this knowledge is kept to a minimum to safeguard confidentiality. Yet, the churches' work is heavily dependent on a sense of voluntarism. Volunteers may direct an every-member visitation. They may be urged to help persuade others to make a pledge. Most attempts to increase the flow of dollars are also perceived as a way of rekindling the enthusiasm of the membership on which the institution depends.

In most Islamic societies, these concepts are foreign. Religion is perceived as an intrinsic part of society that equally affects private and public spheres. Islam is supported by contributions (*zakat*) that are integral with the life of the state. The *zakat* is assessed at one-fortieth of each individual's personal income and is collected as an expected function of government. The lack of such a system of support in the United States presents a tremendous challenge to Muslims, who must depend on a denominational model of organization.

In addition, the *zakat* provides an important link between individuals and the Islamic state. The fact that it cannot exist in the United States raises a profound sense of loss of mooring or reference. This loss is compounded by the absence of Islamic law (*Shari'a*) in the West. Because it is based on the understanding of an ordered society as defined in the Qur'an, by the example of the life of the prophet Muhammad, and by other avenues of Islamic jurisprudence, *Shari'a* provides an additional link between the individual and the state. In its absence, and in the context of a legal system that is divorced from religion, conflict between Muslim values and the demands of life in the United States can often result.

Such conflict also results from the nature of the denominational system. As voluntary associations, denominations are founded on the principle of the separation of church and state. For Muslims in Islamic countries, who see no separation between religion and government, this is an important difference, which limits the authority of their faith. Further, the influence of Christian dominance in the United States often causes a struggle. For example, Christians tend strongly to see clergy as pastors providing spiritual guidance. Most imams, who are primarily worship leaders, would reject such a notion as foreign to their tradition, yet many feel pressure to function in this manner.

In summary, the growth of Islam in the United States, both among born Muslims and among converts, is fully denominational. For each, growth has been different for a variety of reasons. The movement of Islam among converts has been influenced by a few strongly prophetic leaders, such as W.D. Fard, Elijah Muhammad, Warith Deen Muhammad, and Louis

Farrakkhan, who exercised authority in the black community much as Christian preachers do. The national organizations that were formed as a result of the popular appeal of these individuals became authoritarian federations drawing heavily on the leadership of founder figures. Local *masjids,* in turn, drew their authority from the teachings of the national leadership.

Beginning with the formation of a variety of Islamic associations and mosques in the twentieth century, Muslim communities of immigrants developed as both democratic and authoritarian coalitions, depending on local leadership, size, and the historical development of each institution. The trend moved toward the formation of Islamic associations and ultimately toward larger democratic federations, including the Federation of Islamic Associations, the Islamic Society of North America, the Muslim Students' Association, the Council of Imams, and a variety of professional associations.

Observations

This brief overview of Asian religions in the United States yields several observations. First, it has demonstrated that both classical Asian religions that have been transplanted to the United States and new religions that have arisen from the American counterculture have become fully denominational. As denominational organizations, they share a variety of types of structure, ranging from small local constituencies and single founder figures in authoritarian coalitions, for many new religions, to large, nationally based, democratic federations, such as the Islamic Society of North America.

Second, many Asian religions have preferred the autonomy and isolation that the denominational system allows. The reasons include fear of public reaction as well as concern that the process of assimilation would dilute the tradition. For some faiths that have frequently chosen to build new temples away from centers of urban life, as, for example, Chinese Buddhism, the search for privacy has been paramount. For others, the desire for autonomy has decreased as they have grown from smaller coalitions to more regionally based federations. In many instances, this transition has been accompanied by an increasing democratization of the structure, which has led to a greater receptivity to interfaith dialogue.

Third, there is often a struggle between the homogeneous, *Gemeinschaft* orientation of traditions in their original form and the realization that in the United States such a life-style is difficult if not impossible to maintain. This struggle is apparent both for immigrants, who have left a village-centered life, and for converts, who may attempt communally to create a traditional environment.

Hinduism. The struggle is exemplified by the Hare Krishna movement, which, as noted earlier, has magnified, idealized, and more rigidly imposed the homogeneity of the Indian tradition it emulates to help compensate for the threat that its diversity represents in the United States.

All of this has been done in an American denominational milieu in which groups such as the ISKCON are perceived as cults. Because they do not conform to the expected Judeo-Christian pattern of behavior, they are suspect. Yet, in reality, they exhibit the same characteristics that have become typical of other denominational organizations.

The ISKCON thus is caught on the horns of a dilemma. It exists in an environment where its measure of diversity is not accepted. Yet, it has magnified the homogeneity of the Indian life-style it emulates to the point that it exhibits a greater degree of conformity than its prototype. By adopting a uniform mode of life that is overtly communal and quasi-monastic, the movement's isolation is legitimated and its doctrine protected from the inroads of society.

Among Hindu immigrants in the United States, the struggle between diversity and conformity is particularly felt by the youth. Second-generation Indian Americans are frequently torn between two worlds. On the one hand they are encouraged to become Americans. Yet, on the other, they are urged to express Indian values, although many have lived in South Asia for only brief periods, if at all. Hindu organizations frequently deal with these issues by offering summer camps where traditions are reinforced, by encouraging discussions on the conflict of cultures, and by molding the programmatic life of their temples to be both Indian and American.

As already noted, temples have been established as congregational institutions with defined memberships, methods of fund raising, and democratic processes of electing leadership. Throughout the process of adaptation, there has been some loss of those parts of the faith that have not been viable in the United States such as the caste system. The faith struggles with this, with the ongoing assimilation of its members, and hence with its ability to retain a level of orthodoxy that is defined by the parts of the tradition that it has lost.

Buddhism. The Buddhist Churches of America have struggled with assimilation and identity in a similar fashion. For this tradition, which was organized denominationally in Japan, the tendency to adapt to an American model was logical. Yet, as adaptation took place and a greater percentage of members came to be born outside of Japan, the preservation of their heritage became a significant struggle.

Soka Gakkai met the challenge of acceptance in Japan by espousing highly patriotic values. Its vocabulary became identified with civil religion, allowing the tradition to maintain a level of diversity, hidden beneath a veneer of acceptable behavior. In the United States, where Buddhism is much less likely to be understood or accepted, the Nichiren Shoshu Academy has attempted much the same strategy. Espousing patriotic values, the NSA has become highly nationalistic.

Islam. Among Muslim organizations, the utopian ideology of the Islamic state urges a level of conformity that is difficult to achieve in the United States and hence becomes a focus of struggle. Pressures to conform to a pastoral model of religious life, which is foreign to Islam, create an additional source of tension.

Perhaps the most difficult struggle for Muslim immigrants, however, has been the discrimination that they have experienced, particularly following periods of violence against Americans in the Middle East. Such sustained levels of prejudice are often expressed in ignorance of either the global character of the faith or its sixty-year history in the United States.

Muslims are caught in a variety of contradictory expectations. The society in which they live, work, and worship expects them to conform to stereotypes of behavior based on images of Islam that extend as far back as the Crusades. Stereotypes have frequently led to prejudice and discrimination. Further, parents, grandparents, and religious authorities overseas expect them to retain a high level of orthodoxy. Any adaptation of tradition is frowned upon. Finally, the voluntary society within which they have formed Islamic associations and mosques expects very different measures of conformity. Muslims have met these demands by placing a strong emphasis on the role of national organizations that can interface between sources of authority and orthodoxy abroad, maintain a highly denominationalized presence in this country, and speak to the issue of religious discrimination and defamation.

Among converts to Islam, the struggle between the retention of doctrinal orthodoxy and the process of assimilation and denominationalization has been carried on largely by the leadership. Under the guidance of Elijah Muhammad, separation of the movement from society was understood in the context of race. Such isolation also became a way of protecting the faith from the loss of tradition.

His successor and son led the organization in a very different direction that emphasized adaptation to American denominationalism. The name American Muslim Mission indicated an identity as Americans and at the same time a role within the larger, global community of Islam. When it finally dissolved in 1985, Louis Farrakkhan returned the faith to a racial focus and a state of isolation and protection from society.

Civil Religion, Cults, and Continuing Struggle

Robert Bellah's controversial idea of an American civil religion was initially introduced by means of a phrase of Rousseau.[50] Positing a level of

religious behavior directly associated with patriotism and national fervor,
Bellah distinguished the influence of four strains of thought that molded
the civil faith.[51] These, he suggested, were included in the Declaration of
Independence:

> There are four references to God. The first speaks of the "Laws of Nature
> and of Nature's God" which entitle any people to be independent. The
> second is the famous statement that all men "are endowed by their
> Creator with certain inalienable Rights." Here Jefferson is locating the
> fundamental legitimacy of the new nation in a conception of "higher law"
> that is itself based on both classical natural law and Biblical religion. The
> third is an appeal to "the Supreme Judge of the world for the rectitude of
> our intentions," and the last indicates "a firm reliance on the protection
> of divine Providence."[52]

Civil religion evolved as an expression of conformity to and homogeneity of national purpose. It associated the nation's mythology of independence and individual rights with a higher law and with a God whose image
was shaped by deism and by biblical religion. This highly symbolic level of
behavior therefore had much in common with Christianity but also exhibited some important differences.

> The God of the civil religion is not only rather "unitarian," he is also on
> the austere side, much more related to order, law, and right than to
> salvation and love. Even though he is somewhat deist in cast, he is by no
> means simply a watchmaker God. He is actively interested and involved
> in history, with a special concern for America.[53]

Bellah suggested that civil religion has been an active societal force
since the nation's inception, acquiring accretions of myth and symbols.
The imagery surrounding Abraham Lincoln was a formative influence. In
some instances, a symbolic identification was made between Lincoln and
Christ.[54] The martyred President became an agent of the nation's salvation singularly identified with its purpose and with a God-given destiny.
Lincoln's law partner thus described him:

> For fifty years God rolled Abraham Lincoln through his fiery furnace.
> He did it to try Abraham and to purify him for his purposes. This made
> Mr. Lincoln humble, tender, forbearing, sympathetic to suffering, kind,
> sensitive, tolerant; broadening, deepening and widening his whole
> nature; making him the noblest and loveliest character since Jesus
> Christ. . . . I believe that Lincoln was God's chosen one.[55]

Since Bellah's original thesis, the concept of an American civil religion
has engendered substantial debate. This led him to reformulate his original argument restricting the idea of civil religion to "formal symbols and

statements of nationalist theism—for example, 'In God We Trust.'"[56] The reformulation also led to the theory of public theology, that form of the discipline that perceives America as a "new Israel" whose essence and spirit are divinely ordained.[57]

As statements of national theism, civil religion drew its form and substance from a utopian ideal, introduced in chapter 1, the virtuous republic.[58] The republic, both classical and modern, Bellah suggests, has had several components. These include public participation in the process of government and a citizenry that is neither very rich nor very poor but instead exhibits a measure of equality and a concern for the common good. This is in contrast to a conflicting and incompatible ideal, the liberal constitutional state,[59] which allows expressions of self-interest to seek their own accord.

Like the incompatible ideals of the virtuous republic and the liberal constitutional state, American values have reflected a desire for both homogeneity and diversity. At times, different periods have witnessed the ascendancy of one ideal over the other.

The civil faith and the ideals of a virtuous republic were strongly expressed during the 1950s. The decade was characterized by McCarthyism, by an overzealous concern for conformity, and by a rampant desire to homogenize America. Churches grew, the economy prospered, and all that was perceived as antithetical to the notions of God and country was made most unwelcome.

The undoing of such vehement expressions of civil religion was occasioned only by a loss of the nation's credibility brought about by the combination of the Vietnam War and the Watergate debate.[60] During this time, a variety of new religions arose. At the same time, a new ideal of freedom of expression, individualism, and tolerance for diversity captured the nation's interest.

A number of theories have been formulated to explain the decline of civil religion and the subsequent rise of cults during the 1960s. For Bellah, civil religion was corrupted, becoming "an empty and broken shell."[61] Benton Johnson concluded that the public and private sectors have been widely divided, making civil religion untenable and resulting in the rise of more privatistic groups.[62]

Whatever argument is accepted, it is clear that the new religions and the new diversity fulfilled a variety of purposes. Some, such as the Unification Church, generated their own forms of civil religion,[63] using the symbolism of God and country as a means of legitimization. Others, such as the Krishna Consciousness movement, have not looked to the symbols of civil religion or public theology at all. Instead, drawing from the American ideal of the frontier, they found refuge from society, creating their own self-sufficient environments. Still others, by far the most numerous of the new religions, are mainstream Asian faiths transplanted to the United States. The majority of these classical traditions have no affinity for the counterculture and little inclination to proselytize; instead they have quietly (albeit with great internal turmoil) begun to assimilate to the American denominational system. At times they too have attempted to express the civil religion. For example, The Hindu Temple, a major Indian institution in the New York metropolitan area, suggests that the animal carrier (*vahana*) of the god Vishnu can be identified with the American eagle. This attempt to forge links with the very symbol of the nation's identity is a significant adaptation of tradition.

Religious pluralism thus intensified in the 1960s because of the absence of a single viable form of civil religion. It also increased because of a shift in national values that affirmed the right to be different as part of the American experience. The change in national attitude was not, however, without an opposing reaction, which came in the form of an aggressive movement that understood cults as a national menace.

The anticult movement has often been identified as a "cult" in its own right.[64] That is, the emphasis on aggressive opposition to a form of religious behavior, deprogramming, and a defined dogma of its own created a movement not unlike the stereotype of that which it saw as a threat. The anticult movement drew from civil religion and public theology in emphasizing its understanding of the best American values. At the same time, it imposed a level of uniformity that understood Protestantism, Roman Catholicism, and Judaism as virtually the only acceptable forms of mainstream religious expression.

The anticult movement has continued to be a subject of discussion, but its impact on the public consciousness has waned. In its place a growing segment of conservative Christianity—the Moral Majority—has sought to redefine and reestablish civil religion.

In seeking to regenerate civil religion, the Moral Majority has increasingly associated patriotic values with religious piety. The vision of individual salvation has been united with an understanding of America as an agent of God's creative grace. The melding of the symbols of individual and national salvation has been seized by a type of religious practitioner rarely seen in this century, the evangelist-politician.

As an expression of civil religion, the Moral Majority has pleaded its cause through a variety of public issues. It has done so in a similar fashion to earlier manifestations of public theology when a single moral concern was transformed into a national agenda. This was particularly true about the issue of temperance. Ultimately, the sentiments that led to the passage of the Eighteenth Amendment and Prohibition were the culmination of a long battle in which temperance was seen as a hallmark of Christian progress in a chosen land. It was seen to be "a striking victory for the advance of Christian civilization."[65]

The issues on which the Moral Majority has taken stands—abortion, the role of religion in education (the Christian school movement), and prayer in public schools—are conceptualized with the same measure of uniformity, national purpose, and moral passion as the earlier drive for temperance. Each issue has been perceived as a step toward returning America to an understanding of spiritual awareness and divinely inspired destiny that it is perceived to have lost.

What has made each of these issues extraordinarily heated debates, however, has not been just a revitalization of the civil faith but a broader momentum that has reemphasized homogeneity. The drive for uniformity has often rallied the symbols of civil religion at its forefront but has gone far beyond the images of God and country in its mystique.

The Christian right has come back to a vision of America that has drawn on the notion of the virtuous republic and on the homogenizing forces that have sought a unified citizenry working for the public good. It has dipped into the melting pot and pulled out of it a vision of monolingualism, monoculturalism, and unity without diversity. Its evangelizing message of conformity has sought to redefine the American Dream not in terms of freedom of expression and opportunity but as a collective means to a God-given national destiny.

Christian Ecumenism, Interfaith Dialogue, and the Two Values of Unity and Diversity

The two foci in American religion—homogeneity and pluralism—have taken specific form in two historical movements. The first, the ecumenical movement, has been assimilative and has elevated an ideal of unity and union in which diversity is understood as a hindrance to the more important consideration of merger. The second, the interfaith movement, has sought to bridge the isolation and autonomy of the denominational system but has also retained an appreciation of its diversity.

The ecumenical movement has had an important history in the twentieth century. Following the interest in the Social Gospel in the late nineteenth century, which encouraged Christians to work together on the common problems of suffering and injustice, the emphasis shifted from simple cooperation to the desire for a common religious purpose. This conviction was expressed in the organization of the Federal Council of Churches (today the National Council of Churches), which demonstrated its concern for the unity of the American church.

Ecumenism was later given definition by the liberalizing doctrines of Pope John XXIII, who, in 1962, made Protestant-Catholic dialogue a mandate within the Roman Catholic Church. The consequences of this action were far-reaching. Discussions between Catholics and Protestants were initiated in many communities across the United States with no pretentions of working toward union but with concern for a common theological purpose that would bind the fragmented churches together.

The discussions also offered Protestants another model of religious behavior, which informed the dialogue. As Protestantism has historically been characterized by diversity, so Roman Catholicism offered a more homogeneous model. While some might correctly argue that on a diocesan level Catholicism also exhibits diversity, the homogeneity of dogma, the centralization of authority, and the uniformity of the essential ingredients of worship in the Mass all suggest an integrative tradition markedly different from that of Protestantism. Monasticism with its emphasis on conformity and the role of the disciplined community of faith is an important part of the model.

Historically the Roman Catholic model has met with less than enthusiastic reception in the United States from Protestants. By the early 1960s, however, when Protestant fragmentation came to be an increasing problem not only theologically but economically, the Catholic model was seen in a different light. The softening of the nation's attitude to Catholicism was also witnessed by the election of the country's first Catholic President. The time was ripe not to emulate the model, which represented a very different strain of Christendom, but to learn from it, to communicate with its leaders, and in that process, to begin the task of consolidating the Protestant community, which was unable to speak with anything that resembled a single voice.

As Catholic-Protestant discussions continued, so another strain of the ecumenical movement sought organic union. Throughout the twentieth century, American Protestantism felt the impact of a number of denominational mergers, each of which understood union as a corrective balance to the brokenness of the denominational system.

Historian Winthrop Hudson describes the variety of mergers that were initiated between 1900 and 1960:

> Three Methodist bodies came together in 1939 to form the Methodist Church, becoming the United Methodist Church in 1968 with the addition of the Evangelical United Bretheran (German Methodist) Church. In 1958 the United Presbyterian Church joined with the Presbyterian Church, U.S.A. to form the United Presbyterian Church in the U.S.A. In 1961 Unitarians and Universalists united in the Unitarian Universalist Association. Meanwhile the 24 Lutheran groups of 1900 were gradually reduced in number until by 1960 almost all Lutherans (96 percent) belong to three major bodies—the Lutheran Church in America, the American Lutheran Church, and the Lutheran Church-Missouri Synod. The formation of the United Church of Christ in 1957, bringing together the Congregational Christian Churches and the Evangelical and Reformed Church, was the sole merger which bridged traditional denominational lines of division.[66]

In each of these instances, merger resulted in the ability of the denomination to plan more comprehensive programs and in general to increase its longevity and viability.

In 1962, the same year as Vatican II, another bold step in the ecumenical movement was taken. Building on the history of denominational mergers since the turn of the century, the Consultation on Church Union (COCU) sought to bring the mainstream Protestant churches together.[67] Beginning with conversations between leaders of the Presbyterian, Episcopal, and Methodist churches, as well as the United Church of Christ, a plan was conceived that eventually included ten participants. Although the discussions were diminished by the withdrawal of the United Presbyterian Church, interest in COCU was renewed in the 1980s, albeit with some significant changes in direction.

As it has sought both organic union and a common purpose, so the ecumenical movement has depended on self-interest within the denominational system. Urbanization, competition, and the increasing difficulty of funding adequate resources for voluntary organizations (including denominations) have made merger and union a growing necessity. The unification of divergent strains of Christendom has also been understood as theologically important and also as an element of organizational strength and solidarity. Union has been viewed as a correction to a fragmented system that because of its diversity has become out of balance with its original reason for being.

While the ecumenical movement has been a priority within the denominational system, the interfaith movement has not. Its motivation has not come from self-interest, and in this sense, it has been a movement that, while initiated by religious organizations, has become peripheral to their work. By definition, it has excluded any considerations of merger or union. There has been no common purpose or goal, no common identity that all could affirm.

The interfaith movement in the United States was formally initiated with the 1893 Parliament of Religions, described in chapter 2.[68] The parliament was conceived as an initiative of denominations rather than as a product of academic interest. While the event succeeded in attracting many intellectual giants of the day, the incentive for the gathering came from a group of committed church leaders. The parliament became an exercise in encountering diversity in public life. It was not identified as such at the time nor was it held for the purpose of addressing the issue of pluralism. It was seen as way of celebrating religious diversity, or as was more often the case, defending one's role and claim to truth in the midst of it. Yet, the parliament grew into something much more significant. It became a statement of the possibilities for communication in public life.

The parliament was held in the most public of places imaginable, the Chicago World's Fair. The presence of such an event at the largest public gathering of the decade, the Columbian Exposition, and its overwhelming seventeen-day duration put the event directly and uniquely in the context of public life. It was a microcosm of the world in the heart of a North American city. The street from Cairo, the Javanese village, and the Turkish mosque were all parts of the Exposition that enabled even the casual observer to participate in an unparalleled level of religious and cultural diversity in but a few blocks.[69]

The vision that the parliament engendered for public life was thoroughly experiential. It offered its participants a unique opportunity to experience an intense level of profound diversity firsthand. In its seventeen-day duration, its addresses, discussions, and social gatherings provided numerous chances for contact between persons from different religious and cultural backgrounds. Asian presenters, representatives of denominational bodies, and the general public had ample opportunities to interact.

The parliament was more than an exercise in structured interfaith dialogue. Its significance lay rather in what went on behind the scenes. It raised for the first time the understanding that Asian religions were more than just attractive philosophies that had sparked the imagination and peaked the curiosity of such literary giants as Emerson and Thoreau. The presenters gave very personal statements of worldview nurtured by life experience.

Without even being aware of the nature of its legacy, the parliament became a unique model for approaching diversity in public life. Its very existence was a profound statement that the avenues in public life for the experience and understanding of diversity could be expanded in a way that had not hitherto been explored.

Although the vision of the parliament was profound, however, it was also fleeting. As the swell of immigrants increased, the country rebelled against diversity. Public reaction against the presence of large numbers of Indians and Chinese accelerated. Greater demands for restrictive exclusion laws were voiced. In the area of religion, the conservative evangelical movement continued to capture the nation's spirit as did interest in promoting foreign missions abroad and in proselytizing members of other religions.

Perhaps most significantly, the parliament's vision of interfaith conversation failed to gain a foothold in American denominationalism because it was viewed as beyond the self-interest of denominationalism. Where the churches sought a vision of a unified Christian civilization, interfaith dialogue could only offer a chance to improve relationships among vastly different traditions. It became identified as an abstract process whose goals were often intangible and whose vision of American life was not the same as that of the general public. While such significant bodies as the

National Conference on Christians and Jews were formed in subsequent years, few other lasting effects of the movement were realized throughout most of the next century.[70]

This was in distinct contrast to the ecumenical movement, which increased its ability to effect mergers, initiate conversations, and in general, to build a vision of the organic unity of the church. Such a vision carried with it the implication that a unified Christian Church would have greater authority and a clearer perception of truth than a church in diaspora. Ecumenism became a plea for homogeneity and a vehicle for justifying common patterns of theology and praxis. In this regard it evolved as an extension of the assimilative mechanisms of a denominational society that, despite its internal diversity, has assumed a common framework of organization and purpose.

Whether the ecumenical vision of unity is interpreted as parallel to the nation's interest in securing a manifest destiny or as a utopian pursuit of a wider Christian civilization, it has failed to see much possibility in the diversified fabric of America. Seeing diversity as an obstacle to the forward momentum of humankind, it has sought union not so much for the sake of the recipients of the faith as for the achievement of a wider, more authoritative appeal. In the process of voicing a zeal for a common purpose, it has also internalized its goals in the denominations that have affirmed it.

Because it has been extraneous to the denominational system, the interfaith movement has had extreme difficulty in building similar alliances. Instead, the weight of the system has served to keep extremely diverse groups apart rather than to promote their interaction. There has not been nor can there be common ground in interfaith relationships that will increase membership, insure the longevity of churches, increase stewardship, or create additional congregations.

The interfaith movement has remained a vision of pluralism in the midst of a system that, internally diversified, has sought to promote greater homogeneity. As the denominational system has voiced greater and greater interest in merger and assimilation, so the interfaith movement has had to defend simple diversity.

Finally, the pluralist vision of interfaith relations often was not appealing because it remained a perplexing reminder that the world is complex and confusing with few simple answers. The opposing view (which has been dialectical rather than confrontational) affirmed a homogeneous worldview in which the presence of a unified Christian faith was by its very design seen as a decisive step in the progress of the human condition and as a movement closer to God. The pluralist vision of interfaith relationships could only affirm that should the wider ecumenical vision take place, the effect might not be what was once expected. Differences in philosophy, culture, and religion would still abound. Peace would remain an elusive, fleeting ideal. It is because a vision of diversity could ultimately offer no assurances of stability or order that it became a less attractive model. Only when it is built into the viscera of the denominations who tout it, when it is intertwined with their identity and existence, will its dreams be realized.

CHAPTER 5

Pluralism and Conflict

In the 1970s and 1980s, conflict between majority groups and racial and religious minorities in the United States became increasingly common. In a variety of cities, violence erupted. In Boston, police reported attacks on Asian Americans.[1] In Harlem, disputes broke out between Korean shop owners and black residents. Nearby in the Borough of Queens, conflict between Hispanics and Hindus was reported. In Philadelphia, the move of a single black family into a white neighborhood caused intense racial violence.

Unlike the racial conflict in the 1960s, which was precipitated by the injustices experienced by a single, subjugated black minority for more than a century, these incidents reflect a new type of conflict, one that involves religious and racial minorities in a pluralistic society. Yet, disputes have arisen not just because of an increase in diversity. Instead, they reflect a far more complicated pattern of national existence in which conflict is one dimension of human relationship in a society that continues to experience profound change. They also show the continuing tendency of the society to react not just to differences in ethnicity but also to differences in religion.

The clash of the ideologies of plurality and homogeneity has often exacerbated community conflict. This is not because the different ideologies have always coexisted on a local level as much as it is a result of the presence of contradictory visions of the value of diversity in different segments of the population. When one vision is brought to bear against another, conflict can be created, intensified, or prolonged.

Using the clash of ideologies as an interpretive framework, this chapter

seeks to examine the factors that have propelled communities into a kind
and degree of conflict that would not have been anticipated only a few
years ago. It suggests that conflict focused on religion often involves
ethnic issues as well. For example, disputes involving the practice of
Asian religions by immigrants frequently revolve around stereotypes of
Eastern peoples. Thus, when hostages were taken in the American embassy in Iran in 1979, the news media periodically reported references to
an increased level of vandalism against mosques in the United States.
Although these attacks were directed at religious institutions, they also
resulted from a stereotype that all Muslims were much the same and
behaved like the particular Iranians who had seized the embassy.

Similarly, conflicts that are focused on ethnic or racial minorities may
have significant religious overtones. At the turn of the century when large
numbers of Asian Indians entered California, popular sentiment reacted
against the "Hindu" problem. In fact, the vast majority of the immigrant
Indian population was Sikh. The stereotype confused religious and ethnic
designations and was a poignant reminder of the public's inability to tell
the difference.

In addressing these issues, the chapter begins with a brief theoretical
overview. Then it examines several case studies of ethnic and religious
conflict in which the clash of competing ideologies of pluralism and
homogeneity has been part of a multifaceted struggle in a pluralistic
society. The first study looks at the roots of conflict between competing
minority groups in Pennsylvania and California. The second demonstrates
how, in a pluralistic suburban New Jersey town, short-term conflict arose
over the presence of a new religion that the community perceived as a
threat. The third examines conflict in the western part of New Jersey,
where a Hindu minority sought to establish a temple and a school. A
concluding study shows how in a mid-size northeastern Pennsylvania city,
intergroup conflict exists around a segregated model of community life
that has been passed from one generation of residents to another. However, because there has been some accommodation between understandings of pluralism and assimilation, conflict has been minimal and is
perceived as a defined on-going process of intergroup struggle in a stratified and segregated community.

Theoretical Assumptions About Conflict in a Pluralistic Society

Many theories of social conflict are available to the student of pluralism.
Some assume that conflict is within the normal parameters of the social
order, or consensus, while others suggest that it is not. This chapter
follows a dialectical approach in which both order and change are seen to

be interrelated. In particular, the chapter uses William M. Newman's *American Pluralism: A Study of Minority Groups and Social Theory* as a basis for its assumptions.[2]

Newman suggests that conflict is a form of group relationship that reflects a society's struggle over rewards, resources, or values.[3] It is an expected part of human interaction that is not out of the ordinary and may, but more often does not, erupt into violence.

In a stratified or ordered society, conflict often revolves around the quest for rewards or arises because of a difference in values. Max Weber defined three types of societal rewards—class, status, and power.[4] Conflict, then, is a form of social relationship in which there is a struggle over values, resources, or rewards that is frequently manifested in the attempt to gain class, status, or power.[5]

Since the nation has valued both pluralism and assimilation as competing ideologies, it is not surprising that such extreme differences in belief have also produced conflict. The type of struggle that has become characteristic over questions of diversity and uniformity has usually not sought the dissolution of society or of a community but rather has attempted to legitimate one ideology over the other.

Consensus-Bounded and Consensus-Projected Conflict

Newman has termed this kind of struggle, within the established boundaries of society, consensus-bounded. He suggests, "Any instance of social conflict may be viewed as consensus-bounded when that conflict by and large remains within the prescribed institutional framework for conflict of the society and within the norms embodied in those situations."[6] In other words, consensus-bounded conflict takes place within the accepted parameters of society and the institutions that compose it. It is governed by accepted rules of behavior. Thus, those who engage in consensus-bounded conflict may seek to defeat an opposing group by helping to enact legislation, securing a judgment from a recognized source of authority, or working in a variety of other ways that are understood as established means of change.

Consensus-bounded conflict is distinguished from consensus-projecting conflict, in which society's rules are not recognized and may be overturned by other than accepted means. Consensus-projecting conflict seeks to "transcend the routine channels for conflict in the society."[7] It attempts to reorder but usually not to destroy. This type of dispute is frequently employed by minority groups seeking to redress discrimination and to redefine the social order so that it may become equitable and just.

In describing the differences between consensus-bounded and consensus-projecting conflict, Newman uses analogies from American history.[8] His conclusions suggest that on the one hand, sit-ins, demonstrations, and protest movements have usually been seen by the general public as anarchist.[9] They are, in fact, forms of consensus-projecting conflict that do not seek to destroy the society in which they take place but rather to alter it. On the other hand, the civil-rights movement, while employing some of these same techniques, has looked to the courts and the congress as its major arena of battle. As a form of consensus-bounded conflict, it was an attempt to transform the system from within and to utilize the accepted instruments of social change in that process.[10]

While consensus-projecting conflict may be common at times of social upheaval, consensus-bounded struggles are more evident in periods of stability. For example, the same religious traditions that were established during the sixteenth-century Reformation as consensus-projecting movements of profound change, later became in themselves part of the established social order. In the United States, many of these same traditions have employed consensus-bounded conflict as a means of "protecting" communities from the new religions, which they perceived as a threat.

Consensus-bounded conflict is also more likely to occur where groups occupy positions of parity (equality) in regard to rewards—the ability to share in the economic resources that society offers and in social benefits that accrue from them.[11] Consensus-projecting conflict is frequently observed where reward parity does not exist.[12] In other words, minority groups that are deprived of resources are more likely to participate in conflict that seeks to alter or change society. Groups that exhibit greater parity are more likely to utilize accepted means of redress.

Conflict in a religiously and culturally diverse society is related to the degree to which groups are perceived as a source of competition or a threat to the acquisition of social resources or social values.[13] Competition does not inherently produce social unrest. When a group is viewed as a threat, however, particularly in a society where competition and achievement are societal norms, conflict is likely to occur.[14] When conflict occurs over differences in values or religion in a competitive society, the struggle is likely to be intense. This is particularly true of situations in which a minority group does not have reward parity and when it is segregated from the rest of society.[15] Under these conditions, the presence of a vastly different religion may be seen as such a significant threat that efforts may be made to eliminate it quickly and firmly.

An example of this type of conflict was the opposition of American Protestantism to the presence of large numbers of Roman Catholics in the nineteenth century. The anti-Catholic movement emerged as an effective political force that sought to rid Protestantism of what it perceived as a menace. It came at a time when the Roman Catholic Church was experiencing significant growth, becoming the largest church in the nation.[16] The growth had been triggered in part by the presence of large numbers of Irish immigrants, who were (initially) a segregated population that experienced economic disparity. The resulting conflict, initiated by the Protestant majority, was intense and violent.

Conflict and Variables

Conflict in a pluralistic society can be further understood when it is placed in the context of several variables. The first variable is the nature of the minority group itself. Groups may be identified by racial, sexual, or cultural distinctions or by their national origins. Differences in both belief systems and values (as component parts of religion) can become reasons for considering a faith as a potential threat. [17]

Another variable that affects conflict is the degree of integration or segregation that minority groups experience. [18] Some groups, including many of the new religions, are self-segregated, preferring to live apart from the general society. The Krishna Consciousness movement (ISKCON), the Unification Church, and the followers of Guru Rajneesh have segregated themselves from mainstream society by choice. Other groups, including some racial minorities, are segregated by virtue of the wishes of the dominant culture. This has been true of groups that have been geographically isolated through redlining practices and economic subjugation.

Some ethnic minorities have developed the ability to choose either to remain segregated from, or to be integrated into, the society at large. The degree to which this is true is related to the parity or deprivation of reward that the minority experiences. Groups that have less parity are dependent on the will of the dominant group.

This tenet is humorously illustrated by a conversation in the *Garfield* comic strip. Jon asks Garfield if he caught the rat he had been chasing. Garfield responds, "You know, Jon, people should talk more." Again Jon asks the cat, "The rat . . . did you catch the rat?" Once more Garfield's answer is entirely logical, suggesting that "all things can be worked out if you just use reason." Jon asks again, "What happened?" Finally Garfield confesses the real solution, "I gave him territory."[19] As a member of a dominant group, Garfield dictated the spatial arrangement within which a member of a subordinate group would reside.

The degree to which minorities are segregated or integrated may also depend on the values they place on assimilation or pluralism. For example, Asian Indians living in parts of New York City tend to live in close proximity to other persons of the same national and racial heritage. This is supported by the pattern of immigration itself. The extended family is an important vehicle for helping even distant cousins enter the United States. Relatives find sources of employment for new arrivals and provide them with a place to live and with support until they are on their own. Conversely, other members of this highly educated, upwardly mobile minority can afford to move into suburban communities, where they are completely integrated and assimilate at a faster rate, thus suggesting a correlation between the level of integration or segregation and reward parity.[20]

Therefore, yet another variable in the study of conflict is the degree of reward parity that minority groups enjoy, as previously noted.[21] Parity usually refers to economic equality but may also include other resources in the social stratification system.[22] The question of parity may be racial but may be dictated by other concerns as well. A case in point is the women's rights movement, in which gender is the determining factor that historically has governed socioeconomic parity in the marketplace. Because women have been discriminated against, they have been denied pay equivalent to men and as a consequence have experienced other means of subjugation including lack of access to status and power.

Parity may also relate to religion. Members of the new religions have experienced disparity simply by virtue of their association with a "cult." This occurs when an individual leaves the religious community and seeks secular employment. Many former commune members will, because of intense stereotyping, fail to mention this part of their past at all. One observer concluded:

> Many of these young people are college-educated (40 to 60 percent . . .) and have received valuable training during their years in their respective movements—running shops and restaurants, starting newspapers, fund-raising, managing large groups of people, handling accounts, doing legal work, and functioning daily in an antagonistic environment. When they encounter hostility in personnel offices because of their religious past, however, many revise their résumés and avoid mentioning these skills."[23]

A former member of the Unification Church described her experience:

> I interviewed for an entry-level position as a counselor. The interviewer praised my education and fieldwork experience. Then he asked me about the three years I described as "lay missionary" on my résumé. Not wanting to hide anything, I told him I was a member of the Unification Church and explained why I left. At that point I felt that the interviewer regarded me as a strange, impaired, and psychologically drained or deranged individual, even though he had previously perceived me as an articulate, well-educated person. My present job as a probation investigator came about because I didn't admit my past membership. I told them I had traveled extensively for a few years.[24]

A fourth variable is the way conflict is carried on. Conflict may be conducted by either rigid or variable means.[25] Rigid means is the use of a single method of engaging in struggle, while variable means involves the selection of a variety of tactics. The use of rigid or variable means is dependent on the role of the group initiating or responding to the conflict. A privileged group in a stratified society may be able to afford to choose the best single means available to engage in the conflict. A minority in a less beneficial position may be forced to use a variety of means of conflict because it lacks the resources to use a single method.

Conflict and Prejudice

Conflict in any of these variable contexts may be supported by prejudice. Prejudice is the attempt to prejudge a minority based on its distinguishing features and the stereotypes that are perceived from them.[26] Prejudice is also a stereotypical assessment of the worth of the group that may be applied to persons within it. Prejudice reduces the ability to judge or understand an individual apart from the group within which he or she is found. For example, in the 1940s and 1950s, Hollywood produced a variety of films about Orientals that reflected the prejudice of the larger society. In motion pictures such as *Kim* and the popular Charlie Chan series, Oriental people were consistently played by Caucasian actors. In each case, the caricatures were the result of racial stereotypes. Asian Indians were portrayed as either holy men or warriors. Chinese were seen as wise, beguiling, or deceptive. Japanese were viewed as aggressive. The stereotypes in film were visual impressions whose roots were far older. Even such seemingly harmless stories as Andersen's or Grimm's fairy tales contain a variety of stereotypical impressions of Asian peoples, many of which stemmed from the Crusades.

Finally, as a weapon of social conflict, prejudice depends on the size and visibility of a minority group. This dynamic, as the succeeding pages will show, is particularly important in conflicts involving the new religions in the United States. In those communities where members of new religions have increased in numbers and in visibility, their faith is more likely to be seen as a threat and to incur active discrimination.

Discrimination is based on prejudice and is the attempt to neutralize a minority group. It is an act of differential treatment of a group or of an individual who is a member of a group.[27] Discrimination may be social or economic and in both situations puts constraints on minority groups.

Gordon Allport suggests that in pluralistic societies greater opportunity exists for both prejudice and discrimination.[28] The existence of a large number of minority groups frequently provides scapegoats for the society's problems. It also increases the proliferation of stereotypes. Discrimination may actually help to create additional sources of religious and ethnic stereotyping.

Perhaps the most classic example of this syndrome was the practice of occupational discrimination against Jews in Europe during the late Mid-

dle Ages. Because of religious sanctions, most Christians would not
enter the profession of money lending. It became one of the few significant occupations open to Jews, and they were encouraged to enter it
precisely because it was too "dirty" a business for Christians. This
pattern of discrimination soon produced the stereotype of the Jew as a
"money-grubbing" individual, a role into which he had, in fact, been
forced by collective patterns of discrimination.[29]

Whether conflict in a pluralistic society or community is consensus-
bounded or consensus-projecting, whether it employs variable or rigid
means, whether it involves discrimination by a majority against a minority
or antagonisms between competing minority groups, it may be intensified
by the tension that arises between the conflicting views of a pluralistic or
homogeneous society. The following example demonstrates how this occurs when a melting-pot ideology is imposed by an arm of government,
backed by public policy, on a racially segregated community in an intensely pluralistic city.

Conflict Between Minorities in Philadelphia

In Philadelphia in the early 1980s, the refugee resettlement policy of
the Immigration and Naturalization Service (INS) produced immediate
conflict when it was brought to bear on a black community. The policy of
the INS has been one of dispersal of refugees throughout the society, a
policy that has been understood as an expedient way of promoting the
assimilation of persons radically different from mainstream American
citizens. In most cities, the private sector has frequently been utilized to
assist in this process.[30] Many organizations that have taken on the responsibility for resettlement have been religious bodies.

At times, resettlement agencies have continued a process of segregating
the Indo-Chinese populations away from the mainstream. The process has
important historical precedents. In the colonial period, those elements of
society that were deemed unacceptable in church-dominated colonies—
Jews, Quakers, Catholics, and others—found refuge in colonies that were
pluralistic by design. More than a century later, the frontier provided the
same outlet both for those who sought it intentionally, as did the Mormons, and for those who were thrust into it not by their own choice, as
were numerous Indian tribes.

Yet another century later the same process continues. The ghetto,
analogous to the frontier by virtue of its insulation from the mainstream,
has become home for minorities that exhibit racial, cultural, and economic differences from the majority. In such an environment, where
survival is a central concern, conflict has resulted when resettlement
programs have placed one minority in close proximity to another in a
racially segregated area where groups compete to survive.

This was the situation in 1980 in Philadelphia, where an estimated population of 3,000 Hmong had been resettled in a predominantly black neighborhood with catastrophic results.[31] When the Cambodian government became Communist, the Hmong, a mountain people indigenous to Laos, who had been allies of the United States during the war, were persecuted. Many fled to Thailand and eventually were transported as refugees to the United States. As a tribal people, the Hmong are a unique community that exhibits extraordinarily close relationships.

In urban Philadelphia, surrounded by residents of a black neighborhood who did not understand the purpose of the Hmong's resettlement there and who perceived them as an economic threat, the refugees were unable to maintain the closeness of their community. They did not assimilate as the government's plan had hoped. Instead, many retreated into extreme isolation, often giving the impression to friends and relatives who remained in refugee camps in Thailand that life was better there than in the United States. As a final act of loneliness and despair, one elderly grandmother committed suicide in 1984.[32]

Chau Yang explained on a tape recording she had left in the midst of her children's clothing that she was too lonely to continue living. She had been unable to assimilate into the city's fast-paced and often confusing way of life:

> The 74-year-old Hmong refugee, a woman who grew up in a thatched hut in the hills of Laos, had lived since 1982 with her grandson and his family in a rowhouse in the Feltonville section of Philadelphia.
> She spoke no English, she was very scared of the strange world around her, and she got violently ill whenever she rode in a car. And so, she almost never left her house.[33]

The newspapers reported that Chau Yang had attempted to commit suicide once before in Laos, an act that in this traditional southeast Asian Buddhist culture is virtually unknown.[34] Yet, despite her emotional distress, the deed that she finally completed successfully in urban Philadelphia was also for a number of social reasons. It was an "extreme reaction to the intense culture shock and confusion that many Hmong and other recent refugees have felt in America."[35]

In Philadelphia, Chau Yang was completely cut off from her community.

> In Laos, she could have looked forward to an old age of working the family vegetable patch, taking care of the great-grandchildren, gossiping with the other older ladies. In Philadelphia, she spent her last days inside a dark, drafty rowhouse—10 blocks from her nearest Hmong friend.[36]

Her final taped message explained the depth of her loneliness. Her only satisfaction came from calling her sister in California, which, because of the expense, she could do only on occasion.

Unable to read or write, Chau Yang surely never understood the ideological conflict between opposing visions of pluralism and assimilation. She only understood that in order to be happy she needed intense, close contact with one society, her own people. She did not and could not assimilate. At the same time, she could not function in a pluralistic community where ethnic differences were so great that the closest member of her cultural group was ten blocks away. In the end, the differences between the assimilationalist philosophy of the federal resettlement program (and the public policy that supported it), combined with the intensely hostile, pluralistic atmosphere of that part of Philadelphia where she lived, led Chau Yang to take her life.

A year before Chau Yang's death, conflict between Hmong refugees and the blacks in Philadelphia had been exacerbated by the beating of one refugee by three young men. The incident triggered the exodus of large numbers of Hmong from the city. It also reflected a period of escalating tensions and distrust between the two minority communities.

The conflict between the blacks and the Hmong had taken a number of different forms, which included a rent strike as well as court action. Ultimately, when the Hmong were unable to improve their position, many chose to leave.

The struggle developed for several reasons. First, the resettlement policy of the Immigration and Naturalization Service directed that "ethnic enclaves" not be created throughout the nation and that every opportunity be given for rapid assimilation of these tribal people into American society. Little consideration was given to the maintenance of important cultural, religious, and familial ties among the Hmong in their new location.

Second, the community that was targeted for resettlement of the Hmong was demographically homogeneous in a section of Philadelphia that was particularly segregated. Communities that exhibit such patterns of segregation are frequently resistant to the presence of other ethnic or religious groups in significant numbers. Often, other groups are understood as sources of competition for resources.[37] In many areas, race and even religion are seen as strong "turf" issues. Other religioethnic groups are "allowed" to coexist only so long as important cultural and physical boundaries are not broken. When they are, intense struggle may result.

The Hmong were caught between the assimilationist policy of a government agency and the sense of ownership and control of resources by a black population in an intensely segregated, pluralistic city. Like the blacks, their primary concern was not so much to relate to other ethnic groups as to continue their traditional way of life. Yet, it was precisely this similarity that made them a threat to the indigenous community, who understood the presence of the Hmong as an invasion of their domain and a source of competition.

The tragedy was that neither in the public nor in the private sector did organizations involved in refugee resettlement do anything to avert it. Adequate preparations for the arrival of the Hmong that could have averted the conflict were not made. Similarly, the Hmong were not prepared for the situation in which they found themselves. For the black and Hmong communities, both of which sought to protect their identities, and for the government, which administered a broadly based assimilationist policy, the struggle was counterproductive. It set minorities that had experienced high levels of economic disparity against each other. It also demonstrated the way that dominant elements of the society can dictate the social space arrangements of subordinate groups when they exhibit significant levels of reward deprivation.[38]

Minority Difficulties in California

Because the assimilationist ideology is so deeply embedded in the American psyche, clashes similar to the experience of the Hmong in Philadelphia have occurred in other parts of the country as a result of refugee resettlement. In California, for example, the efforts of Indo-Chinese to maintain a sense of identity and to practice traditional occupations as fishermen have produced conflict with the indigenous population.

Particular anxiety developed among fishermen in Moss Landing, California, situated between Santa Cruz and Monterey in the early 1980s.[39] The tension focused on the attempt of the Indo-Chinese to continue their traditional livelihood of fishing and the fear of members of the local fishing industry that they presented a threat to their business.

The conflict finally led to a series of prohibitions. As aliens, the refugees were prohibited from using large commercial fishing boats. Additional legislation forced them to abstain from using nylon gill nets, which they had successfully used to catch kingfish.

The Indo-Chinese had been particularly enterprising. They had fished for kingfish, a shallow-water fish, because most other fishermen had not considered it to be worthwhile. The Vietnamese had sold their catch to California's Oriental population at a low rate of twenty-five cents a pound.[40]

The fisherman's dispute with the Indo-Chinese came on the heels of a sense of rage throughout the state. The Indo-Chinese were perceived as a drain on the state's welfare system. The rage turned into racism. In Sacramento, a homeowners' organization "asked a local grand jury to investigate the possibility of establishing internment camps for Vietnamese refugees."[41]

While such sentiments reflected public resentment against the Vietnamese, they also masked the real reason for the conflict—the growing

fear of competition, which was perceived as a threat to established businesses. This fear was nourished by the prejudice that many persons felt
toward Vietnamese after the war.

> "I personally feel that it's mostly become [sic.] of economic factors,"
> said Duong Bui, an instructor at the Defense Language Institute at
> nearby Fort Ord. But he said another factor was the changing nature of
> Vietnamese immigrants. "In the past, we had well-to-do, educated
> people," he said. "We have a new group now who are not as educated,
> and they are competing for blue-collar jobs."[42]

In some parts of the state, the conflict also included other minority
groups. In San Francisco, for example, Indo-Chinese experienced resistance from the Chinese community. For many of the Chinese who had
lived in the bay area for decades, the newcomers were unwelcome.
Differences in class between the Chinese and Indo-Chinese immigrants
compounded by variations in ethnicity, language, and religion, all contributed to the feelings of resentment.

The conflict demonstrated several points. The primary source of the
dispute was the perception of members of the established fishing industry
in southern California that the Indo-Chinese refugees were both a source
of competition and a threat. This perception became the central issue
even though it was not always logical in that the fish the Indo-Chinese sold
to the Oriental population was peripheral to the indigenous fishing industry. Nevertheless, the community perceived them as a threat and succeeded in lobbying for legislation that prevented the Vietnamese from
using the large nets with which they were familiar.

The conflict, which took various forms over a long period of time,
intensified because of the racial stereotypes that had been applied to
Indo-Chinese refugees throughout the state. Much like the Chinese and
Asian Indians before them, Indo-Chinese were perceived as a backward
Oriental population that was a drain on the state's economy.

The stereotypical image was accelerated by the change in type of Indo-
Chinese refugee. Those who had come earlier included a variety of
intellectual and professional persons. The new arrivals were largely blue-
collar workers. The change placed the newer Vietnamese immigrants in
direct contact with a dominant group that controlled access to the economic resources of the community.

Moreover, the dispute was exacerbated by the fact that one group, the
Chinese, in the best American tradition, had assimilated and had adopted
middle-class values and hence had acquired a level of reward parity. The
Indo-Chinese, who had not yet made such a dramatic transition, clung to
older values and ways of life and suffered reward deprivation. Their
struggle was not so much to become American as it was just to survive.
The two value systems thus were a microcosm of the conflict between
homogeneity and plurality. They exemplified the historical struggle of

ethnic and religious groups to maintain patterns of language and occupation in a larger society that emphasized the loss of tradition in a melting pot. At the same time, they continued the struggle between a dominant and subordinate group that competed for social resources.

The conflict was also increased by the fact that both groups claimed the right to practice an occupation of their choice. For the Indo-Chinese, however, fishing was not a "trade." Rather, in a rural village economy such as that in Vietnam and Cambodia, fishing is the only means of support for persons so poor that they otherwise could not survive. In countries where war has been a regular part of life for decades, the ability to fish was also in many instances the only source of food. This situation differs from fishing in southern California, where the occupation is an industry and where commercial boats regularly bring in large catches. Thus, while the California fishermen sought to protect their rights to their industry, the Indo-Chinese simply continued the one thing that they knew would assure them of survival. Having already endured war, the loss of family, and the trauma of life as refugees, they were entrepreneural and sought the most logical source of market for their fish, the state's Oriental population.

Thus, the struggle also came about because of a clash of values in which neither side understood the basis for the other's claim to the right to fish. The conflict, which was instituted by the majority, was of the consensus-bounded type. Traditional means were used to end the dispute, which was decided through legislation.

Much like the Hmong in Philadelphia, Vietnamese and Cambodian refugees in California had been resettled in the United States through public policy. In other words, the dominant elements of society were able to dictate social space arrangements to a subordinate group that experienced significant reward deprivation.[43] The Indo-Chinese were placed not in a segregated urban environment but in mainstream California communities, where fishing was a highly traditional occupation. Occupational identification thus became the primary "turf" on which the struggle ensued. Because the wider community had no clear vision of the ramifications of either an assimilationist policy or the significance of culturally defined patterns of work and identity, they could not either absorb the refugees or tolerate them on the basis of their occupations or by virtue of their unique cultural differences. The conflict was escalated even further by the prejudice and discrimination that the Indo-Chinese experienced throughout the state.

Conflict Between the Followers of an Itinerant Indian Guru and a New Jersey Borough

Montclair, New Jersey, is a quiet suburban community of approximately 43,000 residents. Barely three miles long, located but fifteen miles from New York City, it presents an appearance of upper-middle-class life that is orderly and without major upheaval or change. The majority of streets are tree lined and generally bordered by large, three-story, wood frame houses, many of them constructed in the 1920s. The two parts of the borough, Montclair and Upper Montclair, each have their own post offices, schools, parks, and churches.

Montclair has maintained a strong progressive image. It was frequently cited in the 1950s as having one of the best public education systems in the nation. More recently, it created one of the first magnet school systems in the country and was successfully integrated. In addition, Upper Montclair, which has historically been dominated by a white Anglo-Saxon Protestant majority, has increasingly become a widely diversified community. It is now quite common to see a mixture of black, Hispanic, and Asian Americans in the area.

Montclair proudly claims a rich heritage of Protestants, Catholics, and Jews and contains more than sixty congregations. Moreover, the borough has achieved a national reputation for its concentration of executives both of denominational bodies and of such national ecumenical agencies as the National Council of Churches, suggesting a progressive image in which religious pluralism is fully accepted. It maintains one of the only carpools of commuting clergy in the country.

Despite its growing diversity, Montclair has all of the characteristics of a melting pot and has emphasized the importance of assimilation. Outside of the historical concentration of the black community in Montclair (rather than in Upper Montclair), the area has few concentrations of ethnic or racial groups. Asian Indians, Chinese, Japanese, Korean, Hispanic, and other populations are instead integrated into the mix. Many of these persons are fully assimilated and retain relatively little of their native languages or traditions. Diversity is tolerated, and even celebrated, in this context, as long as it remains within prescribed limits, which are maintained through community consensus. When such boundaries are exceeded, as the following pages will demonstrate, conflict has resulted. The overarching ideology of the community remains that of homogeneity and is quite opposed to any expression of diversity that is equated with the accumulation of status or power.

The community's emphasis on assimilation and its progressive understanding of controlled cultural differences are shown in the school system. An elementary school, for instance, both teaches English as a second language and offers bilingual education to students whose primary tongue is other than English. Students are thus taught the importance of language and culture. Such innovative approaches as art and music classes (for everyone) in Spanish instead of English help students learn of cultural differences. Yet, the purpose of the curriculum in the eyes of the teachers is to prepare children for the societal mainstream and to insure their proficiency as English-speakers, albeit with knowledge of other tongues. This is in full accord with the nature of the community itself, which is very much in the mainstream of upper-middle-class and upper-class American society.

In 1981, Montclair's progressive attitude toward diversity received its greatest challenge. The occasion was the purchase in April of Kipp's Castle, a mansion, often said to be the largest house in the community, by the followers of Rajneesh, an itinerant Indian guru.[44] The sale of the eighty-year-old, German-style castle, complete with carriage house, followed the opening of the Chidvilas Meditation Center, a store-front operation near the center of the community, by followers of the same guru.

After the sale, rumors abounded. One source claimed to have seen a flatbed truck of portable toilets transported through the area and was sure they were in preparation for a mass rally for thousands of the guru's followers.[45] Other rumors voiced the intention of the sect to buy additional property on the mountain overlooking the two communities. Stories of strange sexual rituals and practices were common.[46]

Eventually, the followers of Rajneesh applied for a tax-exempt status in the community as a religious organization. The application was quickly and quietly withdrawn after community leaders rose in anger. Meetings were held in churches to protest the presence of the group, which was perceived as a distinct threat. "Expert" witnesses, who admitted that they did not know very much about this particular sect, issued dire warnings about the dangers of cults.[47]

Perhaps the community's greatest fear, however, came from the assertions that Guru Rajneesh was a staunch advocate of free sex. When an advertisement appeared in a national news magazine touting a variety of concerns of his followers, including sexual liberation, public resentment soared even higher.[48] One resident interviewed by the *New York Times* claimed that she was panic-stricken, and still another expressed concern about the loss of property values that might result from this latest menace.[49]

Officials responded to the public concern by questioning the tax-exempt status of the property. In particular, they suggested that a revaluation of property would take place within a year in Montclair and in neighboring Verona. Verona officials also announced that health department guidelines would have to be checked to determine how many persons could occupy the house and whether or not the commune was in violation of the law. Concern was particularly expressed that the carriage house on the property was for single-family occupancy only.

By the early summer, community reaction had become so intense that the Rajneesh commune began to look for another location. In July 1981, less than four months after the guru had purchased the property and not even a week after he had left his former headquarters in Poona, India, the group secured new property in Oregon. Acquiring a tract of 64,228 acres near the small town of Antelope for $6 million, the sect then set its eyes on a larger, far more isolated piece of land. The Montclair site was sold.[50]

The continuing history of the sect's activities is well known. Once headquartered in Oregon, the movement attempted to secure a political base. It identified its new location as Rajneeshpuram and sought to influence local government. When the commune offered food and shelter to homeless persons across the nation in 1984 as part of this process, it was popularly condemned as corrupt. Finally, in 1985, Guru Rajneesh was deported on charges of immigration fraud. The public disapproval that continued until the guru's expulsion had many of the same dynamics as the original Montclair experience.

In the face of such an intense public reaction to a religious group in a community that prides itself on its religious and ethnic diversity, one cannot help but wonder why. Montclair had proudly claimed that it was religiously diversified and had churches from a wide variety of denominations. Moreover, the area had become culturally and ethnically integrated. Yet, more excitement was raised in three brief months over the issue of an unconventional Indian guru and his followers than in almost any other community-wide confrontation in the town's recent history.

In response to similar questions, William Newman suggests that the frequency and intensity of conflict are related to the ability of a minority group to share in social rewards.[51] This was certainly true with the Rajneesh community in Montclair, which symbolically announced that it shared in these rewards when it purchased what was reputed to be the largest house in town. The conflict, which was initiated by the majority, remained within the parameters of society and was of the consensus-bounded type. It was of short duration and of rigid means. The Rajneesh commune, which was perceived as a threat to the community, was forced to leave through the application of public pressure brought about through the media and community meetings. Discussions about having the "cult" investigated by the health department and their property evaluation reassessed were well within accepted activities of community government. The town also continued a nationally known pattern of public reaction against religious diversity in which allegations of immorality provided reason for suspicion. In the nineteenth century, similar allegations were made against the Mormons, who were popularly condemned for polygamy.

The incident contained two mutually contradictory visions of diversity. The first, an assimilative view, was dominant in the borough. While the area is substantially more integrated than many other communities in the vicinity, diversity remained diffused. Cultural differences were acceptable as long as those who were different melded into the larger society.

The followers of Guru Rajneesh demonstrated that they valued a segregated existence and did not intend to diffuse their religious and cultural differences into public life. Members of the commune held utopian values drawn from the counterculture of the 1960s. They did not attempt to mix with the community at large and, except for their store-front meditation center, maintained no visible evidence of their presence. When conflict was initiated, they preferred to retreat rather than confront it. The castle was a natural symbol of refuge. The mansion was located away from the urban center and in an area where only those persons who knew of its existence could find it. The castle could not even be seen from the street.

It is also important to note that the conflict was initiated not when the followers of Guru Rajneesh came to Montclair, but a year later, when they purchased property for a commune and religious center. By buying the largest house in town, the sect crossed the boundaries within which diversity was allowed to exist. The purchase not only increased the visibility of the commune but became an expression of its attempt to gain parity. In Montclair, where value is placed on upward mobility, the purchase was seen as a significant concentration of power in the context of extreme diversity.

Thus, the two experiences of diversity were in direct opposition to each other. The concentrated appearance of a religious group whose morality was suspect was not compatible with the community's expectation that religious and cultural differences would be diffused throughout the area. Moreover, when the Rajneesh commune achieved resource parity, the level of segregation it experienced was what it desired and was in contrast to the integrated nature of the community.[52] For the residents, segregation merely reinforced the image of a cult and the perception of a threat. This was enough to raise sufficient alarm to lead to the ouster of the commune.

Conflict Between a Traditional Hindu Sect and a New Jersey Township

In a related example, a mainstream Hindu sect was perceived as a cult in rural New Jersey. Unlike the Rajneesh commune in Montclair, however, the Bochasanwasi Swaminarayan Sanstha has been established in the United States for more than sixteen years. This Vaishnava group, descended from an eighteenth-century bhakti tradition, erected a temple in New York City in 1970. Smaller places of worship were opened across the nation. Its members, followers of the reformer Shri Sahajanand Swami (1781–1830), share a common faith focused on the worship of Krishna.[53] The tradition is conservative, emphasizing the teachings of its founder, who sought to regenerate Vaishnavism in northwest India and to promote moral reform. In the United States, devotees are predominately Gujarati and do not actively seek converts from outside the ethnic community. The total number of adherents in the United States approximates 35,000.

In August 1985 the Sanstha purchased a 162-acre piece of land in Independence Township, a community of 2,900 in Warren County in northwestern New Jersey.[54] Soon afterwards it announced its intention to erect a $1 million temple complex, including a school, a dormitory, houses, and a marble temple within ten years. The total project, which was widely reported in varying accounts, was conceptualized as a major institution.

The site offered several advantages. The location was in a relatively isolated part of the state, where an educational and religious institution could maintain a secluded existence. Further, land was cheaper than it would be in New York City, where the sect already maintained a modest temple. In addition, the area was close to its New York headquarters and could be reached in less than three hours' travel.

The community's reaction to the proposal was swift and decisive. Officials voiced concern that the sect had not made its intentions known at the time of the purchase. Moreover, they vehemently objected to the plan, citing the need to protect their community from unwarranted growth.[55]

As the discussions between the sect and the community ensued, a zoning consideration was raised. Although the area was zoned to allow the type of construction that the sect wished to do, the mayor proposed that the regulations be summarily changed. New restrictions would restrict the area to farms or single-family dwellings on one to two acres of land. Community meetings urged the adoption of these new regulations, which would prohibit the sect's plan from reaching fruition.

Other objections surfaced, including assertions that the temple complex would change the assimilative character of the area. A newspaper article described the population mix:

> Over the last 200 years, ethnic groups have blended without much commotion into this little farming community in the hilly country of northwestern New Jersey.
>
> The first settlers were English, Dutch and German. Then came the Irish. After them, Italians, Poles and Ukrainians arrived and assimilated.[56]

While community leaders protested the drain that the sect's presence would create on public services, a major source of the conflict revolved around the perception that the Indians would not assimilate. A reporter concluded, "Publicly, opponents complain about tax exemptions for the schools and temple, increased traffic on narrow country roads, burdens on police and firefighters and the Swaminarayans isolating themselves and breaking the town's tradition of ethnic assimilation."[57]

The assumption that the sect's presence would destroy the homogeneity of the community was bolstered by the stereotype that the Swaminarayans were a cult. Residents voiced their fear of groups like the followers of Guru Rajneesh.[58] News about the guru's alleged violations of immigration law and deportation heightened the awareness of a potential threat. In response, the president of the Sanstha vehemently denied that his organization was a cult, emphasizing the professional background of many devotees.

Following these outbursts that characterized the initial conflict, the struggle entered a more complicated, less publicized phase. After two unsuccessful attempts by the mayor to have an amendment to the community's zoning ordinance passed (which would have forced the temple to secure approval of the planning board), a series of negotiations began in which the size of the project, engineering requirements, and the approval of local, state, and even federal agencies were all subjects of continuing study and debate.

The initial dispute demonstrated several things. First, it showed the high level of apprehension that often surrounds the establishment of a new religion. Similar incidents have been reported in different sections of the country involving the construction of both temples and mosques. In this instance, the public made little distinction between a religious tradition two hundred years old and a recent movement organized around the teachings of an itinerant Indian guru.

Second, the dispute was accelerated by conflicting visions of homogeneity and plurality. The community clearly valued the diffusion of diversity and acknowledged the importance of assimilation. The presence of a new ethnic group, whose numbers were highly concentrated in a single location, was seen as intolerable. It was an expression of visibility in an area where the tolerance of ethnic and religious diversity was governed by their level of invisibility.

This initial dispute (in what became a prolonged conflict) was of the consensus-bounded type and was brought about through rigid means; the majority sought to prevent a minority from establishing in its midst a level of diversity that was deemed unacceptable. It began by trying to change a zoning regulation, a normal avenue of conflict resolution in a democratic society. Unlike consensus-projecting conflict, which seeks to alter an established order, the struggle never threatened the stability of the area.

Community leaders thus sought an amendment to the zoning law, which at that time allowed both churches and schools to be constructed in a residential area. The amendment made the erection of either facility a conditional use. It would have permitted the Swaminarayan Sanstha to construct only the houses in their projected complex without first gaining approval by the township's planning board.

Members of the sect claimed that the successful attempt to pass a restrictive zoning ordinance was discriminatory. They cited the fact that larger developments, including one of 600 townhouses, were currently under way in the township.

The Hindu community perceived the proposed construction of a school and a temple in yet another way. Their view was shaped by their previous experience in the densely populated community of Flushing, New York, which had been revitalized by large numbers of Asians and where segregated pluralism was a fact of life. Within this remarkably diverse metropolitan area of Koreans, Chinese, Japanese, Asian Indians, and other Oriental peoples, most persons shared a vision of the necessity of ethnic and religious institutions and the need to allow them to develop without interference from the community. Differences in theology, culture, language, and even diet separated communities that might even be of the same nationality. Among the Asian Indians of Flushing the total mosaic was accepted as a pattern of life not unlike that in India. There was no amalgam and no expectation of melting or rapid assimilation such as had historically existed in Independence Township, New Jersey.

In summary, the struggle was initiated by the dominant elements of the community when a Hindu group that had achieved economic parity in a segregated environment sought to erect a facility in an area where segregation was not acknowledged or welcomed and where parity by a minority group was seen as a threat.[59] When a segregated Hindu community was proposed, conflict resulted. The struggle intensified when a vision of diversity, based on the Swaminarayan Sanstha's experience, was imposed on a community where the ideal of the melting pot was quite real. What the community perceived as the onslaught of a cult was also a reaction to an incompatible experience of plurality. The two visions of homogeneity and diversity were placed in direct confrontation.

Conflict and Accommodation in Multiethnic Allentown

The dialectic between assimilation and pluralism has produced intense conflict both in the nation's history and in the life of many communities. While the two opposing visions of diversity in American life have frequently clashed, they have also, albeit less frequently, accommodated each other. The following study of the middle-size Pennsylvania community of Allentown shows how this has occurred and how conflict has, as a result, been shaped by the competition between religious and ethnic groups rather than by confrontation. It demonstrates the historical reasons for the coexistence of regional understandings of both ethnic pluralism and the process of assimilation.

Allentown is known for its suburban life-style, good schools, and proximity to both the Philadelphia and New York metropolitan areas. It is part of a cluster of three cities, including Easton and Bethlehem, which are known as the Greater Lehigh Valley.

Residents of the Lehigh Valley are often heard to comment favorably on the quality of life there. Many appreciate the rural flavor of the area and a slower pace of life than they might find living closer to either of the major metropolitan areas. A number of persons do, in fact, prefer a two-hour commute to both of the major cities to residential life in the megalopolis.

Despite its comfortable "middle America" appearance, Allentown is something of an anomaly. It is an area where over the last 200 years an ethnic minority has become a majority. A visitor immediately notices the area's distinctive Pennsylvania German (known as Pennsylvania Dutch) character. The proliferation of German accents, traditional German foods, farmers' markets, and German clubs attests to the origins of this community from peasant stock in Germany's Palatinate. Although the German character of the city has waned considerably since World War II, residents still recall the difficulty of finding wartime employment for persons who spoke Pennsylvania German.

A Long History of Pluralism

Allentown has had a diversified population for a long time. An understanding of its religious and cultural pluralism begins with the founding of Pennsylvania under William Penn. Pennsylvania, like Rhode Island, was intentionally established as a haven for groups that had been persecuted because of their religious beliefs—in Pennsylvania, a variety of Anabaptist groups, including German Mennonites and English Quakers. The area also developed significant populations of Lutheran and Reformed peoples who had been forced to leave Europe because of political unrest and economic hardship.

There is little doubt that the colonial vision of pluralism has survived in Pennsylvania. Pluralist sentiments are frequently espoused. A Japanese Buddhist, who had lived through the traumatic experience of imprisonment in the relocation camps during World War II, commented, for example, that after the war's end, she had intentionally migrated to Pennsylvania. She contrasted her experience there with the prejudice that she had known on the West Coast, concluding that the tolerance of her religion and ethnicity in Pennsylvania was due to the fact that the state had been settled primarily for reasons of religious tolerance. Although such a statement is a generalization, it reflects an understanding of the state's extreme ethnic and religious diversity and its historical ability to house divergent population groups. This understanding of religious and cultural pluralism has governed the historical development of Allentown.

The most significant attraction for many of the European ethnic groups that came there more recently was industry. Allentown (and the Greater Lehigh Valley) became identified with the manufacture of steel and Portland cement. As a result of this large-scale industry, several cultures became part of the area's expanding mosaic. Scots migrated up and down the Lehigh Canal. A variety of Slovak groups became the backbone of the cement industry. Ukrainians found employment in both steel and cement companies. The largest group, the Pennsylvania Germans, remained primarily agricultural.

Still other ethnic groups came to Allentown because of political turmoil abroad. After the break up of the Austro-Hungarian Empire following World War I, many central European emigrants came to the Lehigh Valley. Others, including the Syrians, were lured by the promise of the American Dream.

Because of the colonial experience in Pennsylvania, the continuing ethnic diversification of communities like Allentown was seen as nothing unusual. While new arrivals were never really welcomed, they were tolerated. The parameters for their acceptance were based on the community's earlier experience with the Pennsylvania Germans, who were able to maintain tightly knit communities in a pattern of segregated pluralism. New groups—blacks, Syrians, Hispanics, and others—sustained this pattern of life with very little interaction with the larger society.

The following pages will describe the evolution of this ethnically diverse area and its pluralistic perception of life. This perception is demonstrated by the emphasis on ethnic segregation, the resistance to interethnic coalitions, and the conflict that has historically occurred within ethnic communities rather than between them. The discussion will also suggest that the melting pot model of community life has evolved as the majority population, the Pennsylvania Germans, have gradually assimilated to American ways. Because they have a long heritage as a minority, they have retained their vision of cultural pluralism. The two ideologies—pluralism and assimilation (melting pot and mosaic)—and the demographic processes that support them have thus coalesced with minimal confrontation or struggle.

The Pennsylvania Germans

German immigrants came to Pennsylvania from the Palatinate for several reasons at different periods in the seventeenth, eighteenth, and nineteenth centuries. For the Amish, the move was to escape religious persecution. For others, economic and political upheavals in Europe made emigration to a new land attractive.

Migrations to the Lehigh Valley took place in three successive periods: between 1683 and 1789 (when Germany was a divided feudal empire); between 1789 and 1871 (during the German Confederation); and between 1871 and the present.[60] In Lehigh County, many of the original German settlements date back to the first migration.

Despite the historicity of the Pennsylvania Germans in Allentown, assimilation has been a long, slow process. Evidences of the strong German character of the area continue. Families with roots in the region for four or five generations still retain a German accent. Only in the last thirty years has the assimilation process dramatically accelerated.

While there has been erosion of language and religion, value systems have been the slowest to change. The cultural perceptions of an agrarian, peasant people continue to have great influence. They not only govern the way in which other ethnic groups are perceived but the manner in which conflict takes place.

In Allentown, and in other areas where the German culture has been dominant, values are often expressed in cultural stereotypes. One of the most prevalent images is that of frugality. As an impoverished peasant people, the Germans in Pennsylvania were forced to economize in order to survive. There were few rich people among the immigrant population. Moreover, if conditions worsened, few persons could afford the cost of return passage to Germany. The only recourse to assure survival was to promote self-sufficiency. As a stereotype, however, the Germans were often identified as "tight fisted." The image of frugality became an accepted and often admired trait within the population and was self-fulfilling.

A more important part of the value system has been the tendency to conserve older patterns of life and to resent the intrusion of modernity. While religious groups such as the Amish have maintained strict prohibitions against worldliness, other Pennsylvania German groups have continued similar conventions without incorporating them in doctrine. For example, in many of the older farming communities surrounding Allentown, luxury items such as color television sets, stereos, and expensive cars are seen as frivolous and unnecessary. Among the more traditional, there is resistance to going to the expense of installing modern kitchen or plumbing facilities, which are seen as extraneous to the basic needs of life.

Life among the Pennsylvania Germans is viewed as a day-by-day affair. Goal setting and long-range planning are foreign to the area, which for two hundred years had depended on a strong survival mentality. For this reason, the use of credit is frowned upon. Pledging in churches is rare. Instead, supporters give what they can week by week.

A visitor cannot help but notice the proliferation of ethnic jokes by the Pennsylvania Germans about themselves and the tendency toward low self-esteem that the jokes reflect. The humor establishes a common relationship among members of the culture and at the same time reinforces the image of a peasant people and reveals vestiges of the prejudice experienced by the German community. There is strong evidence for its continual expression since the earliest migrations.

Evidence of Prejudice. In the seventeenth and eighteenth centuries, Pennsylvania Germans were particularly ostracized because of their peasant origins. Benjamin Franklin was heard to identify them as "Palatinate Boors," in 1751.[61] He went on to write, "Those who come hither are generally of the most ignorant Stupid Sort of their own Nation . . . not being used to Liberty, they know not how to make a modest use of it."[62]

Franklin's sentiments reflected a level of prejudice that came to surround the Pennsylvania German community. In the late eighteenth century and throughout the next 150 years, the principal object of derision was language. A text written in 1858 concluded:

> Never does a German learn the English language like a native. He lacks the expression, the accent, the tone. And if it were not the language—the walk, the bearing, the beard betray the German. . . . He eternally remains a stranger in a strange land, and along with it a hated, a despised stranger.[63]

A state law in 1905 became an additional source of difficulty when the use of languages other than English was prohibited in the classroom.[64] A little more than a decade later when World War I brought the United States into an alliance against Germany, the Pennsylvania Germans experienced profound rejection. Anything of German origin from sauerkraut to Bach was treated with contempt. For Germans who were U.S. citizens, it became a traumatic time. German names were deemphasized. Churches ceased to conduct their liturgies in German and changed to English.

The German community in Allentown reflects the result of this sustained prejudice. It has evolved as a tightly knit, cohesive community. Social and cultural ties are maintained by three institutions: the church, the volunteer fire department, and the German club. Clubs include both German historical societies and fraternal organizations such as the Grundsau Lodge. In each institution, familial ties are important, and membership may continue over several generations.

The closely woven fabric of the German community is augmented by its suspicion of outsiders. The term *Auslander*, or "foreigner," is commonly applied to anyone not from the area. Even persons from other parts of the state may not be accepted completely because of the continuing fear of outside groups. As a numerical majority in the region, and as one of a wide variety of European ethnic groups in the nation, the Pennsylvania Germans experience little discrimination today. Yet, the fear of outsiders remains a significant vestige of several centuries of rejection.

Both the discrimination that the Pennsylvania Germans experienced and their own culture have reinforced their isolation and their historical tendency not to interrelate with other groups. Such cultural factors include patterns of intermarriage and social institutions. In addition, values of frugality, hard work, and a strong survival mentality have helped the Pennsylvania Germans resist both assimilation and change until comparatively recent times.

It is this dynamic of self-sufficiency and inwardness that has not only been used by the Pennsylvania Germans to describe themselves but also has governed the way in which they have perceived other ethnic groups. The emphasis on self-determinism has been applied not only to the dominant German culture in Allentown but equally to other groups. This, coupled with suspicion and mistrust of the outside world, has produced resistance toward interethnic or interreligious alliances.

This overall dynamic has been important in the life of the region. It helps explain why historically the presence of a variety of European ethnic groups (including Austrians, Scots, and several Slovak communities) never posed problems for the Pennsylvania Germans. The emphasis on self-sufficiency insisted that each group had the right to control its own destiny. Differences in cultural orientation and religion were tolerated as long as they were not viewed as a threat. This usually meant that as long as they maintained a level of cultural invisibility in public life, their presence was accepted.

Internal Conflict. Conflict within the Pennsylvania German community has traditionally occurred over two issues—religion and language. It has taken various forms over a long period of time. Through the beginning of the twentieth century, it was not uncommon for churches to divide over the question of retaining German in their services. Disputes became so heated that several new churches in Allentown were formed when an English-advocating minority broke off from the German-speaking majority. Frequently, the new churches were constructed not miles away but within sight of one another as a constant reminder of the struggle.

A more frequent source of conflict was religion itself, that is, between members of the German Reformed and Lutheran faiths. The dominant characteristic of Protestantism in the area has been the division and competition between the Lutheran (Evangelical Lutheran Church in America) and Reformed (United Church of Christ) traditions. Historically, the two faiths have often come into close contact in a unique type of religious institution, the Union Church, once common in the Lehigh Valley. Originally established in the eighteenth and nineteenth centuries, Union churches were built as an affordable way of housing two independent congregations under the same roof. Both Lutherans and Reformed parishioners maintained their own governing boards, committees, choirs, and separate congregations. Worship schedules frequently reflected the isolation of the two congregations rather than their cooperation. Since both congregations were of the same ethnic stock and have often had economic parity in a segregated environment with the same resources (i.e., the shared sanctuary and church building), competition has been intense.[65] Conflict has been precipitated by the natural inclination of each congregation to see the other as a threat.

Because the Union Church was not established as an "ecumenical" endeavor but as a practical measure, it has promoted competition between the two faiths, which must occupy the same space and often compete for the same membership. "Lutheran" and "Reformed" jokes are common, as well as the perception on both sides that the other is lax and not holding up its part of the union. This is especially ironic since members of both traditions come from the same part of Germany and represent the same peasant stock. Both have maintained a strong religious and cultural presence in the Lehigh Valley and, as already indicated, frequently intermarry. Yet, the isolation of both religious traditions continues and is often marked by a high incidence of suspicion and mistrust.

Outside Changes and Assimilation.   Many such traditional aspects of life that have defined the parameters of conflict in the Lehigh Valley have changed significantly in the last twenty-five years. The primary cause has been the growth of the area. Thirty years ago, Allentown was a small city in a predominantly village economy. Farmers' markets, county fairs, and churches were the centers of community life. As the city expanded and as suburban sprawl accelerated, the character of the area was dramatically altered. The fundamental change was the erosion of the agrarian life that once characterized the valley. As highway systems and shopping malls were built, entire villages were consumed or isolated to the degree that they soon lost their viability.

The diffusion of the German community throughout the region, the movement of new people into the area, and the expansion of the suburbs all accelerated the rate of assimilation of the Pennsylvania Germans. Intermarriage with persons outside the area increased. The number of young persons who left the region for education or employment also increased. Among the churches, the number of union arrangements noticeably decreased.

As the Lehigh Valley became more of a melting pot, so assimilation with mainstream America became viewed as desirable. Particularly among younger people, there has been an increased desire not to identify themselves as Pennsylvania Germans but to be seen as mainstream Americans. As further evidence of this attitude, administrators in the school system speak of the importance of helping students from different ethnic backgrounds to assimilate. As a result, English as a second language is an important part of the city's work with the immigrant population, and bilingual education is deemphasized.

Continuing Pluralism

Nevertheless, although Allentown has continued to take on more of the characteristics of a melting pot, the earlier view of a pluralistic society has been retained. This has been due to the ability of the inner city to maintain a distinctive diversified character based on the coexistence of a variety of ethnic groups.

In both areas, city and suburb, conflict follows the historical pattern of long-term struggles between groups who compete for rewards in a segregated environment. The degree of segregation of some ethnic groups is shown on the map in figure 5.1. Of those groups relatively new to the Lehigh Valley, blacks and Hispanics show the highest degree of segregation and also the greatest level of economic disparity. Also highly segregated is the city's Syrian population.

Each of these groups experiences geographical and social isolation. The black and Hispanic populations are tightly clustered in the inner city. While the Syrians are also concentrated nearby (in the first and sixth wards), they have shown greater social mobility and often have achieved greater economic parity.[66] Older members of the Syrian community remain in the "ward." Younger generations have shown an increasing ability to assimilate and to move into the suburbs.

Syrians. In addition to a strong extended-family system, Allentown's Syrian population has been united by a variety of other factors. For instance, most Syrians are from one of two villages in Syria's Christian Valley.[67] Because of the small size and close proximity of these two villages, the majority of families know each other and have friends in common. Many are also interrelated.

In addition, the Syrian community has solidified by establishing closer ties with the Middle East. The formation of an Arab-American cultural association aided in this process. In the 1984 national elections in Syria, Syrian residents of Allentown were allowed to vote even though they were United States citizens. Further, the success of one of the communities' members who entered the 1984 Olympic games (on behalf of Syria) has been a tremendous boost to that minority.

Hispanics. Hispanics in Allentown have not had many of these advantages. The community is fragmented. The majority of persons are Puerto Rican. Yet significant populations of Peruvians, Colombians, Dominicans, Cubans, and other groups have increased the city's diversity. As a result, coalitions between Spanish-speaking peoples have been difficult to form.

An additional barrier for the Hispanic population is language. While many members of the Syrian community understand English, this is not true for a large number of Hispanics. Because of national policies in Puerto Rico, children are not educated bilingually. Once in the United States, there are few opportunities for employment in a middle-size city like Allentown without knowledge of English.

Blacks. Blacks have had even fewer means of gathering solidarity in Allentown. They have not developed extensive community organizations or large numbers of leaders. Unlike the Hispanics or Syrians, there is no

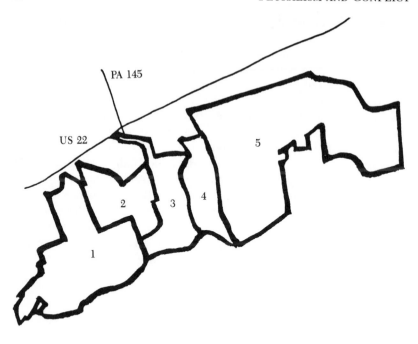

AREA NUMBER	% WHITE NO.	% BLACK NO.	% HISPANIC NO.	% ASIAN/ PACIFIC ISLANDER NO.
1	97.8	.9	1.1	.6
	21,529	208	246	126
2	95.8	1.9	4.0	.4
	17,991	352	747	75
3	86.3	6.9	11.8	.4
	12,634	1,013	1,725	58
4	81.6	5.2	16.8	0.0
	4,569	294	941	
5	93.1	3.3	5.8	.5
	13,933	716	1,231	110

Data are taken from 1980 Census.

Figure 5.1   Racial configuration of the inner city, Allentown, Pennsylvania

extended family to act as a source of support. Many blacks in Allentown live in a tight geographical area in close proximity to their place of employment. Unlike groups who have emigrated to the United States and who live with family members in the inner city by choice, the black population is forced to reside there because of economic, social, and geographical patterns of segregation.

Asians. The arrival of a small Asian population in the city's suburban areas has recently added to the mosaic. The presence of Korean and other Asian minorities in the Lehigh Valley is a phenomenon that has taken place since 1965, when immigration reforms permitted large numbers of Asian peoples to enter the United States for the first time in more than forty years.

Although in the Lehigh Valley their numbers are small, signs of the new emerging minority are easily found and often are surprising. For example, an ad in the Allentown papers in Korean and English asks for single-needle operators for a local knitting mill.[68] Volunteers from a local church were caught off guard when on a door-to-door campaign to obtain new members an Oriental man leaned out of an upstairs window in a suburban development to see what they wanted. When they replied that they were from Hope Church, he responded with the question "What is a church? I am a Buddhist." In another instance, a minister received a telephone call from a Buddhist asking whether or not the sanctuary might be made available for a wedding. The caller also wanted to know if the Christian symbols could be removed prior to the celebration.

Such examples are dramatic signs of the religious diversity in the area. The plurality, however, remains veiled. Most long-term residents are unaware of its existence and still prefer to think of the area as Pennsylvania German.

One of the most noticeable of the new Asian groups are the Indians, who now include more than two hundred families. Most Asian Indians are upwardly mobile, professional persons, who have sought employment in many of the universities and corporations in the area.

As a sign of this community, the first Hindu temple in the Lehigh Valley was erected in 1985.[69] The institution, located between a Pentecostal church and a mainline Protestant church, has neither been the subject of controversy nor has it caused the community any great alarm. There are several reasons for this lack of conflict over the same issue that, just forty miles away in Warren County, New Jersey, has caused considerable unrest.

First, as a middle-class, professional population, the Asian Indians in the Lehigh Valley have rapidly assimilated and have gained economic parity in the same places of work as members of the dominant society. Hence, they are not viewed with undue suspicion. Further, they do not reside in ethnic enclaves as in larger cities like New York and are not segregated from the rest of society. Rather, their economic position has made life in a residential suburban area both tenable and easily affordable. The presence of a temple, built by such a population, is not viewed as threatening. A temple bazaar thus attracted many non-Indians by offering an array of curries and other Indian foods, pizza, hot dogs, Pennsylvania German funnel cakes, and apple butter made with Indian spices.

Second, unlike the Warren County example, this population has settled in the Lehigh Valley gradually. This has meant that they have not become visible rapidly and are not seen as a threat. An indication of the group's low visibility is the Hindu temple itself. Constructed to appear much like secular buildings in the area, its external appearance does not suggest a new or different population.

The demand for the invisibility of minority groups was perhaps best symbolized in the area by the early history of the Jewish community. When Allentown's first synagogue was erected in the heart of the inner city, it was constructed to appear like any other building. The structure, which still stands (and is used by an Orthodox congregation), has few of the distinguishing characteristics commonly associated with synagogues.

Thus, when an Asian Indian community sought to build yet another ethnic, religious institution that blended into the general suburban landscape, it presented little difficulty. The presence of one more ethnic group was not seen as a new or threatening event in an area that historically has been the home for the widest possible variety of persons. The fact that this new group has preferred both to assimilate rapidly and to demonstrate a low level of ethnic visibility decreased public resistance. Perhaps most important, the value structure that undergirded the community's tolerance was historically pluralistic, affirming the right of different ethnic groups to maintain their own traditions as long as they retained a certain measure of invisibility. In nearby Warren County, where a pluralist ideology had not previously existed, the sudden interjection of a plan to concentrate a minority group in the area was perceived as highly threatening.

Maintaining Pluralism. Within this potpourri of peoples (which also includes concentrated populations of Austrians, Italians, and other European groups), the city administration has realized the necessity of maintaining an understanding of cultural pluralism despite the growing assimilationist mentality of the wider area. Overtures to different segments of the ethnic community are common. A city official may make a strategic appearance at a cultural festival. The mayor is often chided for his numerous "flag-raising activities." In each case, ethnicity is not treated lightly but as an important part of Allentown's heritage that has had lasting effects. In short, ethnicity and religion are understood as political realities that are part of an ongoing inner-city mosaic that refuses to melt.

Balancing Pluralism and Homogeneity

The example of Allentown has shown several things. First, it has demonstrated how a minority culture that experienced significant discrimination as a result of its cultural origins and language became a numerical majority. As a majority, it effectively established a mechanism for control (through social institutions such as clubs, churches, and associations) that was only available within the culture. This effectively segregated the Pennsylvania Germans from other ethnic groups that entered the area. Each succeeding minority followed the example of the Pennsylvania Germans by establishing their own cultural centers, churches, and clubs and gaining relative economic parity. As the level of parity increased, so did the ability of each group to assimilate to mainstream America.

Newer groups in the Lehigh Valley, including blacks and Hispanics, have followed a different pattern. Because they exhibit the greatest economic disparity, they have maintained a social distance that reflects the wishes of the dominant society. In other words, they have been the most highly segregated groups at the greatest social distance (the inner city) from the majority. There has also been a greater potential for conflict between these groups and the dominant society than among other minorities. However, in Allentown this has been minimal.

The Asians, in contrast to these more disadvantaged groups, have quickly assimilated in much the same way as their European predecessors. Asian Indians, Chinese, and Japanese are mostly middle-class persons who have achieved full economic parity. Most are integrated with the rest of the community. Conflict with these groups is rare.

Second, the data also suggest that although the Pennsylvania Germans became a numerical majority in Allentown, they continue to function attitudinally as a minority. This is suggested by several factors. The self-image of the culture continues to be negative and to reflect long periods of discrimination. Ethnic jokes are frequently told, often ridiculing the lack of education and traditional patterns of life of German immigrants. Further, the tendency of the Germans to insulate themselves from other ethnic groups and their suspicion of outsiders point to a continuing tendency to see themselves as subjugated.

Third, conflict in the area is most often in the form of long-term struggle of variable means rather than intense, short-term disputes. Both intragroup and intergroup conflict have been defined by a sense of competition. For example, within the Pennsylvania German community, conflict has usually involved retention of German as a liturgical language, as noted earlier, and division between Lutheran and Reformed churches. Intergroup conflict is vividly symbolized by a sign in front of a conservative Christian church that, eschewing diversity, proclaims that the only salvation is in Christ. The sign faces the Jewish Community Center (figure 5.2).

Fourth, because of the area's history of segregated pluralism, ethnic or religious coalitions have been almost nonexistent. An ecumenical organization has until the mid-1980s included only the Protestant community. There has, except in recent years, been a minimum of Christian-Jewish

Figure 5.2   Sign facing the Jewish Community Center, Allentown, Pennsylvania

activities. Even within ethnic communities, coalitions have been difficult
to form. The differing segments of Allentown's Hispanic community, for
example, have been unable to build lasting federations to speak with a
unified voice.

The difficulty of forming coalitions in the area is indicative of the effort
of the dominant German culture to retain its control. This is in keeping
with accepted theory that suggests that socially dominant groups tend to
maintain or increase their dominance.[70] Thus, conflict in Allentown's
ethnic matrix has usually been of the consensus-bounded type that has not
threatened the relative position of the majority.

Finally, in Allentown, the self-image of the population is both pluralistic
and homogeneous. In a very real sense, Allentown embodies both characteristics. Its competitive, pluralistic heritage has forced elected officials
periodically to seek the support of the city's ethnic groups. At the same
time, they readily acknowledge a sense of a more homogeneous mindset
characterized by the nomenclature, the "Greater Lehigh Valley." The
symbols of the Greater Lehigh Valley are the large shopping malls, super
highways, and major corporations that form a network throughout the area
and the contiguous cities of Bethlehem and Easton. These symbols have
also been the source of a loss of identity in those villages and small towns
that have ceased to exist because of the area's rapid growth.

As the younger members of the community often deny the importance
of their ethnic heritage and are drawn to the culture of the Greater Lehigh
Valley, so older generations retain their understanding of a segregated
pluralistic community that has been viable for several hundred years.

Although not restricted to it, the total dynamic is analogous to the demography of city and suburb. Ethnic communities are more concentrated in the inner city. There, power is acquired not through an acknowledgment that ethnicity does not exist but through the ongoing understanding that is an important aspect of community life. In the suburbs, where there is more rapid assimilation, the ideology, like the demography, is that of a melting pot. Conflict often takes the form of the fear of invisible boundaries between the two areas. Persons who do not live in Allentown's inner city are often heard to indicate their unwillingness to venture into the area.

However, because Allentown has been able to balance the plural and assimilative character of its community rather than increase the polarity of the two ideologies, conflict has been minimal. City officials and community leaders understand the double nature of their city. They are aware of the homogeneity of the Greater Lehigh Valley that dominates discussions of economic growth and many aspects of day-to-day life. Yet, they are also keenly aware of racial and religious pluralism—of the separate communities of Hindus, Muslims, Jews, Protestants, and Catholics, which, while often integrated within the rest of the population, have significant differences. They also know the highly segregated, economically deprived racial minorities in the inner city. Behind each domain is a separate and highly distinct vision of America that is the continuing focus of this text.

CHAPTER **6**

Mediation in a Diverse Society

When a *New York Times* reporter interviewed the tenants of an apartment building on Justice Avenue in Elmhurst, New York, he found an environment so incredibly diverse that it was without parallel.[1] What made the area unusual was that there was no common ground for communication. Even those residents who understood some English perceived the world in an entirely different fashion from their neighbors.

Justice Avenue Revisited

The reporter encountered not only overwhelming diversity but also extreme isolation. Not only was each resident noticeably different, but many believed that they were the only foreign-born persons on their floor. Contact with other immigrants was minimal and for many nonexistent.

In pluralistic environments such as Justice Avenue, cultural values often inhibit communication. An Indian woman, for example, might be encouraged to remain in her home and not make friends outside of her immediate family and small circle of peers. Her domain may be inside her apartment, where religious and cultural conventions are painstakingly maintained. Her husband and children are expected to be more Westernized and to assimilate.

As Elmhurst exhibits an unusual kind and degree of pluralism, it also is characterized by a noticeable lack of public, or community, life. Most residents have relatively few ways of experiencing prolonged contact with the wider community. A tiny park with a few benches provides one of the few opportunities for public interaction. Block clubs and civic associations have minimal participation from the full range of ethnic groups in the area. Older residents, who tend to dominate such public institutions as the community board, often express their fear of diversity. Newer immigrants, who are unsure of the nature of public life, refrain from committing themselves to it. Instead, they concentrate on reinforcing ethnic ties and on improving their quality and standard of life. They generally prefer an anonymity that assures safety and security.

Privatization of Life

While Elmhurst is more ethnically diverse than the majority of U.S. cities, it is not more privatized. David Popenoe suggests that both the emphasis on privacy and the narrowing of public life have become increasingly important:

> It is in the privatization of space, because it is so tangible and visible, that the breakdown of the public realm in metropolitan life can most clearly be seen. The American suburb is the extreme case, but privatization is a dominant motif in most of the other ecological zones of the metropolis as well. Streets and sidewalks that once provided public pedestrian interaction and even entertainment have for the most part been abandoned to the utter privacy of the automobile; public parks have fallen into disuse and misuse; town squares have become the most ornamental appendages of commercialism. The American metropolitan apartment dweller lives behind locked doors, using public space mainly as a means of access and egress to desired private loci, not as space in which to linger and utilize for its own sake (save, perhaps, for during the lunch hour at work). And where is the public space in a Houston or a Los Angeles? It does exist, but is overwhelmed by the dominance of essential private spheres.[2]

Popenoe concludes that anonymity in public life is a relatively modern occurrence.[3] In preindustrial, urban societies, there were prescribed norms that dictated patterns of relationships with strangers. Such norms often depended on one's dress.

> In contacts with strangers, one could develop some sense of who they were by how they looked—especially what clothes they wore. Members of the various social classes were identifiable, so were members of guilds, ranks of the church hierarchy, and so on. And just as important as these appearential codes was the fact that the relationship among the different types of people was very closely regulated by social norms. There were clearly prescribed ways of acting toward people based on the appearential signals that they gave off.[4]

Unlike such traditional societies, public life in the United States has become more homogeneous in appearance than its preindustrial counterparts (see figure 6.1). No longer can identity or occupation be determined by patterns of dress. While accepted patterns of executive or blue-collar clothing give an approximate indication of class and social position, they do not offer the specificity of identification possible in preindustrial societies. In village India, for example, it is still possible to determine regional identification through dress. A person's origins in Rajasthan, the Punjab, or Bengal are easily recognized through particular forms of clothing. In addition, names specify caste, region of birth, and religion. In industrial and postindustrial societies such as the United States, names and dress no longer perform this specific a function. A person named Mason, for instance, does not necessarily work with mortar, nor does a person named Wheelwright fashion wagon wheels.

Perhaps the best example of uniformity in public life is the suburbs, where differences are regularly camouflaged behind a veneer of homogeneity. With their rows of neatly trimmed lawns, manicured gardens, and shuttered houses, many communities exhibit remarkable uniformity of appearance. Moreover, uniformity is not just a demographic consideration but is a significant part of the suburban system. The neighbor who disregards or breaks this value structure is rejected. An unshoveled sidewalk, a weed-ridden lawn, and a house badly in need of painting are frequently condemned as unwelcome elements of diversity.

In one northeastern community, this value system precipitated an amusing neighborhood feud. After two neighbors had had a series of

Figure 6.1   Homogeneity in late twentieth-century American architecture, repetition of living units in a condominium complex in northern New Jersey

shouting matches, one of them took a drastic step, the ultimate affront. Against the backdrop of this serene, tree-lined community noted for its row after row of attractive thirty-year-old homes, he painted his house bright red. Such an act of "revenge" caused his neighbor to suffer the utmost of hardships, the regular view of a house that was a source of embarrassment because it was different.

Other visual expressions of uniformity in public life are shopping malls, supermarkets, corporate parks, networks of superhighways, and suburban sprawl. The movement toward greater homogeneity has resulted from advances in communication and travel and a rapidly expanding, multinational, corporate economy.

At the same time that appearance and outward signs of identity in American cities have become more homogeneous, the level of actual diversity has markedly increased. The proliferation of persons from different cultures and ethnic backgrounds has been an important national trend. This increase in actual diversity has combined with the long-standing American emphasis on individualism to produce an ethic that rejects the outward expression of differences in public life but upholds the right of the individual to maintain them privately. Since public life is dominated by homogeneity and often anonymity, and since people desire control of some bit of territory in an increasingly crowded society, they attach great significance to the home as a place for the expression of diversity. As the Justice Avenue apartment house demonstrates, in its isolation the home becomes the area of culturally determined patterns of diet, language, and values. Thus diversity has become highly privatized.[5]

Because differences are privatized, they are diffused, and, most significantly, they are valued only as long as they remain invisible. Whenever they appear in public view, public alarm frequently results. All of this suggests that many Americans experience the contradiction of conformity and diversity as an aspect of the distinction between public and private life.

One of the effects of the combination of increased ethnic and religious diversity and the simultaneous increase in the homogeneity of public life is the reduction of opportunities for the interaction of minority groups. The Justice Avenue apartment, as noted previously, is a significant example of this estrangement and isolation. Each of the residents assumed that he or she was the only foreign-born person on the floor. If the residents had experienced any elements of public life in the building or even in the immediate neighborhood, they would have known otherwise. Instead, their experience was totally conditioned by the private world in which they found themselves, interrupted only by forays into the outside world for work or shopping, but significantly not for interaction with other people in the community.

The question that arises under such conditions of anonymity and isolation is what happens when contact with public life in the wider community cannot be avoided. An encounter with a hospital, a public school, a retirement home, or a police station, for example, may become an instance of complete trauma for the immigrant.

Unless public institutions are increasingly trained to mediate such situations, the experiences of isolation and fear will continue. The remainder of this chapter explores the ramifications of this question and lifts up several models of mediating institutions that can make a difference.

Characteristics of Mediating Institutions

In pluralistic societies, the ability to understand diversity is related to the degree that it can be directly experienced. In South Asia, for example, where extreme communalism (primary loyalty to a religious and ethnic group) has historically caused great enmity among different segments of the population, mutual experience is an important issue. It was no accident, for example, that in India the sixteenth-century Mogul emperor Akbar claimed to have had mystical experiences in several major religions. During his reign, Hindu and Muslim institutions alike became the recipients of royal patronage.[6] As a result of these and other tolerant policies, communal tensions were eased and the empire enjoyed a period of relative stability.

While Akbar was often viewed as eclectic, his approach was strategically quite appropriate in a communal culture. In the United States, far removed from a preindustrial South Asian society, the same principle is also pertinent. The experience of diversity is still an important issue.

A Christian cannot completely understand, for example, what it is to be a Jew unless he or she has had the experience of encountering a member of the tradition, of internalizing that person's personal faith journey, and of appreciating the role of the religion in times of suffering. Part of the function of religion cross-culturally is to help explain, justify, and interpret the meaning of suffering. This dimension is never just an abstraction but is always of the most intimate and personal nature. To understand this function through the medium of experience helps to reduce the effect of stereotypes based on culture or religion.

In a pluralistic society the experience of diversity can also provide a valuable point of entry for initiating a level of intercultural and interreligious communication that otherwise might not take place. This is not to suggest that the experience of diversity can by itself create mutual understanding among different ethnic and religious groups where each maintains a vastly different perception of the world. However, in a pluralistic nation where the societal mainstream often encourages homogeneity in dress, language, religion, and other aspects of behavior, a willingness to experience diversity firsthand can be an important means of developing a receptive environment where continuing communication might begin.

This text has presented the 1893 Parliament of Religions as an example of an experiential approach to religious diversity. The parliament for the first time on North American soil brought representatives of diverse religions and cultures into the same environment, during a mammoth, seventeen-day event. Discussions, formal addresses, and social gatherings all helped participants to learn from one another in a setting that encouraged the direct experience of adherents of religions that hitherto had been approached only as the subject of conversion.

The event was made even more noteworthy by the unfavorable social and political climate within which it took place. In 1893, the majority of Americans had a less than positive image of cultural and religious diversity. Only thirty years before, the country had been ravaged by civil war, partly over the issue of slavery. A few years before, in the wake of the Reconstruction Period, the subjugation of the American Indian had drawn national attention. Beginning in 1882, diversity had once again emerged as a pivotal national issue with the passage of the first Chinese Exclusion Act.

It is an anomaly that in the midst of a period in which diversity was a source of division and oppression, an event could be held that sought instead to help the nation experience and understand it. The parliament was also the first time that religious and cultural diversity were positively experienced on such a broad and inclusive context rather than just studied or debated. In its level of enthusiasm, its ability to encounter diversity without avoiding conflict or confrontation, the parliament became a model for approaching pluralism in public life through the medium of direct, personal experience.

Much as the Parliament of Religions did in late nineteenth-century America, so mediating institutions—schools, hospitals, and interfaith organizations, for example—in the late twentieth century provide a common ground where diverse elements of the population can encounter one another in public life. In the United States pluralism has been privatized, and cultural and religious differences have been most significantly expressed at home or extended into ethnic associations and temples. The model of accepted behavior is visible evidence of assimilation and conformity. Many immigrants, especially women, feel threatened by the outside realm with its suspicion of diversity and retreat to the inside domain to maintain loyalty to their heritage. Under these conditions, mediating agencies, programs, and structures provide a quality of experience and communication that might not otherwise take place. For members of religious and cultural minorities, mediating institutions can help to reduce the apprehension and fear that they have of public life. For members of the mainstream, mediating institutions can help to reduce the impact of cultural stereotypes about minority groups.

Mediating institutions, therefore, provide a middle ground between public and private life and between values of homogeneity and diversity. By accepting and emphasizing elements of ethnicity and religion, they provide a secure atmosphere in which traditions, values, and patterns of life often experienced only in the private home, can be made known in public life and thus help reduce the schizophrenic division between the inside and outside realm.

Mediating institutions deal with the question of identity by maintaining a balance between the competing ideologies of pluralism and assimilation. They affirm the value of ethnicity and at the same time offer a vehicle for helping members of tightly knit ethnic communities to overcome their apprehension of the mainstream, and they assist the society in making sense out of the experience of diversity in public life.

Mediating institutions also recognize that, as many of the social theorists discussed in this text have suggested, pluralism and assimilation are interrelated parts of American life. They demonstrate that if the manner in which these processes are approached emphasizes points of contact rather than ideological polarity, conflict within the society may be reduced.

The remainder of this chapter will discuss models of mediation in mainstream life that have been successful.

Schools as Mediating Institutions

In a high school class in Alhambra, California, a boy from Mexico asked a classmate from the Philippines why he had a Spanish name.[7] For the teacher, this was an opportunity to teach an important history lesson that pertained directly to the cultural identity of her students. She answered the question by presenting a summary of European colonialism and imperialism in the sixteenth century and the legacies of these policies. As the discussion continued, a boy from Venezuela joined in, recognizing many words that were also part of his language. For him, Spanish was a second language, which he had learned as the son of Chinese parents who had emigrated to South America.[8] Despite the extreme cultural differences, language became a common link between classmates who prior to the discussion had had no basis for communication.

Unfortunately, such encounters rarely receive the kind of attention that they deserve. All too few teachers and school administrators are equipped to turn such chance occurrences into productive lessons as this teacher did. Instead of treating the initial query by the Mexican child lightly, she used it as a way to help persons of different cultural origins to understand one another. In the end, the entire class received a valuable lesson not only in world history but in the manner in which persons from diverse cultural backgrounds can gain appreciation and understanding of one another.

The following pages describe programs in two schools, one public and the other private, in which classroom experiences like the one described above are a regular occurrence. They are illustrative of creative ways in which schools can perform an important mediating function.

The United Nations International School

In a suburban section of northern Queens, known for its well-maintained, upper-middle-class homes, is the United Nations International School (UNIS).[9] Founded shortly after the establishment of the UN, the school was designed for children of UN employees. UNIS has evolved into two campuses, one in Jamaica Estates (Queens) and the other in Manhattan.

The Queens campus, which serves kindergarten through the sixth grade, is only a few blocks from Jamaica, a principal stop on the E train. Like the UNIS, the area surrounding the school is extremely diverse. On nearby Hillside Avenue, one can purchase lunch from a Chinese-Spanish restaurant or buy fruits and vegetables from a West Indian market. A Korean runs one of the area's many delicatessens. When asked for coffee and a danish, he responds by querying, "What is a danish?" Other immigrants, many of whom are Hispanic or Asian Indian, also have a minimal knowledge of English.

Historically, the UNIS has had two primary purposes. The first has been the education of the children of UN employees in a way that will prepare them eventually to return to their country of origin. In some instances, for children born here or brought to the United States while very young, this emphasis has meant teaching the very essentials of cultural traditions.

The second purpose, like that of the majority of schools in the country, is to help a broader population of children to understand and to function in the American society of which they are a part. Both the sons and daughters of diplomats and UN personnel, as well as other children from the wider city (many of whom are from families who have immigrated to the United States), are taught to value their ethnic, cultural, and religious heritage. This is not to suggest that the school resists their assimilation into the larger society or refrains from helping them appreciate those things that are uniquely American. An emphasis on sports, for example, is seen as a healthy, productive venture. The uniqueness of the UNIS remains its ability to educate and prepare children to be part of the wider society while emphasizing the significance of their heritage.

The school achieves its objectives through several emphases. Each child learns to become more aware of his or her cultural identity through a variety of ways including celebrations and festivals. On UN Day, each October 24, celebrating the anniversary of the founding of the United Nations, children come to school in the native dress of their country of origin. On Mardi Gras children learn of French traditions and are served French food.

In this and other ways, the UNIS stresses experiential education. Children learn from one another about their own and their classmates' cultural backgrounds. The teachers assist in this process by virtue of the fact that they are an international body themselves and include persons from a wide variety of cultures and ethnic groups. In addition, school plays and assemblies frequently have an intercultural focus with themes such as friendship, interdependence, and the need to build bridges between persons from different backgrounds.

The UNIS offers a unique language program that both helps assimilate children whose primary tongue is not English and at the same time reinforces multilingualism. English as a second language is a continuing part of the curriculum. In addition, French as a second language is taught for those students who already speak English. Instruction in French is carried through all levels of the Jamaica Estates campus. Arabic classes are offered after school for interested students. This effort helps children whose parents are from Arabic-speaking countries to know something of their native tongue.

An example of the school's unique thrust is its music classes. Western classical music is deemphasized. Instead, students are urged to learn something of the music in their indigenous cultures.

In other areas, pupils are also helped to learn more about their family's background. A common exercise at the UNIS is to construct a family tree. Students may be assigned to interview their parents and to explore with them the circumstances under which they emigrated to the United States. During this process, one child discovered that his father left his home riding on a camel!

Through such narratives, pupils come to understand both the experience of immigration and, for children of UN personnel, the difficulties of frequent moves from one culture to another. They may become aware of the interdependence between religion and culture. Questions about ethnicity frequently include references to religion. A holiday may provide opportunities for the teaching staff to describe important variations in rituals as well as cross-cultural practices that are much the same.

Teachers admit that the difficulty with the intercultural emphasis at the UNIS is in going beyond a celebration of diversity to form a sense of community. The Jamaica Estates campus is not a neighborhood school. Students come from a wide geographical area rather than a single neighborhood. While they may socialize at school with classmates from different backgrounds, many do not do so at home. Because of cultural values and stereotypes, children frequently feel parental pressure to form peer groups restricted to the dominant culture. Attempts to deal with this issue are difficult but are made. The school tries to meet with parents to help them understand the importance of cross-cultural communication.

UNIS students build community in yet another way. It is a common exercise for classmates to study cross-cultural festivals. Perhaps the most common is Thanksgiving. Thanksgiving celebrations are practiced the world over at different seasons and with a variety of religious interpretations. Festivals such as this present an opportunity for understanding cultural differences and, at the same time, for realizing the commonality between them. This, in turn, is reinforced by relationships forged during school festivals, ethnic food celebrations, and classes.

UNIS teachers are quick to comment that an experiment such as theirs would not survive without an administration possessing tremendous foresight and vision. Most freely admit that a return to those forms of mainstream public education that they have experienced, where such a vision does not often exist, would be difficult. Many of the teaching staff had little knowledge of the value of this kind of education before coming to the UNIS. Now, they comment that the school has taught them as well as the children. Few would return to another model.

Senn Metropolitan Academy

Senn Academy stands on the fringe of a northeastern Chicago community identified as Uptown. Ironically, Uptown is far from the traditional white Anglo-Saxon Protestant image that its name suggests. It is neither homogeneous nor elitist. Rather, Uptown is an urban "intake" area, a massive resettlement community where persons from as many as forty countries live in a tightly concentrated neighborhood where ethnicity is not an anomaly but a way of life.

In the midst of a residential neighborhood, in Edgewater, near Uptown, Senn Academy is a massive and opposing structure. Built more than half a century ago, it is akin to a giant fortress, worn by time and the thousands of students who have walked its hallways. Yet, despite its archaic and well-worn appearance, Senn Academy is ahead of its time. In the midst of overwhelming diversity, it is a community where teachers and students share an understanding of both plurality and assimilation rarely encountered in American society.

Because of its unique policies and programs, Senn has had remarkably few racial incidents. When Chicago first desegregated its public schools, some tensions were experienced. Since then, as the level of ethnic diversity has dramatically increased, Senn has had a decrease in interracial problems. Administrators now experience more tension within ethnic communities than between groups.

Many of Senn's students have come to the United States against the most difficult of circumstances. A Vietnamese girl, for instance, talks of the time that she and her father left the country, while her mother stayed behind. As an employee of the South Vietnamese government during the war, he had been forced to flee for his life after the Communist victory. The trip to the United States was not easily accomplished. The family spent several years in refugee camps in Hong Kong before finally emigrating. Now, the father and six children live in a three-room apartment in Uptown.

A Cambodian student describes his arduous journey to the United States:

> One night in 1979, I had to leave my country. It was a cold and terrible night. Everybody was upset and cried when they said bye [sic.] to their families and friends. It is hard to explain my feelings: at the time I looked at my parents, I felt they were old and looked different than other days. My mother cried a lot and held my hand. When it was time to get on the boat, I walked over to kiss her and said, "I love you." She was still crying and said, "You must write letters to me." My father hugged me and said, "I don't have anything to tell you, but you are still very young, so you must try hard in everything you do. Good luck to you." I started to cry. I knew I was going to be without my parents for a long time.
>
> I looked around the boat; it was old, dirty. It was 300 feet long, but 700 people were in it. I knew my friend had been standing all night long to give me his place. I smiled at him. I didn't have to say, "Thank you." He understood.[10]

Such accounts are often typical of students who arrive at Senn Academy within twenty-four hours after leaving refugee camps in Southeast Asia. Their resettlement in northeastern Chicago has given Uptown and Edgewater tremendous fluidity. This transitoriness is reflected in Senn. Ten years ago the school included students speaking forty-seven languages. Today the number has been reduced to twenty-six, reflecting the consolidation of some of the Asian populations.

Among the groups that have increased in the community and in the school are the Cambodians. The increase stems from the genocide in that nation and the outpouring of thousands of refugees to neighboring Thailand and eventually to the United States and other countries. As the Cambodian population has increased, so others have declined. Senn used to include a significant number of Hmong, a tribal people indigenous to Laos. This tightly knit community has tended to migrate as a unit and has moved away from the Uptown-Edgewater area.

Senn's unique understanding of pluralism began in the late 1960s. A teacher began to notice the appearance of more and more foreign-born students in the school who did not understand English. The outgrowth of this concern was the initiation of a pioneering effort in multilingual education, which included emphases on both teaching English (TESOL) and bilingual education. Students were thus able to learn English and to become part of the societal mainstream and at the same time to improve their knowledge of their native country's language, culture, and history. After changes in Illinois state law that established requirements for bilingual education, other schools in northwestern Chicago followed Senn's example. Yet, Senn is still perceived as including the most comprehensive program and is frequently sought after by students outside its immediate geographical area. The school's success was recognized by the Ford Foundation, which granted the institution a twenty-thousand-dollar city high school recognition award for TESOL in 1983.

Bilingual classes are offered in a variety of subjects. A class in world history, for example, focuses on Vietnam. Both students and the teacher are refugees and share a common experience. Together, using textbooks printed in Vietnamese, they explore a variety of facets of world civilization and Indo-Chinese history.

The bilingual classes have a remarkable attendance and are amazingly free of disciplinary problems. The overwhelming number of students view the experience as helpful and benefit from the sense of community that contact with their ethnic group provides. For many of these students, the most difficult times are the weekends, when they are either with their families or alone. Family time often provides little freedom to interact with peers. For those students who live alone, frequently on public assistance, the classes may be their only regular source of community.

Teachers in the bilingual and TESOL programs describe their work as far more than instruction. Instead, they frequently assume an important role as counselors. A student who has emotional problems that may not be understood by his or her family receives a sympathetic ear from Senn's teachers. The teaching staff is accustomed to interfacing between students, social workers, psychologists, and families.

The bilingual office is frequently the site of intense counseling between teachers and students. Most teachers are sensitive to this, particularly when the interaction is between persons of the same national origin. In these cases, the common link of language, culture, and nationality provides a basis for in-depth communication that otherwise might be difficult.

Teachers comment that although they often receive students within twenty-four hours after leaving their country, the most difficult emotional times frequently occur after three years. The clash of cultural differences, the lack of adequate family support systems, and pervasive loneliness bring great emotional stress. In such instances, a teacher of the same cultural background can become a significant role model and friend.

Students whose primary language is other than English are initially placed in the TESOL program. Once their degree of English proficiency is ascertained, they are assigned to one of three levels of instruction. This in turn helps the school decide which level bilingual courses they may enter. At Senn, bilingual classes are offered in four languages: Cantonese, Assyrian, Spanish, and Vietnamese. The effort is supplemented by a special program for students with limited English proficiency, which is identified by the initials LEP. Senn's bilingual classes provide a setting where students may be comfortable in their own language and also receive help in improving their English. Both processes proceed along with instruction in civics, social studies, and other areas.

An example of the diversity of Senn's bilingual program is a class in American History taught in Chinese. The teacher does not engage in line-by-line translation. Instead, he alternates between Chinese and English, emphasizing key terms. During a discussion of the Bill of Rights, for example, the teacher stops to explain the concept of freedom of the press. As part of the exercise, the origin of the term press is described. Students learn that the term, which originally described a printing process, now includes a broad range of media including radio, television, magazines, and newspapers. They also are asked to discuss freedom of the press in Taiwan, about which many have firsthand knowledge.

Each bilingual teacher is acutely aware of these needs and of the extreme poverty of many of their students. A clothing rack in the TESOL office stays full. Students know that they may help themselves to the coats and sweaters that have been donated. Even under these conditions, however, many are reluctant to accept charity.

The sense of community and belonging at Senn's bilingual programs is so strong that graduates of the program who are "mainstreamed" into the rest of the student population, frequently return. Many enjoy the company of persons from their country and the sense of community that frequently evolves in the classes. Others who have dropped out from school entirely often ask permission to audit the classes.

The multicultural emphasis at Senn is also reflected in the school's programmatic life. An International Day is regularly celebrated each year. All classes are suspended and in assemblies, students perform dances and songs from their country. The emotions surrounding these activities usually are high, and preparations are carefully made over a period of months. They frequently include a variety of foods, which are sampled in the gymnasium after the performance.

In addition to the international festival, Senn's administration encourages the formation of ethnic clubs. Vietnamese, Cambodian, Afro-American, Hispanic, and Cantonese clubs meet regularly. Each club has a particular cultural function and may celebrate other festivals such as the Chinese New Year. Clubs also reach out into the community. They frequently are linked with ethnic organizations in the Uptown and Edgewater area, helping to increase the sense of cohesiveness among different segments of the population.

In keeping with Senn's emphasis on helping foreign-born students assimilate into the mainstream while at the same time enhancing their identity, teachers frequently impress on their students that it is all right to be different. Classmates are encouraged to talk about the ways in which they differ and are particularly urged to become familiar with cultural traditions unique to their country. A music class, for instance, routinely teaches students songs that have great meaning in their native land. A Cambodian folk song speaks of the trauma that nation has experienced:

> Oh my country where I stay each day
> Since I was young and through the years of school
> From my country I have now escaped
> I don't know when I will return
>
> . . .
>
> I will come back—back to my country
> With independence, I will return. [11]

As the class plays the soft, longing music, accompanied by the solitary voice of a Cambodian girl, many of the refugees remember the trauma of their forced evacuation. The teacher is not only sensitive to this but helps each student to draw his or her feelings out and to remember both the circumstances and the place from which he or she has come. Because of the staff's belief in these efforts, the atmosphere of the school remains one of acceptance of cultural and religious differences and the continuous building of community.

Hospitals as Mediating Institutions

In 1984, Seng Vang came to Philadelphia to visit his family. [12] The subsequent attack on the Hmong refugee and a resulting hospitalization has become a symbol of the trauma that all too often accompanies the way that health care is perceived by many Southeast Asian peoples.

During the course of Seng's visit, he became involved in a street fight with black youths, when, according to Seng, they surrounded his car. A fight started when Seng and members of his family were pulled out of the car. This fight later became the motivating force for the exodus of thousands of Hmong from the city. It symbolized their total rejection of

American urban life, which many saw as more threatening than the country they had left behind.

The Hospital Experience of a Hmong Refugee in Canada

For Seng Vang the incident was only the beginning of a strange and difficult ordeal that found him at odds with the North American culture in which he lived. After release from the University of Pennsylvania Hospital, he returned to Sherbrooke, Quebec, where he had been resettled after his arrival from Cambodia. In a short while, he contracted hepatitis from contaminated blood that he had been given in a transfusion in Philadelphia. He was admitted to a private hospital in Sherbrooke.

The hospitalization proved to be a frightening experience. Seng's wife could visit only infrequently because care of the family's six children consumed most of her time. She spoke little French or English and had difficulty communicating with persons from outside her culture. Only one other Hmong family resided in Sherbrooke.

Seng's discomfort was compounded by other reasons. He greatly distrusted Western medicine. Instead, like thousands of persons from Southeast and East Asia, he looked to the shaman, who he believed could drive the spirits from his body that caused the illness. Responding to these concerns, Seng's wife called his family in Minnesota. A shaman was secured, which the family brought to his bedside. Since Seng had already indicated that he was most unhappy in the hospital and wanted to leave, his doctors convinced him to stay with the understanding that the shaman could continue to treat him.

Seng became gravely ill and then began to respond to the treatment, which his family understood as certain evidence of the shaman's abilities. But then, without warning, as his recovery continued, his doctors ordered a change. A limitation was placed on the number of visitors that Seng could receive because the hospital believed that too many visitors would retard a patient's recovery. In addition, Seng became convinced that a new intravenous bag that the hospital installed would poison him, much as he had been poisoned by a blood transfusion in Philadelphia.

These concerns led Seng's family to believe that he might indeed fare better outside of the institution. The director of professional services soon intervened, concluding that the reason for the limitation of family visitors was personality conflicts between the doctor, who was Haitian, and the Hmong family. After these difficulties were remedied, family visits were increased and matters were improving when the director learned that Seng was also being treated by a shaman. He responded by forbidding the use of herbal teas and other medicines that the shaman had prescribed, saying, "There are the laws here about the medicine, and nobody can get anything that does not come from our pharmacy. This is impossible; it cannot be done."[13]

The removal of the shaman and the herbal medicine convinced Seng and his family that the doctors were trying to kill him. From this perspective, Seng had no other choice but to leave. His original doctor pleaded that he might die if he left. But it was to no avail:

> Release papers were brought in, and with a shaking hand, Seng Vang signed them. Then, he pulled himself up onto his crutches and began to inch his way out of the room. Seeing that he was about to topple over, his family rushed to him and propped him up.
>
> And then, under the solemn gaze of dozens of nurses, doctors, and patients, the group made its painstaking way along the corridor, down the elevator and out the door into the rain.[14]

The story of Seng Vang is an anomaly only in that it caught the attention of a reporter and was catapulted into the national eye. The rejection of Western medicine and the total distrust of doctors, hospital administrators, and procedures that most Americans take for granted is characteristic not only of Hmong, but of refugees from other parts of Asia as well.

The hospital in which Seng was treated is all too typical of institutions that have little training in mediating cultural differences. To be sure, there were doctors who were sensitive to his plight, but they had little understanding of the cultural importance either of the extended family or of the faith put in indigenous folk medicine. Because the institution had no unified policy for dealing with cultural differences, the judgment of individual doctors, nurses, and administrators became decisive and contradictory at different points in the case history.

It could be argued that the hospital was outside of a major metropolitan area that had significant numbers of Southeast Asian people and consequently had few ways to know about Seng's preconceptions of Western medicine. Indeed, in Sherbrooke, there was only one other Hmong family, hardly a reason for the hospital to pursue an in-depth knowledge of Hmong culture.

The difficulty with this position remains that in most major North American cities, hospitals are ill equipped to meet the needs of any of the minorities in their midst. When cultural differences are particularly acute, as in the case of Southeast Asian refugees such as the Hmong, the problems are compounded. For older, first-generation refugees and immigrants who do not assimilate rapidly and who are often unable to communicate outside of their ethnic communities, hospitals are formidable barriers. The vast majority of institutions, whether in the heart of urban areas with large ethnic concentrations or in much smaller communities where ethnicity is diffused, are unable to cope with such profoundly different understandings of health care. Even a sensitive doctor or social worker, as the example of Seng Vang illustrates, may be overruled by a hospital administration that does not understand the significance of cultural differences.

Chinese Patients in a New York City Hospital

The following example describes an institution that is an exception. In 1979 in New York City, the New York Infirmary and Beekman Downtown Hospital merged.[15] The merger led to an increased sensitivity in the policy and the program of the institution to the Chinese community in its immediate neighborhood. Soon after the merger, the hospital began an experimental institutionwide effort to try to meet the cultural needs of its Chinatown patients, who, administrators estimated, made up 30 percent of the total. The remainder were drawn from the financial district and from Little Italy, both in close proximity to the hospital. Traditionally, the hospital had worked well with persons from the Wall Street area. The Chinese were another matter and were the subject of much confusion and misunderstanding.

Under the guidelines of the experiment, the visibility of Chinese in the life of the hospital was increased. A Chinese assistant administrator who had grown up in the area around the hospital was hired. Both Lin Mo and his brother Hugh (now deputy police commissioner) had come to the United States from mainland China with their mother following the death of their father (at the hands of the Chinese Communists in 1951).[16] Growing up in New York's Chinatown, the brothers assimilated quickly and at the same time learned to appreciate their heritage and ethnicity. This combination of persons who are members of a minority by birth and who have successfully assimilated can create bridges between the institutions they administer and the communities to which they relate.

Administrators such as Lin Mo understand that the Chinese view health-care institutions differently from the majority of Americans. For many Chinese the hospital is an object of distrust and fear. The type of medicine it practices is not understood. Most Chinese instead value the advice of traditional herbal doctors. The hospital is seen as a place to die:

> They expect very little. Just a place to die. The Chinese who finally present themselves at the hospital door are beset with medical complications. They have avoided this dread step for so long that they are usually suffering from a combination of diseases: the deadly fears often fulfill the dire prophecy.[17]

Most hospitals would do little to calm these fears. Beekman, however, has taken remarkable care to insure that its Chinese patients will feel at home.

The majority of the hospital's departments now have at least one Chinese on staff. In addition, social workers maintain close ties with Chinatown. Referrals are commonly sought from Chinese community organizations in an extensive outreach effort. The result of such carefully constructed ties has been the gradual development of a sense of ownership among the Chinese, who now feel that this hospital is there not just to serve white, middle-class persons in the financial district but them as well.

A visitor to the hospital immediately notices that signs are printed in English and Chinese. Other evidences of the institution's concern for its Asian patients are also evident. Upon admission, a Chinese patient receives a packet of information, some of which is in Chinese. Chinese television is available for a fee. If the patient speaks no English, he or she is presented with a small blue book, A *Handbook of Phrases for Patients*,[18] provided by the Lions Club of Chinatown. Simple phrases are illustrated in cartoon form and are translated in both English and Chinese.

As evidence of its sensitivity to the needs of Chinese patients, the hospital never serves them cold water. Chinese custom insists that warm water is beneficial for illness. In addition, a Chinese menu offers food to which patients are accustomed. In some instances, when the hospital's kitchen cannot prepare particular delicacies, they are secured from Chinatown.

The signs, the food, the warm water, and television are just the outward indications of the hospital's concern. The efforts to meet the needs of Chinese patients go even further. In some instances, where the treatment with herbal medicines is not deemed to be in conflict with Western medical practices, the herbs are allowed to continue. For many patients, this increases their assurance and trust in the hospital.

Most Chinese have had little or no experience with Western medicine and do not know what to expect. Perhaps their biggest fear is having their blood drawn.[19] Many believe that every time blood is taken a portion of the soul is lost. Since most hospitals routinely perform a myriad of tests in which drawing blood is a common procedure, the level of fear is apt to be quite high. Doctors and nurses are aware of this fear. Chinese social workers communicate with patients in their own dialect, helping to soothe their apprehension and explaining why the drawing of blood is necessary.

Other customs are understood by the staff as well. One of the most important Chinese traditions is the role of the extended family. At times, the needs of the family can conflict with hospital routine. This was illustrated by an elderly woman hospitalized for an apparent stroke.[20] While she had a history of hypertension, she was convinced that her symptoms were caused by a lack of blood. In order to combat the problem, she had secured herbal medicine to increase her blood supply.

The medicine actually increased her blood pressure and the danger of illness. In addition, she consumed a lot of soy sauce, which is high in salt content and thus contributed to the risk of further injury. Once these problems were understood and explained, her medical condition could be made more stable. Yet, other culturally defined problems continued.

Before the woman was admitted, she had been taking care of her grandson, the only son of her son. In Chinese culture, sons are especially favored. A grandchild is a particular source of pride. In this instance, the grandmother's sense of responsibility was compounded by the fact that her daughter-in-law worked and that she herself provided the needed child care.

After the older woman's hospitalization, the daughter-in-law visited every day with her son. The visits were especially meaningful because they continued a relationship that was an important source of stability. However, visits by young children were in violation of the hospital's rules. Understanding the cultural considerations involved, a social worker determined that the best solution would be flexibility. Arrangements were made so that the child could see his grandmother in a way that would not disturb other patients.

In another instance, a terminally ill cancer patient in his thirties was admitted to the hospital.[21] In response to her son's illness, his mother arrived from mainland China. In order to support the family's two children under these difficult conditions, the patient's wife sought employment. However, it was difficult for her to take care of the children and to visit her husband for any length of time. The elderly mother responded to meet this need in a way that was in keeping with her culture. She soon became a common sight in the hospital, taking it on herself to provide her son with constant care. The fact that this was her only son increased her desire to be personally attentive.

At first the staff felt that she was in the way. The mother experienced difficulty as well. She spoke no English and didn't know how to perform many of the tasks that her son needed. The hospital became a constant source of intimidation.

A Chinese social worker mediated the situation by helping the staff understand the mother's needs to be attentive to her son and at the same time by helping her understand the staff's role. In a symbiotic relationship, both family and employees were able to be mutually supportive. The mother would do what was needed and, once trained by the staff, could supplement the care they provided. Her role was encouraged. The staff was also supported in its efforts to provide professional care. The patient benefitted from both approaches.

Such examples demonstrate the way that patients who exhibit significant cultural differences can feel threatened by Western hospitals that are often, by necessity, homogeneous institutions with uniform practices and procedures. The case studies suggest that through the efforts of social workers and other staff, who are sensitive to the needs of diverse patients, an important difference in the effectiveness of the institution can be achieved. Through this kind of mediation, Chinese patients are also helped to assimilate into the society of which they are a part. Their fears of Western medicine may be reduced; and often, the next time hospitalization is required, it is not as traumatic.

The hospital also teaches its Chinese clientele to value their cultural identity by serving Chinese food, offering Chinese television, and making available professional persons who are fluent in a number of dialects. Ethnicity is bolstered by the institution's respect for cultural differences. The hospital celebrates festivals such as Chinese New Year. A close relationship between a mother and son is allowed to continue during a traumatic period much as it would have in China. At the same time, the treatment of Western medicine is not ignored or deterred. Rather, an accommodation between medical and cultural needs is reached. Thus, the institution helps to mediate between extremes.

The program at the New York Infirmary-Beekman Downtown Hospital is unique in mediating the needs of vastly different cultures in the same neighborhood. A social worker at the hospital concludes, "Our program is unique in the city because we don't believe any other hospital has gone to the extent we have to reach out to the community."[22] Of the Chinese patients who come to the institution only as a last resort and, in most instances, leave feeling more assured, many would agree.

Interfaith Mediation

The 1960s was a tumultous time characterized by the Vietnam War, by a societal reaction to it, and by the emergence of civil rights as a national concern. At the same time, America became conscious of pluralism in both the broad spectrum of political opinion and the increasing role of minority groups in public life. Not the least of these areas of diversification was religion.

Two areas of religious pluralism were apparent. The first was a significant increase in adherents of mainstream Asian religions—Hindus, Buddhists, Sikhs, and Muslims. This dramatic change was precipitated by the reforms in immigration law in 1965 and later by the Refugee Act of 1980. For the first time since 1924, the doors of the nation were opened to large numbers of persons from the Eastern Hemisphere. Thousands of immigrants took advantage of these changes to enter the United States, bringing their religious traditions with them.

The second was the increase in "new religions," or cults. The counterculture of the 1960s in its reaction to the war and to established society looked to other faiths. Within the potpourri of religions that rapidly captured the nation's attention was almost every type of tradition imaginable from Americanized forms of the major Asian faiths to such anomalies as a revitalization of the beliefs of ancient Druids. Indian-style ashrams, centers of transcendental meditation, and the Hare Krishna movement all became part of a new vocabulary for most Americans.

What failed to accompany these dramatic changes were ways of helping members of established Western faiths to understand their new neighbors. Long-standing patterns of relationships among American Protestants continued to define pluralism in Christian terms. While the liberalizing trends of Vatican II and a concern for the State of Israel led to increased relations among Protestant bodies and with Roman Catholics and Jews, the overwhelming majority of other faiths remained isolated and alienated from the accepted avenues of interfaith communication.

The vast majority of interfaith councils were unable to respond to the new pluralism. A survey conducted in November 1980 concluded that of more than five hundred interfaith councils,

> twenty years ago . . . eight [were] inter-religious. . . . From 1970 to 1980, during a surge of religious question(s) and experimentation, the number of inter-religious councils tripled in the U.S. from eight to twenty-four. Most of these councils were local, "grass roots" developments, generally unaware of the existence or growth of other similar groups, and, interestingly, not limited to any one geographic area or size of city.[23]

Of these, all included Jewish representatives. Eighteen involved Muslims, five included Sikhs, and four, Hindus. Thirteen councils stated that they were open to anyone in the faith community.[24]

Based on these results, it is easy to see, given the number of Hindu, Buddhist, Sikh, and Muslim organizations in the United States, that the norm has not been for broadly defined, inclusive interfaith organizations. Given the lack of other mediating structures in the society, the opportunities for mutual understanding between religious bodies that exhibit extraordinary differences are small.

The following are examples of two interfaith councils that are more inclusive. They are included here not with the suggestion that they exemplify the best possible illustration of interfaith mediation but rather that they are the most significant examples of the relatively small number of multifaith councils that, by virtue of their inclusivity, attempt mediation at all.

The Berkeley Area Interfaith Council

Probably the most inclusive interfaith agency in the nation is the Berkeley Area Interfaith Council (BAIC) in California. Organized in 1982, the BAIC has attempted to represent the total spectrum of religious organizations in the city. In 1984, it represented twenty-four groups. Included in this array of faiths have been such curiosities as the New Reformed Druids of North America, such traditional mainstream Asian religions as the Berkeley Buddhist Temple, and such recognized Christian institutions as Church Women United.

Since its inception, the BAIC has included a variety of activities. A

Community Concerns Task Force has played an advocacy role on the peace issue and has administered an emergency aid program. A Roundtable of Religions has provided a forum for members of diverse religious traditions. This has been supplemented by a speakers' bureau, in which representatives from member organizations share their faith experiences, and by a World Religions program, which has provided presentations for church groups and community organizations.

A regular part of the BAIC's programmatic life has been an annual Thanksgiving service conducted at the culmination of Interfaith Week. In it the community of Berkeley has formally recognized the religious diversity in its midst and the work of the Interfaith Council.

The Interfaith Conference

In the nation's capital, the Interfaith Conference of Metropolitan Washington (IFC) was organized as a meeting ground for Protestants, Roman Catholics, Jews, and Muslims.[25] The conference conducts programs in the areas of both interfaith dialogue and community service and advocacy.

The IFC maintains a vision of limited religious pluralism. It emphasizes the common Semitic heritage of Judaism, Christianity, and Islam. The three traditions share an understanding of a single God in history, the role of prophets who transmitted elements of revelation, and an emphasis on the covenanting community whose focus in worship and action is primarily congregational. Within this context, the organization helps its constituency speak with a unified voice on a variety of social issues including anti-Semitism.

In 1983, the IFC hosted a seminar in which members shared their experiences as victims of discrimination.[26] Members of the Shaare Tefilah congregation in Silver Spring, Maryland, spoke of their temple being spray painted with anti-Semitic slogans. Following the removal of the slogans, the temple hosted an interfaith service, affirming the solidarity of the religious community. Participants in the seminar also heard the director of the Council of Churches of Greater Washington describe the organization of an ad hoc coalition to protest the marching of the Ku Klux Klan into Washington less than a week after the vandalization of the temple. He said, "People in the coalition gave out food to their Black brothers and sisters at local churches, and a public worship service and seminar were held to educate people about the Klan. Rioting that did occur when the Klan came to D.C. was minimized as a result."[27]

The IFC emphasizes the importance of structured interfaith dialogue. As part of this concern, it frequently provides opportunities for mutual understanding among the divergent traditions. For example, in spring 1983, the IFC hosted an interfaith breakfast with Imam Warith Deen Muhammad, who was then leader of the American Muslim Mission. It has also held convocations on the Middle East conflict in which members of all three faiths have had an opportunity for discussion.

In addition, the IFC holds annual celebrations in which patterns of worship central to the three faiths are highlighted, thus helping members understand their shared covenantal tradition and also appreciate their differences. Beyond the value of the act of worship itself, the celebrations facilitate contact between persons of each persuasion. This grass-roots encounter is experiential rather than didactic and enables persons from vastly different backgrounds to come face to face. The effect of these encounters is often to shatter stereotypes, which, left unchallenged, inhibit communication.

Mediating Strengths and Weaknesses

The model of mediation adopted by both the Interfaith Conference and the Berkeley Area Interfaith Council is one of empowering diverse religious traditions to speak with a single voice in public life. Each organization has tried a number of ways to develop a sense of rapport with its broad constituency that has enabled it to speak with a unified voice. This has commonly been achieved through interfaith dialogue. Dialogue has provided opportunities for exchange of views on theology, scriptures, and mutual problems.

The unanimity achieved through this model has enabled the Interfaith Conference successfully to initiate approaches on social issues affecting their constituency in metropolitan Washington. Programs on hunger, poverty, and housing have been addressed more inclusively and forcefully than any denomination alone could do.

This sense of empowerment was particularly evident when the IFC successfully led a fight for the withdrawal of proposed regulations in the District of Columbia that would have modified property-tax exemptions for religious institutions and other nonprofit organizations.[28] By holding a news conference on behalf of its broad-based constituency, the organization was able to gather enough support to force the city to back down.

Both the Interfaith Conference and the Berkeley Area Interfaith Council help mediate between visions of homogeneity and plurality. They are able to affirm the value of religious diversity. Yet, they are also able to speak with a single homogenous voice on societal issues. However, the degree to which each organization is able to deal with diversity varies. The Berkeley group includes the broad range of religious groups in the community. The Interfaith Conference has restricted its membership to covenantal traditions within the Judeo-Christian-Islamic milieu.

A weakness of both organizations as mediating structures is that by design they strive at times to emphasize the unity and commonality of their constituency more than their diversity. Indeed, it is only through this emphasis of common ground that they are able to take unified positions on issues of global peace, hunger, and poverty. Because the experience of diversity is carefully controlled, it is approached in structured interfaith dialogue whose focus may be more theological or scriptural than cultural or political.

Finally, it should be remembered that the interfaith councils briefly introduced here are more the exceptions than the rule. The vast majority of Councils of Churches across the nation are instruments of Christian dialogue rather than interfaith communication. While diversity is certainly part of their concern, it is usually narrowly defined and subordinated to attempts to bolster an ecumenical and cooperative Christian presence.

Interfaith councils, such as the two examples here, have a different agenda. Within the wider religious community, they perform a mediating function. By enabling their constituency to speak with a common voice on issues affecting a large number of people, they are assimilative, drawing their diverse membership into the mainstream of society. Yet, at the same time, their purpose is not to seek a bland uniformity but instead to allow diversity to exist and to increase ways in which it may be understood. Like mainstream society itself, they are thus agents of the interrelated processes of pluralism and assimilation.

Some Conclusions

In the majority of communities across the United States, there are few ways that a member of a religioethnic minority can experience the major institutions of mainstream life without extraordinary difficulty. Contacts with a welfare office, a courtroom, a hospital, or a mainstream religious institution are all potentially traumatic experiences. There are often few ways of mitigating the difficulties in communication or the cultural stereotypes that accompany such encounters. This is true of both institutions that fail to understand the needs and perceptions of minority communities and the minorities themselves, who often hold a distorted impression of the institutions of American public life.

This text has suggested that in such instances mediating structures can make an important difference. This may happen in three primary ways. First, they provide a way to address diversity experientially by promoting direct contact between different segments of community life. Second, they are not so heavily dependent on either a pluralist or assimilationist ideology that they cannot relate to the opposing view, which may be held by a significant proportion of society. Thus, mediation occurs not just between different persons but between conflicting ideologies built on often contradictory and opposing premises. Finally, mediating institutions bridge the gap between ethnic or religious communities that are alienated from the societal mainstream. They help to forge relationships between the pluralistic private world and the more homogeneous realm of public life.

The way that mediating institutions enable the members of one community to come into direct contact with another is illustrated by the meetings and annual worship celebrations held by the Interfaith Conference. These experiences encourage understanding of common ground and differences.

The manner in which mediating agencies address both assimilationist and pluralist ideologies is exemplified by Chicago's Senn Academy. Senn has an effective English instruction program yet is also a pioneer in bilingual education in the city. Philosophically the two programs are opposed and are hotly debated on a national level. Yet at Senn and similar schools they are quite compatible. As the TESOL classes help foreign-born students to enter the school's mainstream, so simultaneous instruction in their native languages affirms their identity. In addition, Senn's programs, special events such as International Day, encouragement of ethnic clubs, and continuing outreach in diverse neighborhoods all help affirm ethnic differences. Thus, the school carefully charts a course that both helps students to assimilate and at the same time celebrates their identities.

Finally, the way in which mediating institutions help bridge the gap between ethnic communities and public life is illustrated by the New York Infirmary-Beekman Downtown Hospital. Because it is aware of the distrust and fear with which its Chinese patients perceive Western health care, it is able to help them experience a mainstream American institution in a manner that reduces their apprehension. They learn not only that the hospital will help, not harm, them but that it values their ethnicity. The process is one of shattering stereotypes in an important mainstream institution and at the same time accommodating a particular form of ethnicity.

In conclusion, this text has emphasized the profound struggle that has resulted from attempting to identify the American experience or paint the national portrait as one of homogeneity or diversity. It has described the ideologies spawned by each point of view and the debates on issues such as slavery, immigration, and bilingual education that have borrowed many of their arguments. Finally, it has examined some of the effects of this struggle on community conflict.

The human consequences of the clash in ideologies are often felt the most on the grass-roots level. A hospital staff that approaches minorities through different ideological perceptions from theirs may do its clientele more harm than good. A school that emphasizes conformity to the extent that it ignores the needs of substantial numbers of minority students may experience repeated crises and unrest. Short of a transformation in national values and a systematic reduction of the struggle about diversity in American life, the most important measure that can be taken to prevent such tragedies is the work of mediating institutions.

Notes

Chapter 1

1. Dena Kleiman, "Immigrants Encountering Choice Between Friendship and Isolation," *New York Times*, 24 December 1982, B1.

2. Ibid.

3. Robert N. Bellah and Phillip E. Hammond, *Varieties of Civil Religion* (San Francisco: Harper & Row, 1980), 141.

4. Andrew Greeley, *The Denominational Society: A Sociological Approach to Religion in America* (Glenview, Ill.: Scott, Foresman & Co., 1972), 108 ff.

5. Primary research on Kusakabe's life has been done by Rev. Kenryu Tsuji and other leaders of the Buddhist Churches of America.

6. Bellah and Hammond, *Varieties*, 141.

7. William M. Newman, *American Pluralism: A Study of Minority Groups and Social Theory* (New York: Harper & Row, 1973), 54.

8. Kirk Johnson, "Asians Galvanize Sales Activity in Flushing: Influx Spurs Building and Revives a Downtown That Was Languishing," *New York Times*, 29 July 1984, sec. 8, p. 1. See also, Martin Gottlieb, "Asian-Americans Compete to Build Queens Complex," *New York Times*, 10 August 1985, B1, and Marvine Howe, "Hong Kong's Plight Alters Look of Flushing," *New York Times*, 14 April 1984, 1.

9. Ibid.

10. Dena Kleiman, "A Hospital Where Ethnic Change Is Constant," *New York Times*, 6 October 1982, B1.

11. Data for the graphs were obtained from the 1980 Census.

12. Newman, *American Pluralism*, 54.

13. See Tom Brune and Eduardo Camacho, *A Special Report: Race and Poverty in Chicago, Analysis and Data Reflecting Race and Poverty in Chicago Based on the 1980 U.S. Census* (Chicago: The Chicago Reporter and the Center for Community Research and Assistance, 1983).

14. Jorge Casuso and Eduardo Camacho, *Hispanics in Chicago* (Chicago: Community Renewal Society, 1985), 1.

15. Census and neighborhood data for New Orleans were taken from James J. Murphy, Jr., and Dalta M. Williams, *New Orleans Atlas Series 1980 Census, New Orleans Neighborhood Maps* (New Orleans: City of New Orleans, 1984), vol. 5.

16. Ibid.

223

17. Ibid. Note: The percentages listed in this text are calculated from the total actual numbers of each population group listed and differ slightly from those in the *Atlas Series*, which are based on different total neighborhood populations.

18. Ibid.

19. Ari L. Goldman, "2000 Attend Buddhist Cremation Rite in Vermont," *New York Times*, 27 May 1987, A15.

20. "Buddhist Bells Ring Out as Rural Temple Opens," *New York Times*, 12 May 1985, 32.

21. Ibid.

22. William E. Schmidt, "Oak Park, Mich.: Focus of Modern U.S. Diversity," *New York Times*, 20 December 1983, A16.

23. Ibid.

24. Ibid.

25. Ibid.

26. Archdiocese of New York, *Hispanics in New York: Religious, Cultural and Social Experiences* (New York: Archdiocese of New York, Office of Pastoral Research, 1982) 2:143.

27. Ibid.

28. Ibid., 142.

29. Harold Isaacs, *Scratches on Our Minds: American Views of China and India* (New York: John Day Co., 1958; reprint, White Plains, N.Y.: M.E. Sharpe, 1980).

30. Ibid., 42–43.

31. Benjamin B. Ringer, *"We the People" and Others: Duality and America's Treatment of Its Racial Minorities* (New York: Tavistock Publications, 1983), 36–69.

32. Emma Lazarus, "The New Colossus," in *The Poems of Emma Lazarus*, 2 vols. (Boston: Houghton, Mifflin & Co., 1889) 1:202–203.

33. Ibid.

34. Dan Vogel, *Emma Lazarus* (Boston: Twayne Publishers, 1980), 123–135.

35. Lazarus, "The New Colossus."

36. Israel Zangwill, *The Melting Pot* (New York: Macmillan Co., 1917).

37. Ibid., 33.

38. Lazarus, "The New Colossus."

39. Zangwill, *The Melting Pot*. It is important to note that the production of *The Melting Pot* caused a controversy within the Jewish community. While the concept of amalgamation was applauded by Zangwill and his supporters, it was not favorably received by other segments of American Judaism.

40. Gunnar Myrdal, *An American Dilemma* (New York: Harper & Brothers, 1944).

41. Ibid., p. xlvii quoted in *"We the People" and Others*, by Ringer, 241–242.

42. Ringer, *"We the People" and Others*, 242.

43. Ibid.

44. Benjamin B. Ringer, "Summary of 'We the People' and Others," paper, 1982, quoted in *"We the People" and Others*, by Ringer, pp. ix–x.

45. Ibid. Since this text, like Ringer's, is concerned with ideologies and utopias, the use of the word America is unavoidable. The reader should be aware, however, that in other contexts the term is frequently ethnocentric, ignoring the rightful claim of many Central and Southern American nations to the same identification.

46. The works of the following theorists should be consulted to understand a dualistic approach to history and Ringer's position:

Pierre L. van den Berghe, *Race and Racism: A Comparative Perspective* (New York: John Wiley & Sons, 1967). Frantz Fanon, *The Wretched of the Earth* (New

York: Grove Press, 1968). J.S. Furnivall, *Colonial Policy and Practice* (New York: New York University Press, 1956). John Rex, *Race Relations in Sociological Theory* (New York: Schocken Books, 1970). ———, *Race, Colonialism and the City* (London: Routledge & Kegan Paul, 1973). M.G. Smith, *The Plural Society in the British West Indies* (Berkeley: University of California Press, 1965).

47. Robert Bellah, "Religion and Legitimation in the American Republic," in *In Gods We Trust: New Patterns of Religious Pluralism in America*, ed. Thomas Robbins and Dick Anthony (New Brunswick, N.J.: Transaction Books 1981), 35–49. The dual nature of attitudes toward religious diversity in the United States has also been briefly discussed by Raymond B. Williams in "Hinduism in America," *Christian Century*, 11 March 1987, 247–249.

48. Dick Anthony and Thomas Robbins, "Culture Crisis and Contemporary Religion," in *In Gods We Trust*, ed. Robbins and Anthony, 11. The reader should note that Benjamin Ringer suggests that the concept of the People's Domain is found in both the Constitution and in the Declaration of Independence. Robert Bellah argues in a different vein that the principles of the liberal constitutional state are conveyed in the Constitution while those of the virtuous republic are expressed in the Declaration of Independence.

Since the understanding of America in the People's Domain reflects a colonial empire that maximized its use of power, Ringer's suggestion that the concept appears in both of the nation's seminal documents is entirely logical. Bellah, on the other hand, deals with two different utopias that also influenced the way that America was perceived and, as part of the same documents, evolved distinct visions of what the nation could be.

49. Bellah and Hammond, *Varieties*, 9–10.

50. Anthony and Robbins, "Culture Crisis. . . ," 11.

51. Sidney Ahlstrom, *A Religious History of the American People* (New Haven, Conn.: Yale University Press, 1972), 453. See also Frederick Jackson Turner, *The Frontier in American History* (New York: Henry Holt, 1950).

52. Lazarus, "The New Colossus."

53. Kallen's theory is expounded in *Culture and Democracy in the United States: Studies in the Group Psychology of the American Peoples* (New York: Boni & Liveright, 1924; reprint, New York: Arno Press and the New York Times, 1970).

54. Bellah and Hammond,*Varieties*, 9.

55. Ringer, *"We the People" and Others*, 30 ff.

56. Ibid.

57. Ahlstrom, *A Religious History*, 293.

58. Ibid., 422 ff.

59. Martin E. Marty, *Pilgrims in Their Own Land* (Boston: Little, Brown & Co., 1984), 154–158.

60. The ideology of assimilation and the utopia of amalgamation both have generated social theories. A good discussion of the differences between theory, ideology, and utopia is provided by William M. Newman in *American Pluralism: A Study of Minority Groups and Social Theory* (New York: Harper & Row, 1973), 52. Newman suggests that on its simplest level a theory expresses what is, while an ideology indicates what ought to be. An ideology is based on old perceptions from societies that have already been formed. Utopias include new ideas about future societies.

The discussion about the distinction between ideologies and utopias is complex and encompasses a wide body of literature. The classic resource is that of Karl Mannheim, *Ideology and Utopia*, translated by Louis Wirth and Edward Shils (London: Routledge & Kegan Paul, 1936).

61. Newman, *American Pluralism*, 58–59.

62. Zangwill, *The Melting Pot*, 208–209.

63. Robert N. Bellah et al., *Habits of the Heart: Individualism and Commitment in American Life* (Berkeley: University of California Press, 1985), 142–143.

64. Ibid., 142.

65. Details of the Bakke case are found in Terry Eastland and William J. Bennett, *Counting by Race: Equality from the Founding Fathers in Bakke and Weber* (New York: Bune Books, 1979), 3 ff. See also Timothy J. O'Neill, *Bakke and the Politics of Equality: Friends and Foes in the Classroom of Litigation* (Middletown, Conn.: Wesleyan University Press, 1985).

66. See Stuart Taylor, Jr., "High Court Bars a Layoff Method Favoring Blacks; But Majority Backs Some Use of Affirmative Action by Government Employers," *New York Times*, 20 May 1986, 1 and "Excerpts from Opinions on Race-Based Layoffs by a Governmental Body," *New York Times*, 20 May 1986, A21.

67. "Excerpts. . . ," *New York Times*, A21.

68. See Stuart Taylor, Jr., "Affirmative Action Upheld by High Court as a Remedy for Past Job Discrimination: Six Vote for Idea; They Say Individuals Who Suffered No Bias May Sometimes Benefit," *New York Times*, 3 July 1986, 1, and B9.

69. Ibid.

70. Ibid.

71. Ibid., B9.

72. "Balancing Act," *Time*, 6 April 1987, 18–19.

73. See *Porterfield et al. v. Webb, Attorney General of the State of California et al.*, 263 U.S. 225 (1923); *Terrace et al. v. Thompson, Attorney General of the State of Washington*, 263 U.S. 225 (1923); *United States v. Bhagat Singh Thind*, 261 U.S. 204 (1922); *Webb, Attorney General of the State of California et al. v. O'Brien et al.*, 263 U.S. 313 (1923).

74. The pro-life/pro-choice argument has become so vigorous that it has internalized much of the emotion surrounding the debate between the contradictory views of American society. It has also eclipsed much of the Catholic-Protestant dialogue initiated in Vatican II.

75. Charles P. McIlvaine, "Address to the Young Men of the United States on Temperance," *The Temperance Volume; Embracing the Temperance Tracts of the American Tract Society*, no. 244. (New York, n.d.), 5, quoted in *A Christian America: Protestant Hopes and Historical Realities* by Robert T. Handy (New York: Oxford University Press, 1971), 53.

76. Proposition 63 became the "Official State Language Initiative Constitutional Amendment." It is found in section 6, article 3 of the Constitution of California.

77. See Joe Kitta, "The Stigma: The Pennsylvania German Culture Was 'a Stone in the Stomach' of the English," *The Morning Call* [Allentown, Pa], 6 October 1983, D3.

78. Robert Lindsey, "A Patchwork of Rulings on Free Speech at Malls," *New York Times*, 10 February 1986, A12.

79. Bryan Connors, "A Multicultural Curriculum as Action for Social Justice," in *Bilingual and Multicultural Education: Canadian Perspectives*, ed. Stan Shapson and Vincent D'Oyley (Clevedon, Avon, England: Multicultural Matters Ltd., 1984), 104.

80. Ian Wright and Carol LaBar, "Multiculturalism and Morality," in *Bilingual and Multicultural Education* by Shapson and D'Oyley, 112–113.

81. Lois Foster and David Stockley, *Multiculturalism: The Changing Australian Paradigm* (Clevedon, Avon, England: Multicultural Matters Ltd., 1984).

82. M. Cigler, "History and Multicultural Education," *Australian Historical*

Association Bulletin 4 (1975): 23, quoted in *Multiculturalism* by Foster and Stockley, 52–53.

83. Ibid., 55.

84. *Age* (June 29, 1979), 13, quoted in *Multiculturalism* by Foster and Stockley, 58–59.

85. Ibid., 69.

86. Ibid., 78–79.

87. Ibid.

Chapter 2

1. This position is articulated in Robert Handy, *A Christian America: Protestant Hopes and Historical Realities* (New York: Oxford University Press, 1971).

2. See Martin E. Marty, *Pilgrims in Their Own Land: 500 Years of Religion in America* (Boston: Little, Brown & Co., 1984), 30.

3. Ibid., 26.

4. Marty, *Pilgrims in Their Own Land*, 32–35.

5. Tony Hillerman and David Muench, *New Mexico* (Portland, Oreg.: Graphic Arts Center Publishing Co., 1974).

6. Ibid.

7. Ibid.

8. Ibid.

9. Ibid.

10. Marty, *Pilgrims in Their Own Land*, 68–71.

11. Ibid., 76.

12. Comment by Gershom Mendes Seixas in *The Constitutions of the Several Independent States of America* (Philadelphia, 1781), 102, quoted in *The History of the Jews of Philadelphia from Colonial Times to the Age of Jackson* by Maxwell Whiteman and Edwin Wolf, (Philadelphia: Jewish Publication Society of America, 1956; reprint, 1975), 147.

13. Marty, *Pilgrims in Their Own Land*, 64.

14. Handy, *A Christian America*, 12.

15. Benjamin B. Ringer, *"We the People" and Others: Duality and America's Treatment of Its Racial Minorities* (New York: Tavistock Publications, 1983), 54.

16. In *Tombee, Portrait of a Cotton Planter: With The Journal of Thomas B. Chaplin (1822–1890)*, (New York: William Morrow & Co., 1986), editors Theodore Rosengarten and Susan W. Walker demonstrate the manner in which some Southern slaveowners believed that their style of life was completely justifiable on biblical grounds.

17. Details of the Amistad incident and trial cited here appear in Clara Merritt DeBoer, "The Role of Afro-Americans in the Origin and Work of the American Missionary Association: 1839–1877" (Ph.D. diss., Rutgers University, 1973). DeBoer's work is an important reference for any student of the history of the AMA. Older sources include Augustus Field Beard, *A Crusade of Brotherhood: A History of the American Missionary Association* (Boston: Pilgrim Press, 1909) and Fred L. Brownlee, *New Day Ascending* (Boston: Pilgrim Press, 1946).

18. DeBoer, "The Role of Afro-Americans. . . ," 23.

19. J. Taylor Stanley, *A History of Black Congregational Christian Churches of the South* (New York: United Church Press, 1978), 18.

20. Marty, *Pilgrims in Their Own Land*, 238–241.

21. DeBoer, "The Role of the Afro-American. . . ," p. vi ff.

22. DeBoer's work documents the extent to which the AMA developed a cadre

of black leadership as part of the organization's overall design and theological intent.

23. *The American Missionary* 14 (March 1870), quoted in DeBoer, "The Role of the Afro-American. . . ," 313.

24. In addition to its work with freedmen, the AMA also developed missions with American Indian and Oriental populations.

25. Michael E. Strieby to George Whipple, 27 February 1864, Archives of the American Missionary Association No. 86928, Amistad Research Center, New Orleans. Permission to quote Strieby supplied by E. Allen and Helen R. Richardson.

26. *Home Missionary* 23 (November 1850): 160.

27. DeBoer, "The Role of the Afro-American. . . ," 2–3.

28. Office of Assistant Commissioner, Bureau of Refugees, Freedmen and Abandoned Lands, State of Alabama to G. Whipple, 13 March 1866, Archives of the American Missionary Association No. 8, Amistad Research Center, New Orleans.

29. James Gillette to J.R. Shipherd, 28 October 1867, Archives of the American Missionary Association No. 89, Amistad Research Center, New Orleans.

30. DeBoer, "The Role of the Afro-American. . . ," 328.

31. *Congregational Milestones* (New York: ca. 1919), quoted in "The Role of the Afro-American. . . ." by DeBoer, 328.

32. Carleton Beals, *Brass-Knuckle Crusade: The Great Know-Nothing Conspiracy: 1820–1860* (New York: Hastings House Publishers, 1960), 293–294. The later history of the Klan is found in Thomas J. Curran, *Xenophobia and Immigration, 1820–1930* (Boston: Twayne Publishers, 1975), 129–144.

33. DeBoer, "The Role of the Afro-American. . . ," 332–333.

34. *American Missionary*, the official publication of the American Missionary Association, was published in New York City beginning in 1847. In similar fashion the masthead of the *Home Missionary*, journal of the Congregational Home Missionary Society, was (ca. 1905) "Christian Civilization for Our Country."

35. Tract from the American Board of Commissioners for Foreign Missions quoted in the *American Missionary* 1 (December 1846).

36. *American Missionary* 3 (January 1849): 26.

37. DeBoer, "The Role of the Afro-American. . . ," 102.

38. See Sidney E. Ahlstrom, *A Religious History of the American People* (New Haven, Conn.: Yale University Press, 1972), 556. Ahlstrom traces the American anti-Catholic bias to prejudice that extended as far back as the war led by Queen Elizabeth against Philip of Spain.

39. Ibid., 559.

40. Ibid., 555.

41. Ellis's source is *The Acts and Resolves, Public and Private, of the Province of the Massachusetts Bay* (Boston: Wright & Potter, 1869) 1:423–424.

42. John Tracy Ellis, *Documents of American Catholic History* (Milwaukee: Bruce Publishing Co., 1932), 119.

43. Ibid.

44. L.H. Butterfield, ed., *Diary and Autobiography of John Adams*, 4 vols. (Cambridge, Mass.: Harvard University Press, Belknap Press, 1961) 1:219–220.

45. Ibid., 220.

46. Lyman Beecher's autobiography is found in Barbara M. Cross, ed., *The Autobiography of Lyman Beecher*, 2 vols. (Cambridge, Mass.: Harvard University Press, Belknap Press, 1961).

47. Sydney Ahlstrom suggests the tract was published in 1835. See Ahlstrom, *A Religious History*, 560.

48. Ibid., 565.

49. Ellis, *Documents*, 311. Ellis calls attention to "A Plan for the Western Colonization of Catholic Immigrants." Similar sentiments appeared in the Boston *Pilot* on March 15, 1856.

50. Ahlstrom, *A Religious History*, 567.

51. Ibid., 565.

52. Hughes was the first archbishop of New York and was in the forefront of a variety of issues affecting the Catholic Church. See Beals, *Brass-Knuckle Crusade*, 77.

53. Ellis, *Documents*, 263–265.

54. Ibid., 473.

55. Jay P. Dolan, "Catholic Attitudes Toward Protestants," in *Uncivil Religion: Interreligious Hostility in America*, ed. Robert N. Bellah and Frederick E. Greenspahn (New York: Crossroad, 1987), 75. See also Ahlstrom, *A Religious History*, 853–854.

56. Ahlstrom, *A Religious History*, 557. The antagonism that the public felt for the Mormon Church continued well into the twentieth century. A tract entitled "The Mormon Mind" written by Rev. Clayton S. Rice, assistant superintendent of the Idaho Congregational Conference in 1923, bemoaned the difficulties of conversion. The Mormon faith was seen as pagan. Rice concluded:

> Ultimately Truth must win. A long, slow process of attrition, taking scores of years, may grind away the theological crudities of the Mormon Church, while an equally long process of assimilation may bring to her the real Christianity of the Christ. But, oh—the weary years wasted in the process, and oh—the long-suffering people, wandering in darkness!

57. Henry E. Fritz, *The Movement for Indian Assimilation, 1860–1890* (Philadelphia: University of Pennsylvania Press, 1963), 16. Fritz suggests that in the 1830s government policy toward American Indians changed. The major objective now became the removal of Indians from land that could be made available for settlement. With the decline of European designs on America, interest decreased in securing allies among the Indian population or in forming relationships at all. Additional insight into the role of the churches with the American Indian is found in Clyde A. Milner II and Floyd A. O'Neil, eds., *Churchmen and the Western Indians: 1820–1920* (Norman: University of Oklahoma Press, 1985).

58. Ringer, *"We The People" and Others*, 136.

59. Reginald Horsman, *Race and Manifest Destiny: The Origins of American Racial Anglo-Saxonism* (Cambridge, Mass.: Harvard University Press, 1981), 207.

60. Charles Darwin, *On the Origin of Species by Means of Natural Selection* (New York: Appleton & Co., 1871).

61. Marty, *Pilgrims in Their Own Land*, 307.

62. Fritz, *The Movement for Indian Assimilation*, 34–38.

63. Ibid., 56–58.

64. Ibid., 57.

65. Ibid., 76–79.

66. Ibid., 87–108.

67. Blanchet to Parker, 8 July 1871. Quoted in *The Movement for Indian Assimilation*, by Fritz, 89.

68. Emma Lazarus, "The New Colossus," in *The Poems of Emma Lazarus*, 2 vols. (Boston: Houghton, Mifflin & Co., 1889) 1:202–203, quoted in *Emma Lazarus* by Dan Vogel (Boston: Twayne Publishers, 1980), 158.

69. Ibid.

70. Mary Roberts Coolidge, *Chinese Immigration* (New York: Henry Holt & Co., 1909; reprint, New York: Arno Press and the New York Times, 1969), 423.

71. David G. Bromley and Anson D. Shupe, Jr., *Strange Gods: The Great American Cult Scare* (Boston: Beacon Press, 1981), 10.

72. Merle Curti, *The Making of an American Community: A Case Study of Democracy in a Frontier County* (Stanford, Calif.: Stanford University Press, 1959).

73. Franklyn Curtiss-Wedge, *History of Trempealeau County, Wisconsin* (Chicago and Winona, 1917), 78, quoted in *The Making of An American Community* by Curti, 98.

74. Ibid.

75. Curti, *The Making of An American Community*, 100.

76. Ibid., 138.

77. Henry Bradshaw Fearon, *Sketches of America* (London: 1818), 148–151, quoted in *Historical Aspects of the Immigration Problem: Select Documents* by Edith Abbott (Chicago: University of Chicago Press, 1926; reprint, New York: Arno Press and the New York Times, 1969), 212–213.

78. *Report of the Minnesota Board of Immigration* (1871), 61–69, quoted in *Historical Aspects* by Abbott, 167–172.

79. Ibid., 171–172.

80. Tamara K. Hareven and Randolph Langenbach, *Amoskeag: Life and Work in an American Factory-City* (New York: Pantheon Books, 1978).

81. Ibid., 385.

82. This observation was originally made by Oscar Handlin in *The Newcomers* (Cambridge, Mass.: Harvard University Press, 1959), 33. See also Ira Rosenwaike, *Population History of New York City* (Syracuse, N.Y.: Syracuse University Press, 1972), 83.

83. Rosenwaike, *Population History*, 82–85.

84. Eric E. Hirshler, ed., *Jews from Germany in the United States* (New York: Farrar, Straus & Cudahy, 1955), 51, quoted in *A Religious History* by Ahlstrom, 580.

85. Ahlstrom, *A Religious History*, 974.

86. Ibid., 973–974.

87. Jonathan D. Sarna, "Jewish-Christian Hostility in the United States: Perceptions from a Jewish Point of View," in *Uncivil Religion: Interreligious Hostility in America*, ed. Robert N. Bellah and Frederick E. Greenspahn (New York: Crossroad, 1987), 7.

88. I.N. Phelps Stokes, *The Iconography of Manhattan Island: 1498–1909* (New York: Robert H. Dodd, 1915; reprint, 6 vols., New York: Arno Press, 1967) 3:651.

89. Minnie J. Reynolds, "Why Despise the Immigrant," *Home Missionary* 79 (December 1905): 223–224.

90. Ibid.

91. W. Montgomery, "What Shall We Do for the Immigrant," *Home Missionary* 79 (December 1905):233.

92. Immigration data for the period before 1924 are compiled in Jeremiah W. Jenks and W. Jett Lauch, *The Immigration Problem: A Study of American Immigration Conditions and Needs* (New York: Funk & Wagnalls Co., 1922).

93. Julian Samora and Patricia Vandel Simon, *A History of the Mexican American People* (London: University of Notre Dame Press, 1977), 136.

94. Ibid., 139.

95. Beneath the concern over breaking the law the drive for deportation of wetbacks was an exclusionary reaction that sought to rid the nation of unwanted

diversity. Leaders of the movement voiced their concerns: "While little could be done about braceros, there was something that could be done about the 'wetbacks.' After all, had not the media, labor leaders, and now the Justice Department said that the 'illegals' had created 'a grave social problem involving murder, prostitution, robbery, and a gigantic narcotics infiltration [as well as] a malignant threat to the growth of our society'?" *Burners' Weekly Magazine*, 24 October 1953, 63, quoted in *Operation Wetback: The Mass Deportation of Mexican Undocumented Workers in 1954* by Juan Ramon Garcia (Westport, Conn.: Greenwood Press, 1980) 159.

The exclusionists' plan achieved much of what it had desired. By the end of "Operation Wetback" the Immigration and Naturalization Service boasted that in California alone 540,000 illegal aliens had been deported. Garcia, *Operation Wetback*, 199. Large figures were also reported in other southwestern states. The action, taken by an established arm of the United States government, was a visible reminder of the call for cultural homogeneity by a segment of the nation that understood diversity as an expendable tool for economic gain but at the same time rejected its full presence in society. It was also a portent of the continuing debate in the next thirty years.

96. Garcia, *Operation Wetback*, 172.

97. *As a Chinaman Saw Us: Passages From His Letters to a Friend at Home* (New York: D. Appleton and Co., 1904), 92.

98. Ibid., p. viii.

99. Ringer, "*We the People*," 108–115.

100. U.S. Public Statutes at Large I:414, quoted in "*We the People*," by Ringer, 115.

101. William L. Tung, *The Chinese in America 1820–1974* (Dobbs Ferry, N.Y.: Oceana Publications, 1974), 18.

102. Ibid., 25.

103. *As a Chinaman Saw Us*, 281.

104. Ibid., 287–288.

105. *Journal of the General Conference of the Methodist Episcopal Church* (1900), 63–64, quoted in *A Christian America* by Handy, 144.

106. Ibid., 75.

107. W.A.P. Martin, "America's Duty to China," in *The World's Parliament of Religions: An Illustrated and Popular Story of the World's First Parliament of Religions Held in Chicago in Connection With the Columbian Exposition of 1893*, ed. John Henry Barrows, 2 vols. (Chicago: Parliament Publishing Co., 1893) 2:1144.

108. "American Matters of Interest," *The Illustrated News of the World*, 5 March 1892, 243.

109. James W. Shepp and Daniel B. Shepp, *Shepp's World's Fair Photographed: Being a Collection of Original Copyrighted Photographs* (Chicago: Globe Bible Publishing Co., 1893), 500.

110. "American Matters. . . ," 243.

111. "Visitors From Many Lands: East Indian Delegates to the Congress of Religions," *New York Times*, 3 September 1893, 2.

112. Ibid.

113. Ibid.

114. Barrows, *The World's Parliament* 1:44.

115. Ibid. 1:19.

116. Ibid. 1:20–22.

117. See Abbé J.A. Dubois, *Hindu Manners, Customs and Ceremonies* (Oxford: Clarendon Press, 1906; reprint, 1959).

118. Max Müller, *Sacred Books of the East* (Oxford, England: Oxford University Press, 1886; reprint, 50 vols., Motilal Banarsidass, 1964).

119. Edwin Arnold, *The Light of Asia or the Great Renunciation (Mahabhinishkramana) Being the Life and Teaching of Gautama Prince of India and Founder of Buddhism* (Boston: Roberts Brothers, 1887).

120. Richard T. Ely, "Christianity as a Social Force," in *The World's Parliament*, ed. Barrows 2:1059.

121. Rev. Antoinette Brown Blackwell, "Women and the Pulpit," *The World's Parliament*, ed. Barrows 2:1150.

122. Alexander Mohammed Webb, "The Spirit of Islam" in Barrows, *The World's Parliament* 2:989.

123. Swami Vivekananda, "Hinduism," in Barrows, *The World's Parliament* 2:975–976.

124. Ibid. 1:107.

125. Ibid. 2:1560.

126. Ibid.

127. A.J. Moulder, State Superintendent of Public Instruction for California, 1859, quoted in *Chinese Immigration* by Coolidge, 69.

128. Coolidge, *Chinese Immigration*, 72.

129. Tung, *The Chinese in America*, 9.

130. Coolidge, *Chinese Immigration*, 75–76.

131. Tung, *The Chinese In America*, 13, 15.

Chapter 3

1. Howard F. Stein and Robert F. Hill, *The Ethnic Imperative: Examining the New White Ethnic Movement* (University Park: Pennsylvania State University Press, 1977).

2. Ibid., 50.

3. Ibid.

4. Robert T. Handy, *A Christian America: Protestant Hopes and Historical Realities* (New York: Oxford University Press, 1971), 18.

5. Ibid.

6. Stein and Hill, *The Ethnic Imperative*, 53.

7. See Frederick Jackson Turner, *The Frontier in American History* (New York: Henry Holt, 1950).

8. Horace Bushnell, *Barbarism the First Danger*, quoted in *A Christian America* by Handy, 27.

9. Sydney E. Ahlstrom, *A Religious History of the American People* (New Haven, Conn.: Yale University Press, 1972), 387. It should also be noted that the Awakenings were not without opposition. The oratory of the first Awakening's greatest prophet, Jonathan Edwards, for example, brought about a surge of liberality among some Congregationalists. See Handy, *A Christian America*, 19.

10. See Winthrop S. Hudson, *Religion in America: An Historical Account of the Development of American Religious Life* (New York: Charles Scribner's Sons, 1981), 103–104.

11. Horatio Alger, Jr., *Struggling Upward and Other Works* (New York: Crown Publishers, 1945), p. viii.

12. Ibid.

13. Ibid., p. x.

14. Ibid., 151 ff.

15. Ibid., xi.

16. See E. Digby Baltzell, *The Protestant Establishment: Aristocracy and Caste in America* (New York: Random House, 1964), 4.

17. Ibid., 6.

18. Stein and Hill, *The Ethnic Imperative*, 59.

19. J. Hector St. John Crèvecoeur (Michel-Guillaume Jean de Crèvecoeur), *Letters from an American Farmer* (New York: Fox, Duffield & Co., 1904), 54–55, quoted in *Beyond the Melting Pot*, by Glazer and Moynihan, 288.

20. Israel Zangwill, *The Melting Pot* (New York: Macmillan, 1909).

21. Ibid.

22. Ibid., 203.

23. Ibid.

24. Ibid., 33.

25. Ibid.

26. Ibid., 184.

27. Ibid.

28. Ibid.

29. Ibid., 208. In the afterword to *The Melting Pot*, Zangwill indicates the contempt that the play received from some Jewish leaders.

30. See pps. 202–203 for Zangwill's concerns about this group.

31. Zangwill, *The Melting Pot*, 209.

32. Ibid.

33. In using the term cultural pluralism, Kallen understood a unique relationship between culture and democracy. He states: "Democracy is an essential prerequisite to culture, that culture can be and sometimes is a fine flowering of democracy, and that the history of the relation of the two in the United States exhibits this fact."

See *Culture and Democracy in the United States: Studies in the Group Psychology of the American Peoples* (New York: Boni & Liveright, 1924; reprint, New York: Arno Press and the New York Times, 1970), 11.

34. William M. Newman, *American Pluralism: A Study of Minority Groups and Social Theory* (New York: Harper & Row, 1973), 67.

35. Horace M. Kallen, *Culture and Democracy in the United States*. The reader is also referred to Horace M. Kallen, *Cultural Pluralism and the American Idea* (Philadelphia: University of Pennsylvania Press, 1956).

36. Kallen, *Culture and Democracy*, 23–24.

37. The Johnson Read Act of 1924 cemented a national origins quota system into place, a policy that remained essentially unchanged until 1965.

38. Kallen, *Culture and Democracy*, 144.

39. Ibid., 147–148.

40. Emory S. Bogardus, *Essentials of Americanization* (Los Angeles: University of Southern California Press, 1919; rev. ed., 1923), 15.

41. Ibid., 21.

42. The Palmer raids are described in Newman, *American Pluralism*, 37–38 and 62.

43. Ibid., 177.

44. Ibid., 169.

45. Kallen, *Culture and Democracy*, 43.

46. Ibid., 124.

47. E.L. Doctorow, *Ragtime* (New York: Bantam Books, 1983).

48. See Louis Adamic, *From Many Lands* (New York: Harper & Brothers for Friendship Press, 1940).

49. Ibid., p. ix.

50. Ibid., 185 ff.

51. Ibid., 184. The "Hymn" was circulated in 1916 in newspapers in the eastern United States and in California.

52. Ibid., 189.

53. Ibid., 147 ff.

54. Will Herberg, *Protestant, Catholic, Jew.* Rev. ed. (New York: Doubleday & Co., 1955).

55. H. Richard Niebuhr, *The Social Sources of Denominationalism* (New York: Henry Holt & Co., 1929).

56. Oscar Handlin, *The Uprooted* (New York: Grosset & Dunlap, 1951). Herberg also drew on the earlier work of Ruby Jo Reeves Kennedy. See "Single or Triple Melting Pot? Intermarriage Trends in New Haven, 1870–1940," in *American Journal of Sociology* 58 (January 1944): 331–339.

57. Herberg, *Protestant, Catholic, Jew*, 53.

58. Andrew M. Greeley and William C. McCready, *Ethnicity in the United States: A Preliminary Reconnaissance* (New York: John Wiley & Sons, 1974). The reader is also referred to Andrew Greeley, *Why Can't They Be Like Us?* (New York: E.P. Dutton, 1971).

59. Andrew M. Greeley, *The Denominational Society: A Sociological Approach to Religion in America* (Glenview, Ill.: Scott, Foresman & Co., 1972).

60. Nathan Glazer and Daniel P. Moynihan, *Beyond the Melting Pot: The Negroes, Puerto Ricans, Jews, Italians, and Irish of New York City* (Cambridge, Mass.: M.I.T. Press, 1963; reprint, 1970).

61. Nathan Glazer and Daniel P. Moynihan, *Ethnicity, Theory and Experience* (Cambridge, Mass.: Harvard University Press, 1975).

62. William Newman, *American Pluralism: A Study of Minority Groups and Social Theory* (New York: Harper & Row, 1973).

63. Michael Novak, *The Rise of the Unmeltable Ethnics* (New York: Macmillan, 1971).

64. Milton Gordon, *Assimilation in American Life* (New York: Oxford University Press, 1964). The reader is also directed to a substantial body of other literature on assimilation, including: Isaac B. Berkson, *Theories of Americanization: Critical Study* (New York: Arno Press, 1969); Julius Drachsler, *Democracy and Assimilation: The Blending of Immigrant Heritages in America* (Westport, Conn.: Negro University Press, 1920; reprint, 1971); Kallen, *Cultural Pluralism and the American Idea* (Philadelphia: University of Pennsylvania Press, 1956); Stanley Lieberson, *Ethnic Patterns in American Cities* (New York: Free Press, 1963).

65. Harold Isaacs, *Scratches on Our Minds: American Images of China and India* (New York: John Day Co., 1958; reprint, White Plains, N.Y.: M.E. Sharp, 1980).

66. Glazer and Moynihan, *Beyond the Melting Pot*, 1963.

67. Glazer and Moynihan, *Ethnicity, Theory and Experience*.

68. Ibid., 5.

69. Ibid., 16.

70. Crèvecoeur, *Letters* in *Beyond the Melting Pot* by Glazer and Moynihan, p. xxiii.

71. See Newman, *American Pluralism*, 79.

72. Ibid. Glazer and Moynihan continue to suggest that as minority groups are initially assimilated into American life, they relate to one another in a new pattern of social pluralism. This, in turn, provides opportunity for increased assimilation as they enter the political process. See p. 86.

73. Greeley and McCready, *Ethnicity*, 3.

74. Newman, *American Pluralism*, 83.

75. Gordon, *Assimilation in American Life*.
76. Newman, *American Pluralism*, 83.
77. Gordon, *Assimilation in American Life*. See also, Newman, *American Pluralism*, 83.
78. Novak, *The Rise of the Unmeltable Ethnics*.
79. Ibid., p. xxii.
80. Ibid., 80.
81. Ibid., 291.
82. Stein and Hill, *The Ethnic Imperative*.
83. *Ibid., p. ix*.
84. *Ibid., 5*.
85. *Ibid., 274–275*.
86. *Ibid., 163*.

Chapter 4

1. The term new religion is applied by a variety of researchers including Benton Johnson, Thomas Robbins, and Dick Anthony. The designation of cults as alternative forms of religion is advanced by J. Gordon Melton and Robert L. Moore in *The Cult Experience: Responding to the New Religious Pluralism* (New York: Pilgrim Press, 1982), 17.

2. Andrew Greeley argues that denominations are found in only a few countries including Canada, the United States, Holland, and Switzerland. He suggests that a denominational society is characterized "neither by an established church nor protesting sect" and is pluralistic, composed of "multiple quasi-equal ecclesiastical organizations which are not a halfway house between a sect and the Church but actually a social organizational adjustment to the fact of religious pluralism." See Andrew Greeley, *The Denominational Society: A Sociological Approach to Religion in America* (Glenview, Ill.: Scott, Foresman & Co., 1972), 1.

3. See David A. Roozen, William McKinney, and Jackson W. Carroll, *Varieties of Religious Presence: Mission in Public Life* (New York: Pilgrim Press, 1984), 30.

4. See Greeley, *The Denominational Society*, 178, 184.

5. Sidney E. Mead, "Denominationalism: The Shape of Protestantism," in *Denominationalism*, ed. Russell E. Richey (Nashville, Tenn.: Abingdon Press, 1977), 71. Another way of identifying the "like-hearted" and "like-minded" behavior that Mead describes is to suggest that denominations are assimilative, reflecting the social order of which they are a part. At the same time they are pluralistic, demonstrating the nation's historical diversity. In similar fashion, the beliefs and ideologies that have informed American denominationalism are indicative of the conformity and plurality that have characterized its function.

6. A *"Gemeinschaft* society is one in which human living is guided in part by traditional, sacred, and ascriptive norms of behavior," and typically is characterized by peasant villages. It is differentiated from *Gesellschaft* societies, identified by "achievement, universality, rationality, and secularity." See Greeley, *The Denominational Society*, 2, note 4.

7. Mead, "Denominationalism. . . ," 80.

8. Ross P. Scherer, *American Denominational Organization: A Sociological View* (Pasadena, Calif.: William Carey Library, 1980), 15.

9. Roozen, McKinney, and Carroll, *Varieties*, 26.

10. Ibid., 26–27. The authors discuss some of the ideas of sociologist David Moberg.

11. Mead, "Denominationalism. . . ," 71.

12. See Timothy L. Smith, "Congregation, State, and Denomination: The Forming of the American Religious Structure," in *Denominationalism*, ed. Richey, 47 ff.

13. See Greeley, *The Denominational Society* and Martin E. Marty, "Ethnicity: The Skeleton of Religion in America," in *Denominationalism*, ed. Richey, 251–272.

14. Greeley, *The Denominational Society*, 117.

15. H. Richard Niebuhr, *The Social Sources of Denominationalism* (New York: Henry Holt, 1929; reprint, Hamden, Conn.: Shoe String Press, 1954), 25, quoted in *Denominationalism*, ed. Richey, 11.

16. The interest in congregations as single-cell organizations is particularly articulated by the Fuller School of Theology.

17. Gary P. Burkart, "Patterns of Protestant Organization," in *American Denominational Organization*, ed. Scherer, 36–83.

18. Ibid., 14.

19. Ibid., 44.

20. Ibid.

21. Ibid., 44–45.

22. Ibid., 45.

23. For a description of the Krishna Consciousness movement and the history of ISKCON see Robert S. Ellwood, Jr., *Religious and Spiritual Groups in Modern America* (Englewood Cliffs, N.J.: Prentice-Hall, 1973), 239 ff.

24. This figure was estimated by the organization during interviews with leaders of the New Vrindaban community in 1985.

25. Batuk Vora, "Internal Conflicts, Charges, and Suit Bedevil Krishnas," *India Abroad*, 25 July 1986, 1.

26. Ibid.

27. Ibid.

28. Lynn Hudson, "Scandal and Fight for Control Boil Over at Krishna Center," *India Abroad*, 29 May 1987, 1.

29. Lynn Hudson, "Splendid Krishna Palace, Shocking Charges," *India Abroad*, 5 June 1987, 16.

30. For a description of Hinduism as practiced by Asian Indians in the United States see E. Allen Richardson, *East Comes West: Asian Religions and Cultures in North America* (New York: Pilgrim Press, 1985).

31. For a guide to Indian voluntary associations in the United States see Thomas Abraham, *North American Directory and Reference Guide of Asian Indian Businesses and Independent Professional Practitioners* (New York: Indian Enterprises of the West, 1984).

32. See Emma McCloy Layman, *Buddhism in America* (Chicago: Nelson-Hall, 1976).

33. Ibid., 117–139. Details about the organization and structure of the Nicheren Shoshu Academy are taken from Layman's observations.

34. Ibid., 134.

35. *The World Tribune*, the publication of the Nicheren Shoshu Academy, is published weekly in Santa Monica, California.

36. Layman, *Buddhism in America*, 127–130.

37. Ibid., 127.

38. See T.C. Tsao, ed., *The Buddhist Association of the United States: 20th Anniversary* (Bronx, N.Y.: Buddhist Association of the United States, 1984), 46.

39. Ibid.

40. *Buddhist Churches of America*, 2 vols. (San Francisco: Buddhist Churches of America, 1974) 1:45.

41. Ibid., 53.

42. Tetsuden Kashima, *Buddhism in America: The Social Organization of an Ethnic Religious Institution* (Westport, Conn.: Greenwood Press, 1977), 167 ff.

43. *Buddhist Churches of America*, 62 ff.

44. Ibid., 65 ff. See also p. 82 ff. for a description of the meeting in 1973 between leaders of the Hompa Hongwanji and the BCA, which gave the North American denomination still greater autonomy.

45. C. Eric Lincoln, *The Black Muslims in America* (Boston: Beacon Press, 1961), 10.

46. Ibid., 11 (from an interview with Sister Carrie Mohammad).

47. Ibid., 119.

48. Khalil Abdel Alim, "The Growth and Development of Al-Islam in America," paper presented to a conference on The World of Islam from Morocco to Indonesia, Johns Hopkins University, School of International Studies, 13–14 June 1980, 6.

49. Umhau Wolf, "The Islamic Federation, 1952: 'Muslims in the American Mid-West,'" in *The Muslim World* 50 (January 1960): 42–43, quoted in *The Arabs in America, 1492–1977: A Chronology and Fact Book,* ed. Beverlee Turner Mehdi (Dobbs Ferry, N.Y.: Oceana Publications, 1978), 103.

50. Robert N. Bellah, "Civil Religion in America," in *Religion in America,* ed. William G. McLoughlin and Robert N. Bellah (Boston: Houghton Mifflin Co., 1968), 3–23. An important contribution to the concept of civil religion was made by Emile Durkheim. See Robert N. Bellah and Philip E. Hammond, *Varieties of Civil Religion* (San Francisco: Harper & Row, 1980), 138 ff.

51. Bellah, "Civil Religion in America," 8.

52. Ibid.

53. Ibid., 9.

54. Ibid., 11–13.

55. Sherwood Eddy, *The Kingdom of God and the American Dream* (New York, 1941), 162, quoted in "Civil Religion in America," by Bellah, 13.

56. Thomas Robbins and Dick Anthony, eds., *In Gods We Trust: New Patterns of Religious Pluralism in America* (New Brunswick, N.J.: Transaction Books, 1981), 10.

57. Ibid.

58. Robert N. Bellah, "Religion and Legitimation in the American Republic," in *In Gods We Trust,* ed. Robbins and Anthony, 35–49.

59. Ibid.

60. Dick Anthony and Thomas Robbins, "Culture Crisis and Contemporary Religion," in *In Gods We Trust,* ed. Robbins and Anthony, 11.

61. Ibid., 10. Bellah's argument appears in Robert N. Bellah, *The Broken Covenant* (New York: Seabury, 1975).

62. See Benton Johnson, "A Sociological Perspective on the New Religions," in *In Gods We Trust,* ed. Robbins and Anthony, 51–66.

63. Anthony and Robbins, "Culture Crisis. . . ," 19.

64. A bibliographic study of this phenomenon is found in Anson D. Shupe, Jr., David G. Bromley, and Donna L. Oliver, *The Anti-Cult Movement in America: A Bibliography and Historical Survey* (New York: Garland Publishing, 1984).

65. Handy, *A Christian America,* 151.

66. Winthrop S. Hudson, *Religion in America: A Historical Account of the Development of American Religious Life* (New York: Charles Scribner's Sons, 1965; reprint, 1981), 392.

67. Ibid., 391.

68. A transcript of the parliament is found in John Henry Barrows, ed., *The*

World's Parliament of Religions: An Illustrated and Popular Story of the World's First Parliament of Religions Held in Chicago in Connection with the Columbian Exposition of 1893 (Chicago: Parliament Publishing Co., 1893).

69. See James W. Shepp and Daniel B. Shepp, *Shepp's World's Fair Photographed: Being a Collection of Original Copyrighted Photographs* (Chicago: Globe Bible Publishing Co., 1893).

70. A survey compiled by Bettina Bentrup Gray in November 1980 has demonstrated the comparatively small number of interfaith councils with a broad representation in the United States.

Chapter 5

1. See "Assaults on Asian Immigrants Increase in Boston," *New York Times,* 11 August 1983, A11.

2. William M. Newman, *American Pluralism: A Study of Minority Groups and Social Theory* (New York: Harper & Row, 1973). The reader is also referred to other conflict theorists. In addition to the classical works of Marx and Durkheim, the following sources have become standard: Lewis Coser, *The Functions of Social Conflict* (New York: Free Press, 1965); Ralf Dahrendorf, *Class and Class Conflict in an Industrial Society* (Stanford, Calif.: Stanford University Press, 1959).

3. Newman, *American Pluralism,* 110.

4. "Class, Status, Party," in *From Max Weber,* trans. and ed. Hans Gerth and C. Wright Mills (New York: Oxford University Press, 1946), cited in *American Pluralism,* by Newman, 110.

5. Newman, *American Pluralism,* 110.

6. Ibid., 119.

7. Ibid.

8. Ibid., 120.

9. Ibid.

10. Ibid.

11. Ibid., 141. Proposition 5 concludes: "The greater the degree to which a social group occupies a position of reward parity, the greater the likelihood that conflicts initiated by that group will be the consensus-bounded type."

12. Ibid., 142. Proposition 6 concludes, "The greater the degree to which a social group occupies a position of reward deprivation, the greater the likelihood that conflicts initiated by that group will be of the consensus-projecting type."

13. Ibid., 112 and 115. Proposition 1 concludes, "The frequency of intergroup conflict in societies is directly proportional to the degree to which different social groups view each other as competitive threats to their social resources, to resources that they wish to obtain, or to their basic social values." Proposition 2 concludes, "The degree to which social groups view each other as competitive threats, and therefore the frequency of social conflict between them, is directly proportional to the degree to which competition and achievement are prescribed norms in society."

14. Ibid.

15. Ibid., 158.

16. Sidney E. Ahlstrom, *A Religious History of the American People* (New Haven, Conn.: Yale University Press, 1972), 555.

17. Richard M. Merelman and Robert N. Bellah have suggested that such differences may also be understood as distinctions in boundaries. Boundaries are formed by expressions of group identity and are also influenced by the role of the individual. Merelman and Bellah suggest that in cultures or religious groups that

are loosely bounded, group membership is fluid, unlike tightly bounded cultures or groups where it is fixed. See Richard M. Merelman, *Making Something of Ourselves: On Culture and Politics in the United States* (Berkeley: University of California Press, 1984) and Robert N. Bellah, "Competing Visions of the Role of Religion in American Society," in *Uncivil Religion: Interreligious Hostility in America*, ed. Robert N. Bellah and Frederick E. Greenspahn (New York: Crossroad, 1987), 219–232.

18. In discussing conflict in a pluralistic society, Newman advances twenty-six propositions. Of these, fourteen are particularly relevant to this discussion and include variables of integration, segregation, reward parity, reward deprivation, frequency and intensity of conflict, and degree of violence. These are ordered as follows (*American Pluralism*, 157–178):

> The greater the degree of reward disparity and social segregation between a dominant and a subordinate group, the greater the likelihood that conflicts between them will be relatively infrequent. (Proposition #13)

> The greater the degree of reward disparity and social segregation between a dominant and a subordinate group, the greater the likelihood that conflicts between them will be relatively intense. (Proposition #14)

> The greater the degree of reward disparity and social segregation between a dominant and a subordinate group, the greater the likelihood that conflicts between them will be violent. (Proposition #15)

> The greater the degree of reward parity and social integration between a dominant and a subordinate group, the greater the likelihood that conflicts between them will be relatively frequent. (Proposition #16)

> The greater the degree of reward parity and social integration between a dominant and a subordinate group, the greater the likelihood that conflicts between them will not be intense. (Proposition #17)

> The greater the degree of reward parity and social integration between a dominant and subordinate group, the greater the likelihood that conflicts between them will not be violent. (Proposition #18)

> The greater the degree of reward parity and social segregation between a dominant and a subordinate group, the greater the likelihood that conflicts between them will be relatively infrequent. (Proposition #19)

> The greater the degree of reward parity and social segregation between a dominant and a subordinate group, the greater the likelihood that conflicts between them will be initiated by the dominant group. (Proposition #20)

> The greater the degree of reward parity and social segregation between a dominant and a subordinate group, the greater the likelihood that the conflicts between them will be relatively intense. (Proposition #21)

> The greater the degree of reward parity and social segregation between a dominant and a subordinate group, the greater the likelihood that conflicts between them will be violent. (Proposition #22)

> The greater the degree of reward disparity and social integration between a dominant and a subordinate group, the greater the likelihood

that social conflicts between them will be initiated by the subordinate group. (Proposition #23)

The greater the degree of reward deprivation and social integration between a dominant and a subordinate group, the greater the likelihood that conflicts between them will be relatively infrequent. (Proposition #24)

The greater the degree of reward deprivation and social integration between a dominant and a subordinate group, the greater the likelihood that conflicts between them will be intense. (Proposition #25)

The greater the degree of reward disparity and social integration between a dominant and a subordinate group, the greater the likelihood the conflicts between them will be violent. (Proposition #26)

19. Jim Davis, "Garfield," *Morning Call* [Allentown, Pa.], 23 August 1986.
20. The correlation is reflected in propositions 11–26.
21. Newman, *American Pluralism,* 133 ff., 141 ff., 151 ff.
22. Ibid., 133.
23. Denis Collins, "Ex-Cultists Need Not Apply," *Across the Board* 21 (December 1984): 60.
24. Ibid.
25. See Newman, *American Pluralism,* 124–125. Newman also suggests a number of assumptions about rigid and variable means of conflict (pp. 145–148):

The greater the degree to which a social group occupies a position of reward deprivation, the greater the likelihood that its initiation of rigid-means conflict will be predicated upon its lack of alternative means and/or the failure of previously employed means of conflict. (Proposition #7)

The greater the degree to which a social group occupies a position of reward parity, the greater the likelihood that its initiation of rigid-means conflict will be predicated upon its ability to affect the social structure. (Proposition #8)

The greater the degree to which a social group occupies a position of reward deprivation, the greater the likelihood that its use of variable-means conflict techniques will be predicated upon its inability to employ effectively any single tactic. (Proposition #9)

The greater the degree to which a social group occupies a position of reward parity, the greater the likelihood that its use of variable-means conflict techniques will be predicated upon the relative deprivation of conflict for group members. (Proposition #10).

26. See Newman, *American Pluralism,* 196. Newman defines prejudice as "any set of ideas and beliefs that negatively prejudge groups or individuals on the basis of real or alleged group traits or characteristics" (p. 196). He also suggests that prejudice includes four component parts. He says, "It is cognitive, collective or group-based, prejudgmental, and always consists of a negative evaluation of an out-group even if positive and desirable group traits are involved" (p. 199).
27. See Newman, *American Pluralism,* 199.
28. In addition to Newman's work the reader is referred to a number of recognized sources on prejudice and discrimination. These include: Gordon Allport, *The Nature of Prejudice* (Reading, Mass.: Addison-Wesley, 1954); Bruno

Bettelheim and Morris Janowitz, *Dynamics of Prejudice* (New York: Harper & Row, 1950); ———— ————, *Social Change and Prejudice* (New York: Free Press, 1964); Robert MacIver, ed., *Discrimination and National Welfare* (New York: Harper & Row, 1949).

29. Newman, *American Pluralism*, 232.

30. A description of some of the problems in the resettlement is given in Murray Dubin and Marc Kaufman, "For Many Refugees, Quiet Despair in a New Land," *Philadelphia Inquirer*, 28 April 1985, 1.

31. See Marc Kaufman, "New Year for Beleaguered People: In West Phila., the Hmong Come Together to be Hmong," *Philadelphia Inquirer*, 25 November 1984, 2-B.

32. See Marc Kaufman, "A Fatal Collision of Old and New: Laotian Immigrant Finds a Final Refuge in Suicide," *Philadelphia Inquirer*, 20 March 1985, 1.

33. Ibid.

34. Ibid.

35. Ibid.

36. Ibid.

37. See Propositions 1 and 2.

38. This is supported by Proposition #11, which states (*American Pluralism*, 151), "The greater the degree to which a subordinate group occupies a position of reward deprivation, the greater the likelihood that the social-space arrangements between it and the dominant group will represent the desires of the dominant group."

39. See Robert Lindsey, "Vietnamese Fishermen Stir Bitterness on Coast," *New York Times*, 8 July 1982, A12.

40. Ibid.

41. Ibid.

42. Ibid.

43. See Proposition #11.

44. Michael Corey, "Castle Bought," *Montclair Times* (N.J.), 18 June 1981, 1.

45. William E. Geist, "Cult in Castle Troubling Montclair," *New York Times*, 16 September 1981, B1.

46. Michael Corey, "Rumors and Concerns Continue to Shroud Rajneesh Mountain Castle—Eyewitnesses Report on Activities in India," *Montclair Times* (N.J.), 25 June 1981, 1.

47. Ibid.

48. The advertisement appeared in *Time* magazine. See Geist, "Cult in Castle. . ."

49. Geist, "Cult in Castle. . ."

50. Ibid.

51. See Propositions #5 ff.

52. See Proposition #12.

53. For more information on the Swaminarayan Sanstha see H.T. Dave, *Life and Philosophy of Shree Swaminarayan* (London: George Allen & Unwin Ltd., 1974).

54. See Robert Hanley, "Hindu Sect's Plans for 162-Acre Compound Jar Town in Jersey," *New York Times*, 3 February 1986, B7. This article is also cited by Raymond B. Williams, "Hinduism in America," *Christian Century*, 11 March 1987, 247–249.

55. Ibid.

56. Ibid.

57. Ibid.

58. Ibid.

59. Newman suggests that when a subordinate group acquires parity and also is segregated, conflict will be infrequent, intense, violent, and often will be initiated by the dominant group. See Propositions 19–22.

60. Frank Whelan, "The Immigrations, America the Land of Freedom," *Morning Call* [Allentown, Pa.], 6 October 1983, D2. An important source for understanding the Pennsylvania German culture is William T. Parsons, *The Pennsylvania Dutch: A Persistent Minority* (Boston: Twayne Publishers, 1976). A comprehensive history of Allentown, Pennsylvania, is Mahlon H. Hellerich, ed., *Allentown 1762–1987: A 225-Year History* (Allentown, Pa.: Lehigh County Historical Society, 1987).

61. "The First 300 Years, Historical Highlights," *Morning Call* [Allentown, Pa.], 6 October 1983, D8.

62. Joe Kita, "The Stigma, The Pennsylvania German Culture Was 'a Stone in the Stomach' of the English," *Morning Call* [Allentown, Pa.], 6 October 1983, D3.

63. Ibid.

64. Ibid.

65. Competition for the same resources combined with equality or parity among the same groups is a frequent cause of conflict.

66. George Olsen, "They're Known as 'The Wards,' Many Success Stories Began in These Old Neighborhoods," *Morning Call* [Allentown, Pa.], 26 September 1985, B1.

67. A history of Allentown's Syrian population is found in Mary Ann Fay, "Allentown, Pennsylvania—Fertile Valley," in *Taking Root Bearing Fruit: The Arab-American Experience*, ed. James Zogby (Washington, D.C.: ADC Reports, 1984), 27–31.

68. The ad appeared in *Morning Call* [Allentown, Pa.] March 10, 1984.

69. The temple is identified as Shantiniketan and is located near the city's airport.

70. See Newman, *American Pluralism*, 140. Proposition #3 states (p. 140), "Socially dominant groups generally attempt to maintain or increase their position of dominance over other groups in society."

Chapter 6

1. Dena Kleiman, "Immigrants Encountering Choice Between Friendship and Isolation," *New York Times*, 24 December 1982, B1.

2. David Popenoe, *Public Pleasure, Public Plight: American Metropolitan Community Life in Comparative Perspective* (New Brunswick, N.J.: Transaction Books, 1985), 117.

3. Ibid., 116 ff. Popenoe suggests that on the eve of the Revolution, an observer in Philadelphia noted that the vitality of American society was occasioned by a sense of community and a lack of anonymity—in order words, by the strength of public life.

4. Ibid., 118–119.

5. Popenoe has an excellent discussion about privatization. See chapter 7, pp. 111–142. An example of the privatization of diversity is the tendency of immigrant groups to retain their primary language at home and to use English in public life. The same pattern is also evident among some black Americans who may speak standard English at work and use black dialect at home.

6. E. Allen Richardson, "Mughal and Rajput Patronage of the Bhakti Sect of

the Maharajas, the Vallabha Sampradaya, 1640–1760 A.D." (Ph.D. Diss., University of Arizona, 1979).

7. Interview with Carol Fujita, from Mark Keppel High School, Alhambra, Calif., 29 June 1985.

8. The relationship between China and Spanish-speaking countries has some interesting historical associations. Spanish trade routes to China in the sixteenth century began in Mexico, continued to Manilla and China, returning to Acapulco. The currency for the China trade was the Mexican silver dollar.

9. Interviews with administrators and teachers at the UNIS were conducted in 1986. See also "247 Pupils, 77 Nations in 1 School," *New York Times*, 22 December 1985.

10. Vien, "My Trip From Vietnam to Hong Kong," paper presented to English III class, Senn Metropolitan Academy, Chicago, 1982–1983.

11. The Cambodian song was translated into English as part of a music class at Senn Academy.

12. Marc Kaufman, "Cultures in Conflict: Hmong Rejects Hospital Care," *Philadelphia Inquirer*, 5 October 1984, 1.

13. Ibid., 2A.

14. Ibid.

15. Interviews at the New York Infirmary-Beekman Downtown Hospital were conducted in March 1986. See also Edward A. Gargan, "Hospital Speaks Patients' Language," *New York Times*, 25 July 1983, B1.

16. Marvine Howe, "A Senior City Police Officer Pursues His Roots in China," *New York Times*, 14 November 1985, B1.

17. Kenneth Gross, "A Final Touch of Compassion," *Newsday*, 3 July 1983.

18. Lions Club of Chinatown, N.Y., *Handbook of Phrases for Patients of N.Y. Infirmary-Beekman Hospital* (New York, n.d.).

19. Edward A. Gargan, "Hospital Speaks Patients' Language," *New York Times*, 25 July 1983, B1.

20. Interview with social worker Teresa Tam, New York Infirmary-Beekman Downtown Hospital, March 1986.

21. Ibid.

22. Joyce White, "When Chinatown Needs Medical Care," *Daily News*, 4 March 1983, M1 and M3.

23. The survey was conducted by Bettina Bentrup Gray in conjunction with the Berkeley Area Interfaith Council in November 1980.

24. Ibid.

25. Interviews at the Interfaith Conference were conducted in March 1986.

26. Ibid.

27. Mary Grayken, "Panel Tells How to Prevent, Respond to Incidents of Group Hate-Violence," *Interfaith Connector* (Washington, D.C.: Interfaith Conference of Metropolitan Washington, Spring 1983).

28. See Interfaith Conference of Metropolitan Washington, "IFC Leads Successful Fight; District Withdraws Tax Changes," *Interfaith Connector*, Spring 1985.

Bibliography

"A Plan for the Western Colonization of Catholic Immigrants. . ." Quoted in *Documents of American Catholic History*, by John Tracy Ellis, 311. Milwaukee: Bruce Publishing Co., 1962.

Abbott, Edith. *Historical Aspects of the Immigration Problem, Select Documents*. Chicago: University of Chicago Press, 1926. Reprint. New York: Arno Press and the New York Times, 1969.

Abraham, Thomas. *North American Directory and Reference Guide of Asian Indian Businesses and Independent Professional Practitioners*. New York: Onida Enterprises of the West, 1984.

The Acts and Resolves, Public and Private, of the Province of the Massachusetts Bay. Boston: Wright & Potter, 1869, 1:423–424.

Adamic, Louis. *From Many Lands*. New York: Harper & Brothers for Friendship Press, 1940.

Age, 29 June 1979, 13. Quoted in *Multiculturalism: The Changing Australian Paradigm*, by Lois Foster and David Stockley, 58–59. Clevedon, Avon, England: Multicultural Matters Ltd., 1984.

Ahlstrom, Sidney E. *A Religious History of the American People*. New Haven, Conn.: Yale University Press, 1972.

Alger, Horatio, Jr. *Struggling Upward and Other Works*. New York: Crown Publishers, 1945.

Alim, Khalil Abdel. "The Growth and Development of Al-Islam in America." Paper presented at a conference, The World of Islam from Morocco to Indonesia. Johns Hopkins University, School of International Studies, 13–14 June 1980.

Allport, Gordon. *The Nature of Prejudice*. Reading, Mass.: Addison-Wesley, 1954.

"American Matters of Interest." *The Illustrated News of the World*, 12 March 1892, 243.

American Missionary 1 (December 1846).

American Missionary 3 (January 1849): 26.

American Missionary 14 (March 1870). Quoted in "The Role of Afro-Americans in the Origin and Work of the American Missionary Association: 1839–1877," by Clara Merritt DeBoer. Ph.D. diss., Rutgers University, 1973.

Anthony, Dick, and Thomas Robbins. "Culture Crisis and Contemporary Religion." In *In Gods We Trust: New Patterns of Religious Pluralism in America*, edited by Thomas Robbins and Dick Anthony, 9–31. New Brunswick, N.J.: Transaction Books, 1981.

Archdiocese of New York. *Hispanics in New York: Religious, Cultural and Social Experiences*. 2 vols. New York: Archdiocese of New York, Office of Pastoral Research, 1982.

Arnold, Edwin. *The Light of Asia or the Great Renunciation (Mahâbhinishkramana) Being the Life and Teaching of Gautama Prince of India and Founder of Buddhism*. Boston: Roberts Brothers, 1887.

As a Chinaman Saw Us: Passages from His Letters to a Friend at Home. New York: D.A. Appleton & Co., 1904.

"Assaults on Asian Immigrants Increase in Boston." *New York Times*, 11 August 1983, A11.

Assistant Commissioner, Bureau of Refugees, Freedmen and Abandoned Lands, State of Alabama to George Whipple. 13 March 1866. New Orleans. Amistad Research Center. Archives of the American Missionary Association, no. 8.

"Balancing Act: In a Sweeping Decision the High Court Expands Affirmative Action." *Time*, 6 April 1987, 18–19.

Baltzell, E. Digby. *The Protestant Establishment: Aristocracy and Caste in America*. New York: Random House, 1964.

Barrows, John Henry, ed. *The World's Parliament of Religions: An Illustrated and Popular Story of the World's First Parliament of Religions Held in Chicago in Connection with the Columbian Exposition of 1893*. 2 vols. Chicago: Parliament Publishing Co., 1893.

Beals, Carleton. *Brass-Knuckle Crusade: The Great Know-Nothing Conspiracy: 1820–1860*. New York: Hastings House Publishers, 1960.

Beard, Augustus Field. *A Crusade of Brotherhood: A History of the American Missionary Association*. Boston: Pilgrim Press. 1909.

Bellah, Robert N. *The Broken Covenant*. New York: Seabury Press, 1975.

———. "Civil Religion in America." *Daedalus* 96 (1967): 1–21.

———. "Civil Religion in America." In *Religion in America*, edited by William G. McLoughlin and Robert N. Bellah, 3–23. Boston: Houghton Mifflin Co., 1968.

———. "Competing Visions of the Role of Religion in American Society." In *Uncivil Religion: Interreligious Hostility in America*, edited by Bellah and Frederick E. Greenspahn, 219–232. New York: Crossroad, 1987.

———. "Religion and Legitimation in the American Republic." In *In Gods We Trust: New Patterns of Religious Pluralism in America*, edited by Thomas Robbins and Dick Anthony, 35–49. New Brunswick, N.J.: Transaction Books, 1981.

———, and Frederick E. Greenspahn, eds., *Uncivil Religion: Interreligious Hostility in America*. New York: Crossroad, 1987.

———, and Phillip E. Hammond. *Varieties of Civil Religion*. San Francisco: Harper & Row, 1980.

———, et al. *Habits of the Heart: Individualism and Commitment in American Life*. Berkeley: University of California Press, 1985.

Berger, Peter. *The Sacred Canopy*. New York: Doubleday, 1967.

Berkson, Issac B. *Theories of Americanization: Critical Study*. New York: Arno Press, 1969.

Berry, Brewton. *Race and Ethnic Relations*. Boston: Houghton Mifflin, 1951.

Bettelheim, Bruno, and Morris Janowitz. *Dynamics of Prejudice*. New York: Harper & Row, 1950.

——— ———. *Social Change and Prejudice*. New York: Free Press, 1964.

Blackwell, Rev. Antoinette Brown. "Women and the Pulpit," In *The World's Parliament of Religions: An Illustrated and Popular Story of the World's First Parliament of Religions Held in Chicago in Connection with the Columbian*

Exposition of 1893, edited by John Henry Barrows, 2: 1148–1150. Chicago: Parliament Publishing Co., 1893.

Blalock, Hubert M., Jr. *Toward a Theory of Minority-Group Relations*. New York: Capricorn Books, 1967.

Blanchett, F.N. to Parker. 8 July 1871. Quoted in *The Movement for Indian Assimilation, 1860–1890*, by Henry E. Fritz, 87. Philadelphia: University of Pennsylvania Press, 1963.

Bogardus, Emory S. *Essentials of Americanization*. Los Angeles: University of Southern California Press, rev. ed., 1923.

Bromley, David G., and Anson D. Shupe, Jr. *Strange Gods: The Great American Cult Scare*. Boston: Beacon Press, 1981.

Brownlee, Fred L. *New Day Ascending*. Boston: Pilgrim Press, 1946.

Brune, Tom, and Eduardo Camacho. *A Special Report: Race and Poverty in Chicago, Analysis and Data Reflecting Race and Poverty in Chicago Based on the 1980 U.S. Census*. Chicago: *Chicago Reporter* and Center for Community Research and Assistance [1983].

Bryce, James. *The American Commonwealth*. 2 vols. New York: 1910.

"Buddhist Bells Ring Out as Rural Temple Opens." *New York Times*, 12 May 1985, 32.

Buddhist Churches of America. 2 vols. San Francisco: Buddhist Churches of America, 1974.

Burkart, Gary P. "Patterns of Protestant Organization." In *American Denominational Organization: A Sociological View*, edited by Ross P. Scherer, 36–83. Pasadena, Calif.: William Carey Library, 1980.

Burners' Weekly Magazine, 24 October 1953, 63.

Bushnell, Horace. *Barbarism the First Danger*, n.d.

Butterfield, L.H., ed. *Diary and Autobiography of John Adams*. 4 vols. Cambridge, Mass.: Harvard University Press, Belknap Press, 1961.

Cafferty, Pastora San Juan, and William C. McCready. *Hispanics in the United States: A New Social Agenda*. New Brunswick, N.J.: Transaction Books, 1985.

Camacho, Eduardo. *A Special Report: Race and Poverty in Chicago, Analysis and Data Reflecting Race and Poverty in Chicago Based on the 1980 U.S. Census*. Chicago: *Chicago Reporter* and Center for Community Research and Assistance, 1983.

Casuso, Jorge, and Eduardo Camacho. *Hispanics in Chicago*. Chicago: Community Renewal Society, 1985.

Chicago Fact Book Consortium. *Local Community Fact Book Chicago Metropolitan Area Based on the 1970 and 1980 Censuses*. Chicago: Chicago Review Press, 1984.

Chicago Reporter. Chicago: Community Renewal Society.

Child, Irvin L. *Toward a Theory of Minority-Group Relations*. New Haven, Conn.: Yale University Press, 1943.

Cigler, M. "History and Multicultural Education." In *Australian Historical Association Bulletin* 4 (1975): 23. Quoted in *Multiculturalism: The Changing Australian Paradigm*, by Lois Foster and David Stockley, 52–53. Clevedon, Avon, England: Multicultural Matters Ltd., 1984.

"Class, Status, Party." In *From Max Weber*. Translated and edited by Hans Girth and C. Wright Mills. New York: Oxford University Press, 1946.

Collins, Denis. "Ex-cultists Need Not Apply." *Across the Board* 21 (December 1984): 60.

Colton, Calvin. *Manual for Emigrants to America*. London: F. Westley and A.H. Davis, 1832. Reprint. New York: Arno Press and the New York Times, 1969.

Connors, Bryan. "A Multicultural Curriculum as Action for Social Justice." In *Bilingual and Multicultural Education: Canadian Perspectives*, edited by Stan Shapson and Vincent D'Oyley, 104–111. Clevedon, Avon, England: Multicultural Matters Ltd., 1984.

Coolidge, Mary Roberts. *Chinese Immigration*. New York: Henry Holt & Co., 1909. Reprint. New York: Arno Press and the New York Times, 1969.

Corey, Michael. "Castle Bought." *Montclair* [N.J.] *Times* 18 June 1981, 1.

———. "Rumors and Concerns Continue to Shroud Rajneesh Mountain Castle: Eyewitnesses Report on Activities in India." *Verona-Cedar Grove* [N.J.] *Times*, 25 June 1981, 1.

Coser, Lewis. *The Functions of Social Conflict*. New York: Free Press, 1956.

de Crèvecoeur, J. Hector St. John. *Letters from an American Farmer*. New York: Fox, Duffield & Co., 1904. Quoted in *Beyond the Melting Pot: The Negroes, Puerto Ricans, Jews, Italians, and Irish of New York City*, edited by Nathan Glazer and Daniel P. Moynihan, 288. Cambridge, Mass.: MIT Press. 1963. Reprint 1970.

Cross, Barbara M., ed. *The Autobiography of Lyman Beecher*. 2 vols. Cambridge, Mass.: Harvard University Press, Belknap Press, 1961.

Curran, Thomas J. *Xenophobia and Immigration, 1820–1930*. Boston: Twayne Publishers, 1975.

Curti, Merle. *The Making of an American Community: A Case Study of Democracy in a Frontier County*. Stanford, Calif.: Stanford University Press, 1959.

Curtiss-Wedge, Franklyn. *History of Trempealeau County, Wisconsin*. Chicago and Winona, 1917. Quoted in *The Making of An American Community: A Case Study of Democracy in a Frontier County*, by Merle Curti, 78. Stanford, Calif.: Stanford University Press, 1959.

Darwin, Charles. *On the Origin of Species by Means of Natural Selection*. New York: Appleton & Co., 1871.

Dave, H.T. *Life and Philosophy of Shree Swaminarayan*. London: George Allen & Unwin Ltd., 1974.

Davis, Jim. "Garfield." *Morning Call* [Allentown, Pa.], 23 August 1986.

DeBoer, Clara Merritt. "The Role of Afro-Americans in the Origin and Work of American Missionary Association: 1839–1877." Ph.D. diss. Rutgers University, 1973.

Doctorow, E.L. *Ragtime*. New York: Bantam Books, 1980.

Dolan, Jay P. "Catholic Attitudes Toward Protestants." In *Uncivil Religion*, edited by Bellah and Greenspahn, 72–85. New York: Crossroad, 1987.

Drachsler, Julius. *Democracy and Assimilation: The Blending of Immigrant Heritages in America*. Westport, Conn.: Negro University Press, 1920. Reprint. 1971.

Dubin, Murray, and Marc Kaufman. "For Many Refugees, Quiet Despair in a New Land." *Philadelphia Inquirer*, 28 April 1985, 1.

Dubois, Abbé J.A. *Hindu Manners, Customs and Ceremonies*. Translated by Henry K. Beauchamp. Oxford, England: Clarendon Press, 1906. Reprint. 1959.

Eastland, Terry, and William J. Bennett. *Counting by Race: Equality from the Founding Fathers to Bakke and Weber*. New York: Bune Books, 1979.

Eddy, Sherwood. *The Kingdom of God and the American Dream*. New York: 1941, 162. Quoted in *Religion in America*, edited by William G. McLoughlin and Robert N. Bellah, 13. Boston: Houghton Mifflin Co., 1968.

Ellis, John Tracy. *Documents of American Catholic History*. Milwaukee: Bruce Publishing Co., 1962.

Ellwood, Robert S., Jr. *Religious and Spiritual Groups in Modern America*. Englewood Cliffs, N.J.: Prentice-Hall, 1973.

Ely, Richard T. "Christianity as a Social Force." In *The World's Parliament of Religions: An Illustrated and Popular Story of the World's First Parliament of Religions Held in Chicago in Connection with the Columbian Exposition of 1893*, 2: 1056–1061, edited by John Henry Barrows. Chicago: Parliament Publishing Co., 1893.

"Excerpts from Justices' Opinions in Affirmative Action Cases." *New York Times*, 3 July 1986, B8.

"Excerpts from Opinions on Race-Based Layoffs by a Governmental Body." *New York Times*, 20 May 1986, A21.

Fanon, Frantz. *The Wretched of the Earth*. New York: Grove Press, 1968.

Fay, Mary Ann. "Allentown, Pennsylvania-Fertile Valley." In *Taking Root Bearing Fruit: The Arab-American Experience*, edited by James Zogby, 27–31. Washington, D.C.: ADC Reports, 1984.

Fearon, Henry Bradshaw. *Sketches of America*. London: 1818. Cited in *Historical Aspects of the Immigration Problem: Select Documents*, by Edith Abbott. Chicago: University of Chicago Press, 1926. Reprint. New York: Arno Press and the New York Times, 1969.

"The First 300 Years, Historical Highlights." *Morning Call* [Allentown, Pa.], 6 October 1983, D3.

Fishman, Joshua A., et al. *Ethnicity in Action: The Community Resources of Ethnic Languages in the United States*. Binghampton, N.Y.: Bilingual Press, 1985.

Foster, Lois, and David Stockley. *Multiculturalism: The Changing Australian Paradigm*. Clevedon, Avon, England: Multicultural Matters Ltd., 1984.

Franklyn, John Hope, Thomas F. Pettigrew, and Raymond W. Mack. *Ethnicity in American Life*. New York: Anti-Defamation League of B'nai B'rith, 1971.

Fritz, Henry E. *The Movement for Indian Assimilation, 1860–1890*. Philadelphia: University of Pennsylvania Press, 1963.

Fujita, Carol. Mark Keppel High School, Alhambra, Calif. Interview, 29 June 1985.

Furnivall, J.S. *Colonial Policy and Practice*. New York: New York University Press, 1956.

Garcia, Juan Ramon. *Operation Wetback: The Mass Deportation of Mexican Undocumented Workers in 1954*. Westport, Conn.: Greenwood Press, 1980.

Garcia, Richard A. *The Chicanos in America 1540–1974: A Chronology and Fact Book*. Dobbs Ferry, N.Y.: Oceana Publications, 1975.

Gargan, Edward A. "Hospital Speaks Patients' Language." *New York Times*, 25 July 1983, B1.

Geist, William E. "Cult in Castle Troubling Montclair." *New York Times*, 16 September 1981, B1.

Capt. James Gillette to Rev. J.R. Shipherd. 28 October 1867. New Orleans: Amistad Research Center. Archives of the American Missionary Association, No. 89.

Glazer, Nathan, ed. *Clamor at the Gates: The New American Immigration*. San Francisco: Institute for Contemporary Studies, 1985.

Glazer, Nathan, and Daniel P. Moynihan. *Beyond the Melting Pot: The Negroes, Puerto Ricans, Jews, Italians, and Irish of New York City*. Cambridge, Mass.: MIT Press, 1963. Reprint. 1970.

——— ———, eds. *Ethnicity: Theory and Experience*. Cambridge, Mass.: Harvard University Press, 1975.

Goldman, Ari L. "2000 Attend Buddhist Cremation Rite in Vermont." *New York Times*, 27 May 1987, A15.

Gordon, Milton. *Assimilation in American Life*. New York: Oxford University Press, 1964.

Gottlieb, Martin. "Asian-Americans Compete to Build Queens Complex." *New York Times,* 10 August 1985, B1.

Gray, Bettina Bentrup. Data from Survey of Interfaith Councils. San Francisco: 1980.

Grayken, Mary. "Panel Tells How to Prevent, Respond to Incidents of Group Hate-Violence." *Interfaith Connector* (Interfaith Conference of Metropolitan Washington), spring 1983.

Greeley, Andrew M. *The Denominational Society: A Sociological Approach to Religion in America.* Glenview, Ill.: Scott, Foresman & Co., 1972.

———. *Why Can't They Be Like Us?* New York: E.P. Dutton, 1971.

Greeley, Andrew M., and William C. McCready. *Ethnicity in the United States: A Preliminary Reconnaissance.* New York: John Wiley & Sons, 1974.

Gremillion, Joseph, and William Ryan, eds. *World Faiths and the New World Order: A Muslim-Jewish-Christian Search Begins.* Lisbon: Interreligious Peace Colloquium, 1977.

Grodt, Rod. "'Parsonage' Not Exempt." *Montclair* [N.J.] *Times,* 15 October 1981, 1.

———. "Religious Sect's Presence Prompts Council Concern." *Montclair* [N.J.] *Times,* 23 July 1981, 1.

Gross, Kenneth. "A Final Touch of Compassion." *Newsday,* 3 July 1983.

Handlin, Oscar. *Race and Nationality in American Life.* Garden City, N.Y.: Doubleday, 1957.

———. *The Newcomers.* Cambridge, Mass.: Harvard University Press, 1959.

———. *The Uprooted.* New York: Grosset & Dunlap, 1951.

Handy, Robert T. *A Christian America: Protestant Hopes and Historical Realities.* New York: Oxford University Press, 1971.

Hanley, Robert. "Hindu Sect's Plans for 162-Acre Compound Jar Town in Jersey." *New York Times,* 3 February 1986, B7.

Hareven, Tamara K., and Randolph Langenbach. *Amoskeag: Life and Work in an American Factory-City.* New York: Pantheon Books, 1978.

Hellerich, Mahlon H., ed. *Allentown 1762–1987: A 225-Year History.* Allentown, Pa.: Lehigh County Historical Society, 1987.

Herberg, Will. *Protestant-Catholic-Jew.* Garden City, N.Y.: Doubleday, 1955.

Hillerman, Tony, and David Muench. *New Mexico.* Portland, Ore.: Graphic Arts Center Publishing Co., 1974.

Hirshler, Eric E., ed. *Jews from Germany in the United States.* New York: Farrar, Straus & Cudahy, 1955.

"History of Schools for the Colored Population." In *Special Report of the Commissioner of Education on the Improvement of Public Schools in the District of Columbia,* 1871. Reprint. New York: Arno Press and the New York Times, 1969.

Home Missionary 23 (November 1850): 160.

Horsman, Reginald. *Race and Manifest Destiny: The Origins of American Anglo-Saxonism.* Cambridge, Mass.: Harvard University Press, 1981.

Hosch, Harmon M. *Attitudes Toward Bilingual Education: A View from the Border: Studies in Language and Linguistics 1984–1985.* El Paso: University of Texas, Texas Western Press, 1984.

Howe, Marvine. "A Senior City Police Officer Pursues His Roots in China." *New York Times,* 14 November 1985, B1.

———. "Hong Kong's Plight Alters Look of Flushing." *New York Times,* 14 April 1984, 1.

Hudson, Lynn. "Scandal and Fight for Control Boil Over at Krishna Center." *India Abroad,* 29 May 1987, 1.

Hudson, Winthrop S. *Religion in America: An Historical Account of the Develop-ment of American Religious Life*. New York: Charles Scribner's Sons, 1965.

"IFC Leads Successful Fight; District Withdraws Tax Changes." *Interfaith Con-nector* (Interfaith Conference of Metropolitan Washington), spring 1985.

Interfaith Conference of Metropolitan Washington, Washington, D.C. Interviews, March 1986.

International Society for Krishna Consciousness, New Vrindaban, W. Va. Inter-views, October 1985.

Isaacs, Harold. *Scratches on Our Minds: American Views of China and India*. New York: John Day Co., 1958. Reprint. White Plains, N.Y.: M.E. Sharpe, 1980.

Jenks, W., and W. Jett Lauch. *The Immigration Problem: A Study of American Immigration Conditions and Needs*. New York: Funk & Wagnalls Co., 1922.

Johnson, Benton. "A Sociological Perspective on the New Religions." In *In Gods We Trust: New Patterns of Religious Pluralism in America*, edited by Thomas Robbins and Dick Anthony, 51–66. New Brunswick, N.J.: Transaction, 1981.

Johnson, Kirk. "Asians Galvanize Sales Activity in Flushing: Influx Spurs Building and Revives a Downtown That Was Languishing." *New York Times*, 29 July 1984. sec. 8, p. 1.

Jones, Howard. *Mutiny on the* Amistad: *The Saga of the Slave Revolt and Its Impact on American Abolition, Law and Diplomacy*. New York: Oxford Univer-sity Press, 1987.

Journal of the General Conference of the Methodist Episcopal Church, 1900. Quoted in *A Christian America: Protestant Hopes and Historical Realities*, by Robert T. Handy, 144. New York: Oxford University Press, 1971.

Kallen, Horace M. *Culture and Democracy in the United States: Studies in the Group Psychology of the American Peoples*. New York: Boni & Liveright, 1924. Reprint. New York: Arno Press and the New York Times, 1970.

———. "Democracy Versus the Melting Pot." *The Nation* 100 (18, 25 February 1915): 190–194, 217–222.

———. *Cultural Pluralism and the American Idea*. Philadelphia: University of Pennsylvania Press, 1956.

Kapp, Friedrich, *Immigration and the Commissioners of Emigration*. New York: Nation Press, 1870. Reprint. New York: Arno Press and the New York Times, 1969.

Kashima, Tetsuden. *Buddhism in America: The Social Organization of an Ethnic Religious Institution*. Westport, Conn.: Greenwood Press, 1977.

Kaufman, Marc. "A Fatal Collision of Old and New: Laotian Immigrant Finds a Final Refuge in Suicide." *Philadelphia Inquirer*, 20 March 1985, 1.

———. "Case Against Refugee Rent Strikers is Dropped." *Philadelphia Inquirer*, 31 July 1985, 7B.

———. "Cultures in Conflict: Hmong Rejects Hospital Care." *Philadelphia In-quirer*, 5 October 1981, 1.

———. "New Year for Beleaguered People: In West Phila., the Hmong Come Together to be Hmong." *Philadelphia Inquirer*, 25 November 1984, 2-B.

———. "Refugees Stage a Rent Strike: Gingerly, Tenants Protest State of West Phila. Building." *Philadelphia Inquirer*, 18 July 1985, B-1.

———. "Rent Strike Gets Quick Results for Asian Refugees." *Philadelphia In-quirer*, 7 November 1985, 18-BP.

———. "Trial Starts in Beating of Hmong Man in '84." *Philadelphia Inquirer*, 18 January 1986, 1-B.

Kennedy, Ruby Jo Reeves. "Single or Triple Melting Pot? Intermarriage Trends in

New Haven, 1870–1940." In *American Journal of Sociology* 58 (January 1944): 331–339.

Killian, Lewis, and Charles Grigg. *Racial Crisis in America*. Englewood Cliffs, N.J.: Prentice-Hall, 1964.

King, Wayne. "Red-Clad Disciples of an Indian Guru Build a Farm Community in Oregon." *New York Times*. 26 September 1981.

Kita, Joe. "The Stigma: The Pennsylvania German Culture was 'a Stone in the Stomach' of the English." *Morning Call* [Allentown, Pa.], 6 October 1983, D3. D3.

Kleiman, Dena. "A Hospital Where Ethnic Change Is Constant," *New York Times*, 6 October 1982, B1.

———. "Immigrants Encountering Choice Between Friendship and Isolation," *New York Times*, 24 December 1982, B1.

Kramer, Judith. *The American Minority Community*. New York: Appleton, 1970.

Kuper, Leo, and M. G. Smith, eds. *Pluralism in Africa*. Berkeley: University of California Press, 1969.

Layman, Emma McCloy. *Buddhism in America*. Chicago: Nelson-Hall, 1976.

Lazarus, Emma. *The Poems of Emma Lazarus*. 2 vols. Boston: Houghton, Mifflin & Co., 1889.

Learsi, Rufus. *The Jews in America: A History*. Karp, Abraham J. *Epilogue American Jewry 1954–1971*. New York: Ktau Publishing House, 1972.

Leggett, John. *Class, Race and Labor*. New York: Oxford University Press, 1968.

Lejeune, Robert, ed. *Class and Conflict in American Society*. Chicago: Markham Publishing Co., 1972.

Lenski, Gerhard. *Power and Privilege*. Garden City, N.Y.: Doubleday, 1966.

———. *The Religious Factor*. Garden City, N.Y.: Doubleday, 1961.

Lieberson, Stanley. *Ethnic Patterns in American Cities*. New York: Free Press, 1963.

Lincoln, C. Eric. *The Black Muslims in America*. Boston: Beacon Press, 1961.

Lindsey, Robert. "A Patchwork of Rulings on Free Speech at Malls." *New York Times*, 10 February 1986, A12.

———. "Vietnamese Fishermen Stir Bitterness on Coast." *New York Times*, 8 July 1982, A12.

Lions Club of Chinatown, New York. *Handbook of Phrases for Patients of New York Infirmary-Beekman Hospital*. New York: n.d.

MacIver, Robert, ed. *Discrimination and National Welfare*. New York: Harper & Row, 1949.

Mannheim, Karl. *Ideology and Utopia*. Translated by Louis Wirth and Edward Shils. London: Routledge & Kegan Paul, 1936.

Manschreck, Clyde L., and Barbara Brown Zikmund, eds. *The American Religious Experiment: Piety and Practicality*. Chicago: Exploration Press, 1976.

Martin, W.A.P. "America's Duty to China." In *The World's Parliament of Religions: An Illustrated and Popular Story of the World's First Parliament of Religions Held in Chicago in Connection with the Columbian Exposition of 1893*, edited by John Henry Barrows, 2:1137–1144. Chicago: Parliament Publishing Co., 1893.

Marty, Martin E. "Ethnicity: The Skeleton of Religion in America." In *Denominationalism*, edited by Russell Richey, 251–272. Nashville, Tenn.: Abingdon Press, 1977.

———. *Pilgrims in Their Own Land: 500 Years of Religion in America*. Boston: Little, Brown & Co., 1984.

McCoy, Charles. *When Gods Change: Hope for Theology*. Nashville, Tenn.: Abingdon Press, 1980.

McIlvaine, Charles P. "Address to the Young Men of the United States on Temperance." In *The Temperance Volume: Embracing the Temperance Tracts of the American Tract Society.* no. 244. New York: n.d. Quoted in *A Christian America: Protestant Hopes and Historical Realities,* by Robert T. Handy, 53. New York: Oxford University Press, 1971.

Mead, Sidney E. "Denominationalism: The Shape of Protestantism." In *Denominationalism,* edited by Russell Richey, 70–105. Nashville, Tenn.: Abingdon Press, 1977.

Merelman, Richard M. *Making Something of Ourselves: On Culture and Politics in the United States.* Berkeley: University of California Press, 1984.

Milner, Clyde A., III, and Floyd A. O'Neal, eds. *Churchmen and the Western Indians: 1820–1920.* Norman: University of Oklahoma Press, 1985.

Montgomery, M.W. "What Shall We Do for the Immigrant [sic.]." *Home Missionary* 79 (December 1905): 233.

Morrison, Joan, and Charlotte Fox Zabusky. *American Mosaic: The Immigrant Experience in the Words of Those Who Lived It.* New York: E.P. Dutton, 1980.

Müller, Max, ed. *Sacred Books of the East.* 50 vols. Oxford, England: Oxford University Press, 1886. Reprint. Motilal Banarsidass, 1964.

Murphy, James J., Jr., and Dalta M. Williams. *New Orleans Atlas Series 1980 Census, New Orleans Neighborhood Maps.* vol. 5, New Orleans: City of New Orleans, 1984.

Myrdal, Gunnar. *An American Dilemma.* New York: Harper & Brothers, 1944.

"New Castle Owners Draw Media Interest: First Time Look at Rajneesh Property." *Montclair* [N.J.] *Times.* 2 July 1981, sec. 2, p. 51.

New York Infirmary-Beekman Downtown Hospital, New York. Interviews, March 1986.

Newman, William M. *American Pluralism: A Study of Minority Groups and Social Theory.* New York: Harper & Row, 1973.

Niebuhr, Richard H. *The Social Sources of Denominationalism.* New York: Henry Holt, 1929. Reprint. Hamden, Conn.: Shoe String Press, 1954.

"No! Cry Brooklyn Pastors; International Prize Fight Must Not be Fought; Officials Denounced from the Pulpit; the Times Applauded for Its Battle to Save the City of Churches from Disgrace; Rebuke for the Lawbreakers." *New York Times,* 2 October 1893, 1.

Novak, Michael. *The Rise of the Unmeltable Ethnics.* New York: Macmillan, 1971.

Olsen, George. "They're Known as 'the Wards,' Many Success Stories Began in These Old Neighborhoods." *Morning Call* [Allentown, Pa.], 26 September 1985, B1.

O'Neill, Timothy J. *Bakke and the Politics of Equality: Friends and Foes in the Classroom of Litigation.* Middletown, Conn.: Wesleyan University Press, 1985.

Parsons, Talcott. *The Social System.* New York: Free Press, 1951.

Parsons, William T. *The Pennsylvania Dutch: A Persistent Minority.* Boston: Twayne Publishers, 1976.

Polenberg, Richard. *One Nation Divisible: Class, Race and Ethnicity in the United States Since 1938.* New York: Viking Press, 1980.

Popenoe, David. *Private Pleasure, Public Plight: American Metropolitan Community Life in Comparative Perspective.* New Brunswick, N.J.: Transaction Books, 1985.

Report of the Minnesota Board of Immigration, 1871. Quoted in *Historical Aspects of the Immigration Problem; Select Documents,* by Edith Abbott, 167–172. Chicago: University of Chicago Press, 1926. Reprint. New York: Arno Press and the New York Times, 1969.

Rex, John. *Race Relations in Sociological Theory*. New York: Schocken Books, 1970.

———. *Race, Colonialism and the City*. London: Routledge & Kegan Paul, 1973.

Rice, Clayton S. "The Mormon Mind." New York: Home Missions Council and Council of Women for Home Missions, 1923. New Orleans. Amistad Research Center. Archives of the American Missionary Association, no. A1476.

Rich, Andrea L. *Interracial Communication*. New York: Harper & Row, 1974.

Richardson, E. Allen. *East Comes West: Asian Religions and Cultures in North America*. New York: Pilgrim Press, 1985.

———. "Mughal and Rajput Patronage of the Bhakti Sect of the Maharajas, the Vallabha Sampradaya, 1640–1760 A.D." Ph.D. diss. University of Arizona, 1979.

Richey, Russell, ed. *Denominationalism*. Nashville, Tenn.: Abingdon Press, 1977.

Ringer, Benjamin B. "Summary of 'We the People' and Others." Paper. 1982. Quoted in *"We the People" and Others: Duality and America's Treatment of its Racial Minorities*, by Benjamin B. Ringer, pp. ix–x. New York: Tavistock Publications, 1983.

———. *"We the People" and Others: Duality and America's Treatment of its Racial Minorities*. New York: Tavistock Publications, 1983.

Robbins, Thomas, and Dick Anthony, eds. *In Gods We Trust: New Patterns of Religious Pluralism in America*. New Brunswick, N.J.: Transaction Books, 1981.

Roozen, David A., William McKinney, and Jackson W. Carroll. *Varieties of Religious Presence: Mission in Public Life*. New York: Pilgrim Press, 1984.

Rosengarten, Theodore, and Susan W. Walker, eds. *Tombee, Portrait of a Cotton Planter: with the Journal of Thomas B. Chaplin (1822–1890)*. New York: William Morrow & Co., 1986.

Rosenwaike, Ira. *Population History of New York City*. Syracuse, N.Y.: Syracuse University Press, 1972.

Samora, Julian, and Patricia Vandel Simon. *A History of the Mexican American People*. London: University of Notre Dame Press, 1977.

Sandoval, Moises, ed. *Fronteras: A History of the Latin American Church in the USA Since 1513*. 11 vols. San Antonio, Tex.: Mexican American Cultural Center, 1983. vol. 10, *Hispanics in the United States*.

Saran, Parmatma. *The Asian Indian Experience in the United States*. Cambridge, Mass.: Schenkman Publishing Co., 1985.

Sarna, Jonathan D. "Jewish-Christian Hostility in the United States: Perceptions from a Jewish Point of View." In *Uncivil Religion* by Bellah and Greenspahn, 7. New York: Crossroad, 1987.

Scherer, Ross P., ed. *American Denominational Organization: A Sociological View*. Pasadena, Calif.: William Carey Library, 1980.

Schermerhorn, Richard. *Comparative Ethnic Relations*. New York: Random House, 1970.

Schmidt, William E. "Oak Park, Mich.: Focus of Modern U.S. Diversity," *New York Times*, 20 December 1983, A16.

Segal, Bernard E., ed. *Racial and Ethnic Relations*. New York: T.Y. Crowell, 1966.

Seixas, Gershom Mendes. *The Constitutions of the Several Independent States of America*. Philadelphia: 1781. Quoted in *The History of the Jews of Philadelphia from Colonial Times to the Age of Jackson*, by Edwin Wolf and Maxwell Whiteman, 147. Philadelphia: Jewish Publication Society of America, 1956. Reprint. 1975.

Shapson, Stan, and Vincent D'Oyley. *Bilingual and Multicultural Education:*

Canadian Perspectives. Clevedon, Avon, England: Multicultural Matters Ltd., 1984.

Shepp, James W., and Daniel B. Shepp. *Shepp's World's Fair Photographed: Being a Collection of Original Copyrighted Photographs*. Chicago: Globe Bible Publishing Co., 1893.

Shibutani, Tomatso, and Kiah Kwan. *Ethnic Stratification*. New York: Macmillan, 1965.

Shriver, Donald W. "The Pain and Promise of Pluralism." *Christian Century* (March 26, 1980): 345–350.

Shupe, Anson D., Jr., David G. Bromley, and Donna L. Oliver. *The Anti-Cult Movement in America: A Bibliography and Historical Survey*. New York: Garland Publishing, 1984.

Simpson, George, and J. Milton Yinger. *Racial and Cultural Minorities*. New York: Harper & Row, 1972.

Smith, M.G. *The Plural Society in the British West Indies*. Berkeley: University of California Press, 1965.

Smith, Timothy L. "Congregation, State, and Denomination: The Forming of the American Religious Structure." In *Denominationalism*, edited by Russell E. Richey, 47–67. Nashville, Tenn.: Abingdon Press, 1977.

Sontag, Frederick, ed. *God: The Contemporary Discussion*. New York: Rose of Sharon Press, 1982.

Sowell, Thomas. *The Economics and Politics of Race: An International Perspective*. New York: Quill, 1983.

———. *Ethnic America: A History*. New York: Basic Books, 1981.

Stanley, J. Taylor. *A History of Black Congregational Christian Churches of the South*. New York: United Church Press, 1978.

Stein, Howard F., and Robert F. Hill. *The Ethnic Imperative: Examining the New White Ethnic Movement*. University Park: Penn State Press, 1977.

——— ———. "The Limits of Ethnicity." *American Scholar* (Spring 1977): 181–189.

Steinberg, Stephen. *The Ethnic Myth: Race, Ethnicity and Class in America*. New York: Atheneum, 1981.

Stokes, Isaac Phelps Newton. *The Iconography of Manhattan Island*. 6 vols. New York: Robert H. Dodd, 1915. Reprint. New York: Arno Press, 1967.

Michael E. Strieby to George Whipple. 27 February 1964. New Orleans. Amistad Research Center. Archives of the American Missionary Association, no. 86928.

Tam, Teresa. New York Infirmary-Beekman Downtown Hospital, New York. Interview, March 1986.

Taylor, Stuart, Jr. "Affirmative Action Upheld by High Court as a Remedy for Past Job Discrimination: Six Vote for Idea; They Say Individuals Who Suffered No Bias May Sometimes Benefit." *New York Times*, 3 July 1986, 1.

———. "High Court Bars a Layoff Method Favoring Blacks; But Majority Backs Some use of Affirmative Action by Government Employees." *New York Times*, 20 May 1986, 1.

Tracy, David. *The Analogical Imagination: Christian Theology and the Culture of Pluralism*. New York: Crossroad, 1981.

Tsao, T.C., ed. *The Buddhist Association of the United States: 20th Anniversary*. Bronx, N.Y.: Buddhist Association of the United States, 1984.

Tung, William L. *The Chinese in America 1820–1973: A Chronology and Fact Book*. Dobbs Ferry, N.Y.: Oceana Publications, 1974.

Turner, Frederick Jackson. *The Frontier in American History*. New York: Henry Holt, 1950.

"247 Pupils, 77 Nations in 1 School." *New York Times*, 22 December 1985.

United Nations International School, New York. Interview with teachers, March 1986.

Van den Berghe, Pierre L. *Race and Racism: A Comparative Perspective*. New York: John Wiley & Sons, 1967.

——. *Race, Colonialism and the City*. London: Routledge & Kegan Paul, 1973.

Vien. "My Trip from Vietnam to Hong Kong." Paper presented to English III Class, Senn Metropolitan Academy, Chicago, 1982–1983.

"Visitors from Many Lands: East Indian Delegates to the Congress of Religions." *New York Times*, 3 September 1893, 2.

Vivekananda, Sivami. "Hinduism." In *The World's Parliament of Religions: An Illustrated and Popular Story of the World's First Parliament of Religions Held in Chicago in Connection With the Columbian Exposition of 1893*, edited by John Henry Barrows, 2 : 968–978. Chicago: Parliament Publishing Co., 1893.

Vogel, Dan. *Emma Lazarus*. Boston: Twayne Publishers, 1980.

Vora, Batuk. "Internal Conflicts, Changes and Suit Bedevil Krishnas." *India Abroad*, 25 July 1986, 1.

Warner, Lloyd, and Leo Srole. *The Social System of American Ethnic Groups*. New Haven, Conn.: Yale University Press, 1945.

Webb, Alexander Mohammed. "The Spirit of Islam." In *The World's Parliament of Religions: An Illustrated and Popular Story of the World's First Parliament of Religions Held in Chicago in Connection with the Columbian Exposition of 1893*, edited by John Henry Barrows, 2: 989–996. Chicago: Parliament Publishing Co., 1893.

Weber, Max. *The Protestant Ethic and the Spirit of Capitalism*. Translated by Talcott Parsons. London: George Allen & Unwin, Ltd., 1930.

Weiss, Mitchell. "Town Residents Resent Sight of Refugees." *Dayton* [Ohio] *Daily News*, 16 July 1986.

Whelan, Frank. "The Immigrations, America the Land of Freedom." *Morning Call* (Allentown, Pa.), 6 October 1983, D2.

White, Joyce. "When Chinatown Needs Medical Care." *Daily News*. 4 March 1983, M1 and M3.

"Why Despise the Immigrant." *Home Missionary* 79 (December 1905): 223–224.

Williams, Raymond B., "Hinduism in America." *Christian Century*, 11 March 1987.

Williams, Robin Murphy, Jr. *Mutual Accommodation: Ethnic Conflict and Cooperation*. Minneapolis: University of Minnesota Press, 1977.

Wirth, Louis. *The Ghetto*. Chicago: University of Chicago Press, 1958.

Wolf, Umhau. "The Islamic Federation, 1952: 'Muslims in the American Midwest.'" in *The Muslim World* 50 (January 1960): 42–43. Quoted in *The Arabs in America 1492–1977: A Chronology and Fact Book*, edited by Beverlee Turner Mehdi, 103. Dobbs Ferry, N.Y.: Oceana Publications, 1978.

Woodall, Martha. "Suit: School District Aids Asians Inadequately." *Philadelphia Inquirer*, 31 December 1985, 4-B.

Wright, Ian, and Carol LaBar. "Multiculturalism and Morality." In *Bilingual and Multicultural Education: Canadian Perspectives*, by Stan Shapson and Vincent D'Oyley, 112–129. Clevedon, Avon, England: Multicultural Matters Ltd., 1984.

Zangwill, Israel. *The Melting Pot*. New York: Macmillan, 1909.

Zogby, James, ed. *Taking Root Bearing Fruit: The Arab-American Experience*. Washington, D.C.: ADC Reports, 1984.

Zorbaugh, Harvey. *The Gold Coast and the Slum*. Chicago: University of Chicago Press, 1929.

United States Federal Statutes—Selected Acts

"An act to establish an uniform rule of naturalization." *Statutes at Large*, vol. 1 (1790).

"An act to establish an uniform rule of naturalization, and to repeal the act heretofore passed on that subject." *Statutes at Large*, vol. 1 (1795).

"An act to execute certain treaty stipulations relating to Chinese." *Statutes at Large*, vol. 22 (1882).

"An act to amend an act entitled 'An act to execute certain treaty stipulations relating to Chinese,' approved May sixth, eighteen hundred and eighty-two." *Statutes at Large*, vol. 23 (1884).

"An act to prohibit the coming of Chinese laborers to the United States." *Statutes at Large*, vol. 25 (1888).

"An act to supplement an act entitled 'An act to execute certain treaty stipulations relating to Chinese,' approved the sixth day of May, eighteen hundred and eighty-two." *Statutes at Large*, vol. 25 (1888).

"An act making an appropriation for the enforcement of the Chinese exclusion act." *Statutes at Large*, vol. 25 (1888).

"An act to prohibit the coming of Chinese persons into the United States." *Statutes at Large*, vol. 27 (1892).

"An act to amend an act entitled 'An act to prohibit the coming of Chinese persons into the United States,' approved May fifth, eighteen hundred and ninety-two." *Statutes at Large*, vol. 28 (1893).

"Joint resolution of Congress extending anti-Chinese legislation to Hawaii." *Statutes at Large*, vol. 30 (1898).

"An act making appropriations for sundry civil expenses of the Government for the fiscal year ending June thirtieth, nineteen hundred and one, and for other purposes." *Statutes at Large*, vol. 31 (1900). See p. 610 for a provision for enforcement of the Chinese Exclusion laws.

"An act to provide a government for the territory of Hawaii." *Statutes at Large*, vol. 31 (1900). This statute required Chinese in the Hawaiian Islands to obtain certificates of residence.

"An act supplementary to an act entitled 'An act to prohibit the coming of Chinese persons into the United States,' approved May fifth, eighteen hundred and ninety-two, and fixing the compensation of commissioners in such cases." *Statutes at Large*, vol. 31 (1901).

"An act to prohibit the coming into and to regulate the residence within the United States, its territories, and all territory under its jurisdiction, and the District of Columbia, of Chinese and persons of Chinese descent." *Statutes at Large*, vol. 32 (1902).

"An act to establish the Department of Commerce and Labor." *Statutes at Large*, vol. 32 (1903). See p. 828 for a reaffirmation of the Chinese Exclusion laws.

Amendment to "An act to prohibit the coming into and to regulate the residence within the United States, its territories, and all territory under its jurisdiction, and the District of Columbia, of Chinese and persons of Chinese descent." *Statutes at Large*, vol. 33 (1904).

"An act to regulate the immigration of aliens into the United States." *Statutes at Large*, vol. 34 (1907).

"An act to regulate the immigration of aliens to, and the residence of aliens in, the United States." *Statutes at Large*, vol. 39 (1917).

"An act to limit the immigration of aliens into the United States." *Statutes at Large*, vol. 42 (1921).

"An act to limit the immigration of aliens into the United States, and for other purposes." *Statutes at Large*, vol. 43 (1924).

"An act to repeal the Chinese Exclusion Acts, to establish quotas, and for other purposes." *Statutes at Large*, vol. 57 (1943).

"An act to authorize the admission into the United States of persons of races indigenous to India, and persons of races indigenous to the Philippine Islands, to make them racially eligible for naturalization, and for other purposes." *Statutes at Large*, vol. 60 (1946).

"Immigration and Nationality Act." *Statutes at Large*, vol. 66 (1952).

"Civil Rights Act of 1964." *Statutes at Large*, vol. 78 (1964).

"An act to amend the Immigration and Nationality Act, and for other purposes." *Statutes at Large*, vol. 79 (1965).

"Refugee Act of 1980." *Statutes at Large*, vol. 94 (1980).

"Immigration Reform and Control Act of 1986." *Statutes at Large*, vol. 100 (1986).

"Official State Language Initiative Constitutional Amendment," Proposition 63, Section 6, Article 3, Constitution of California (1986).

Supreme Court Decisions—Selected Cases

Chae Chan Ping v. United States. 130 U.S. 581 (1889).

Fong Yue Ting v. United States, Wong Quan v. United States, Lee Joe v. United States. 149 U.S. 698 (1893).

United States v. Wong Kim Ark. 169 U.S. 649 (1898).

United States v. Bhagat Singh Thind. 261 U.S. 204 (1922).

Terrace et al. v. Thompson, Attorney General of the State of Washington. 263 U.S. 225 (1923).

Porterfield et al. v. Webb, Attorney General of the State of California et al. 263 U.S. 225 (1923).

Webb, Attorney General of the State of California, et al. v. O'Brien et al. 271 U.S. 323 (1926).

Regents of the University of California v. Bakke. 438 U.S. 265 (1978).

United Steelworkers of America, AFL-CIO-CLC v. Weber et al. 443 U.S. 193 (1979).

Fullilove et al. v. Klutznick, Secretary of Commerce, et al. 448 U.S. 448 (1980).

Firefighters Local Union No. 1784 v. Stotts et al. 467 U.S. 561 (1984).

Wendy Wygant et al., Petitioners v. Jackson Board of Education, etc., et al. 476 U.S. ——— (1986).

Local Number 93, International Association of Firefighters, AFL-CIO, CLC, Petitioner v. City of Cleveland et al. 478 U.S. ——— (1986).

Local 28 of the Sheet Metal Workers' International Association and Local 28 Joint Apprenticeship Committee v. Equal Employment Opportunity Commission et al. 478 U.S. ——— (1986).

Paul E. Johnson, Petitioner v. Transportation Agency, Santa Clara County, California, et al. 480 U.S. ——— (1987).

Index